Who Owns CBI

The Naked Truth

Who Owns CBI

The Naked Truth

B.R. Lall, IPS (Retd.)
Former : Joint Director–CBI
Director General of Police, Haryana

Manas Publications
New Delhi-110 002 (INDIA)

MANAS PUBLICATIONS
(Publishers-Distributors-Importers-Exporters)
4402/5-A, Ansari Road (Opp. HDFC Bank)
Darya Ganj, New Delhi - 110 002 (India)
Phones: Off.: 011-23260783, 23265523,
Res.: 011-23842660
E-mail: manaspublications@gmail.com
manaspub6@gmail.com
www.manaspublications.in

2018

ISBN 81-7049-293-9 **(10 Digit ISBN)**
978-81-7049-293-1 **(13 Digit ISBN)**

Rs. 495/-

Designed at
Manas Publications

Printed in India at
RK Offsets, Delhi
and published by Mrs Suman Lata for
Manas Publications, 4402/5-A,
Ansari Road (Opp HDFC Bank),
Darya Ganj, New Delhi - 110002 (INDIA)

DEDICATED TO

The teeming millions whom corruption deprives of two square meals despite toiling day and night

Contents

List of Abbreviations

AC-HQ Zone	Anti-Corruption Head-Quarter Zone
AD CBI	Additional Director CBI
AG	Attorney General/Accountant General
AHD	Animal Husbandry Department
AHD Scam	Animal Husbandry Department Scam (Bihar)
ALA	Additional Legal Advisor (CBI)
BHEL	Bharat Heavy Electricals Ltd.
CAG	Comptroller and Auditor General (of India)
CAT	Central Administrative Tribunal
CBI	Central Bureau of Investigation
Cr PC	The Code of Criminal Procedure
CVC	Central Vigilance Commissioner
DDO	Drawing and Disbursing Officer
DIG	Deputy Inspector General of Police
Director/DCBI	Director CBI
DLA	Deputy Legal Advisor (CBI)
DO letter	Demi Official Letter
DPIO	Deputy Principal Information Officer
DSPE	Delhi Special Police Establishment
FD	Finance Department
FERA	Foreign Exchange Regulations Act
FIR	First Information Report
GDP	Gross Domestic Product
GNP	Gross National Product

Hawala Case	Famous Jain Hawala Case
ICAC	Independent Commission Against Corruption
IO	Investigating Officer
JD	Joint Director (of the rank of Inspector General of Police)
JE	Junior Engineer (of Public Works Department)
JJ Colony	Jhuggi Jhonperi Colony (rehabilitation colony)—special colonies constructed for the evacuee slum dwellers of Delhi
JPC	Joint Parliamentary Committee
LA	Legal Advisor (CBI)
LoC	Letter of Credit
LoC Scam	Letter of Credit Scandal (Assam)
LR	Letter Rogatory
MLA	Member of Legislative Assembly (of an Indian State)
MP	Member of Parliament (India)
PC Act	Prevention of Corruption Act
PE	Preliminary Enquiry
PIL	Public Interest Litigation
PM	Prime Minister (of India)
PMH	Prime Minister's House
PMO	Prime Minister's Office
PP	Public Prosecutor
PVNR	PV Narasimha Rao, Prime Minister of India 1991-1996
RC	Registered Case – used in CBI for FIR
SAIL	Steel Authority of India Ltd.
SD CBI	Special Director CBI
SLP	Special Leave Petition
SP	Superintendent of Police
Sr. PP	Senior Public Prosecutor
TADA	Terrorist and Disruptive Activities Act

Preface

I am not a professional writer, nor do I have any claim to be an academician. As a simple policeman, I was happy enforcing the laws equitably, impartially, firmly and strictly, when posted in Central Bureau of Investigation (CBI) in the mid-nineties. However, such action is not cherished in the country, when it affects the higher echelons of the society, particularly in corruption related cases, as corruption has made deep inroads into the high places, where it is viewed as a perquisite or a by-product of the system. This mindset has given rise to a class of parasites, who survive on corruption and will go to any extent to resist any effort for change. The elite have acquired a mindset that they are superior, out of a different world, can do anything and get away as they are above the law.

The investigating agencies have failed to storm the citadel of corrupt high and mighty, because of their own mindset that they have to guard the privileged. The agencies feel helpless, directionless and absolutely impotent when faced with these elements. I was a witness to the shocking drama, when those entrusted with the task of apprehending the culprits, themselves devised strategies to ensure that the big fish slipped out of the net, unharmed. I strongly protested against these shady going-ons, but was neutralised, and when still I insisted, I was shunted out of the CBI—a normal practice.

The Jain Hawala Case is a stance in view. It was a mind-boggling Rs. 1000 crore scam. Involvement of the Supreme Court enthused the people and public euphoria remained high during 1995 and 1996. At last there appeared a distinct possibility that top politicians and bureaucrats would finally be made accountable for their alleged criminal activities. However, the insiders were aware of what was going on in the CBI and knew that the euphoria would be short-lived. When the chargesheets (filed blindly) started falling like ninepins in the courts, a pall of gloom descended. A despondent nation was once again rudely reminded that the powerful elite could not be touched as they were beyond the reach of the law.

I firmly believe that the fight against the canker of corruption can be successfully fought from within the criminal justice system. The mindset of the officials as also the public has to undergo a radical change, treating corruption like any other crime and the corrupt like any other ordinary criminal, instead of creating a smoke screen of moral and ethical or other hyperboles in dealing with this category of criminals. Crime has to be fought by the law, and the law alone. Morality may assist law wherever possible, feasible and convenient, but cannot substitute it.

This work is intended as a mirror to various players indulging in this sordid drama as also those who are duty-bound to prevent and fight corruption. It is an analysis of corruption, of related issues and of criminal justice system. It also proposes to delve deep into the mindset of various constituents of the system, as also the people, their rulers, their public servants and the consequent corruption-friendly environ that has been generated. I am of the firm conviction that it is possible to contain corruption by a combination of well meaning and effective executive and the criminal justice system of the country. The executive has to create and provide the necessary infrastructure and grant freedom to act so that the criminal justice system can fight the evil effectively and successfully.

The reader may kindly excuse me for use of first-person style, particularly in the first few chapters, but all the authentic first hand frontal accounts and experiences can better be narrated in the first-person only.

B.R. Lall

1

Introduction

"No Sir, we cannot and should not discriminate between the criminals. The laws of corruption should operate more stringently against the higher-ups. If a serving Prime Minister turns corrupt, it is far more serious a matter and if he is not even investigated, the country would be drowned deep into the mire of corruption."

My chain of arguments for investigating all the persons, named in the diaries and the statements of Jains, against whom there was *prima facie* material in the Jain Hawala Case, cut no ice with the boss K. Vijay Rama Rao, the then CBI director, who firmly believed that the serving Prime Minister could not and should not be touched. The controversy continued for long, from March 13th, to July 25th, 1995. My deputy, who was on the same wavelength as myself, was repatriated by the end of May and ultimately I, the leader of the team investigating the Hawala case was divested of investigations of the case and later transferred from that seat to another, not concerned with important cases and in particular the VIPs. I was thought to be too risky for handling VIP material, in the investigations of which one was expected to conceal more and expose less.

As I faced imminent ouster from CBI itself, I was in a nostalgic mood on 23rd December 1996, reflecting over the events of the past thirty-two months. My transfer order was expected any day, any time; and perhaps that may bring my dream of taking the fight against corruption to high places, to an end.

I had realised as early as 1959 when I was a college student, that there was widespread corruption at the grassroots level all around. Thirty-five years later, in 1994, when I learnt about having been picked up for deputation to CBI, my joy knew no bounds. My wife and my daughters were very happy that at last I had an opportunity to do something concrete on the ground, instead of arguing endlessly in the drawing room: how bad the corruption was, how it was retarding economic progress, distorting income and wealth distribution, breaking the social fabric and destroying the nation. By then, my wife had already been inflicted with such stuff for the past 17 years. Both my children had grown up in an environ of endless analysis of corruption and the corrupt, its ill-effects and measures to control it, but they felt helpless in the helplessness of their father.

On reporting to the CBI on 26th April 1994, I was placed as Joint Director to head the Anti-Corruption Head-Quarter (AC-HQ) Zone, dealing with the most important VIP and super VIP cases. This zone was thought to be the flagship of the CBI, so the great responsibility had been placed on my shoulders.

The cases were really sensitive and super sensitive. The Jain Hawala case was already being investigated as part of another case under Terrorist and Disruptive Activities Act (TADA). Four cases were pending against V. Krishnamurthy who had held important assignments like Member Planning Commission, Secretary Heavy Industries, Chairman Maruti Udyog, Chairman Steel Authority of India Ltd. (SAIL) and Chairman Bharat Heavy Electricals Ltd. (BHEL). The most serious of the cases against him was regarding the allegations of having received millions of dollars as kickbacks abroad. At the first stance, it was clear that several spokes were being put in the wheels of investigations and it did not take long to sense that efforts were already on to scuttle the case.

In May 1994 the investigations of Assam Letter of Credit (LoC) Scandal were also assigned to this zone. The evidence very soon led the investigations to the door of the then Assam Chief Minister, Hiteshwar Saikia, making addition to the list of important cases.

I soon realised that in CBI dealings were not equitable. It was dealing differently with people in power, people not in power and people out of power or favour. The CBI was functioning like any other department of the government, carrying out executive commands rather than working impartially and fearlessly upholding the Law of the Land.

The feeling became stronger with every passing day, and so also the struggle against the powers that be, ultimately culminating in my ouster. It was an unprecedented offence in the annals of the CBI to proceed against the big VIPs in power, whereas, my team and I were going ahead against the highest possible VIPs, not sparing anyone. Strong action against even the worst accused is foreign to Indian ethos. It constitutes deviant behaviour on the part of a civil servant and is almost forbidden if the accused happens to be from higher echelons of society. My insistence on complete investigation, that too with searches against these privileged people, was enough to activate the powers to get rid of a nonconformist like me, notwithstanding whatever the mundane law books may say about upholding laws, enforcing them impartially and equitably.

I committed yet another audacity at the CBI conference, held from 20th to 22nd November 1996, by advocating for complete truth and transparency in the functioning of the CBI and brought the subject of complete investigations against the high and mighty in the open. The very mention of these two-fold officially paraded virtues of Truth and Transparency, was considered a sacrilege when brought into the open discussions. Director Joginder Singh flew into an uncontrollable rage at the conference itself. The next day I brought these very issues into the focus in the same conference before the then Prime Minister Deve Gowda (issues such as the CBI's failure to investigate the "Big" people: how CBI skirted and scuttled investigations, and how so many scams remained uninvestigated and consequently unsolved), Gowda also took offence at such a plain talk. In his speech, he decried all efforts at fighting corruption by all concerned, by the Lokayukt, The Lokpal, the Judiciary and predicted that Judicial activism would make no difference to control the corruption. He emphasised that no country in the world was free from corruption and that no efforts would be successful in fight against it.

Just four weeks later, on 23rd December, I knew that my repatriation had already been approved by the Appointments Committee of the Cabinet (ACC) in utter disregard of rules, procedures, and safeguards that our constitution and legal system are ostensibly supposed to uphold. It became widely known in CBI as well and demoralized the CBI cadres dinning the eternal message into their ears that respect the privileged and do not be stupid to touch those who are "beyond the laws".

The question foremost in my mind has always been, how this nation can effectively control corruption at high places. I had always wished to be in such a position as could enable me to fight and wage a war against it. The opportunity to fight came in April 1994 and it was all over in December 1996 in less than three years! I had gone to the CBI not for a job but with a mission, and that was all over!

The society has constantly been in turmoil; the youth has been directionless; the corruption has stunted their growth and ensured their unending exploitation. The number of people below the poverty line has always been very high. In a rating of 223 countries on index of Human Development, as compiled by World Bank in its Development Report, 2000-2001, the position of India is 153. All sorts of countries, big or small, European, Asian or African, with hot climate or cold climate, communist or capitalist, are placed above us. We keep on picking up various lame excuses suitable for each occasion, whereas the world keeps marching forward very fast. The nature has blessed us with its richest bounties, but it is unfortunate, that we continue to slog in poverty. Our performance, both in the fields of agriculture and industry, is much below the world standards. The costs of all our products are high, so our wares are not competitive in the international market.

Reasons are not far to seek. Our farmer does not get inputs like water, seeds, fertilizers, insecticides and the pesticides in time and of requisite quality. Whatever inputs he gets, are priced very high and still there is always a question mark on their quality. The common thread running through all these factors is greed, which is defined as corruption when indulged in by officials and black marketing, tax evasion etc., when indulged in by non-officials.

The agencies to enforce laws do exist with CBI at the head, but are normally dormant and turn inert when it comes to taking action against the powerful sections of the society. They are the people who by and large corner the resources by exploiting and bleeding the nation. This privileged section loots its own countrymen in various ways and spends luxuriously both at home and abroad.

Mahatma Gandhi was extremely worried and had lamented about this corrupt mindset as early as 1921 and his lament grew sharper and more frequent after independence. He was pained at the corruption of the members of the Interim Government before Independence. In his address to Constructive Works Committee on 12.12.1947, Gandhiji said[1], "...Today politics has become corrupt. Anybody who gets into politics gets contaminated...But in general there is so much corruption today that it frightens me." Every word of concern that worried the father of our nation, has come true.

In 1951, Government of India appointed a committee under the chairmanship of A.D. Gorwala to took into why Indian administration was not able to implement various programmes efficiently and effectively. The committee after deliberating, amongst other factors, found corruption ruling the roost and being perpetuated by the higher ups culminating into a nexus between the Politicians, the Businessmen and the Bureaucrats. The committee noted[2], "Dangerous as the association of politics with wealth is at any time, it becomes particularly dangerous when wealth takes the form of large industrial and speculative interests...." Regarding public servants, the committee perceived even the entertainment degenerating into corruption.[3]" It is not unusual to find in the central capital and elsewhere, public servants being entertained by individuals or firms who have, have had, or are likely to have, request to make to them. There is no special reason why such entertainment should be accepted." The committee felt that those who spend either on politicians or on civil servants will surely extract returns in different forms. The committee quoted the Hyderabad Economic Committee Report,[4] "the rich man will not pay unless he gets some return, and the poor, except under duress."

The CBI – as Chief Enforcement Agency

The boldest and the most serious attack on corruption that was ever mounted in this Republic was with registration of the Jain Hawala Case on 4th March 1995, by the CBI, against S.K. Jain, his brothers and 115 others named in their diaries, under the directions of apex court, which itself monitored the investigations directly. It roused great public expectations and the citizen, who had so far viewed the corruption at high places with helpless abandon, suddenly saw himself as a part and parcel of the crusade. But everything fell back to square one when the charges against the accused persons started falling in 1997 on the ground that there was no evidence and evidence of the diary entry was not admissible. The nation settled back, but with intense despondence that nothing could be done in this country against this deeply entrenched vice amongst the big.

The post-mortem began in the aftermath of the Hawala case. Various viewpoints were expressed leading to several misconceptions, that the case failed because of lack of evidence, that CBI found no evidence but chargesheeted the accused persons under pressure from judiciary that was breathing fire, that there was terrorist angle impinging on national security which was not looked into and that the FERA (Foreign Exchange Regulation Act) violation angle was suppressed.

I headed the team investigating the Hawala case from May 1994 when I joined CBI to June 1995 when I was removed from the scene. I discovered that in the CBI, naked uncovering of facts was neither acceptable, nor would it be tolerated beyond certain limits. The unwritten rule was that certain persons were not to be touched and if the line of investigation reached them, the investigations should be diluted, diverted or dropped and scuttled in due course. As per routine, if during the course of investigations, the name of the Prime Minister or the Union Ministers cropped up, the investigations would just be stopped or deflected without naming them. Such cases could be registered initially as the names of such dignitaries did not occur till then, but sprang up later on. The CBI felt shy of fighting corruption at high places, though it had the requisite skills, but it lacked the mental make-up, direction, courage, guts or the will. The CBI top brass was *ipso facto* seized with this mindset.

The mindset of the administration in general and enforcement/investigation agencies in particular, is that select the victim down the line, follow him up and spare the higher sections. This mindset, coupled with our social and sociological attitudes on corruption, has perpetuated this chronic evil. The corruption in its train has ushered in other related evils of smuggling, black-marketing, theft, pilferage, tax evasion and mis-appropriation, creating black or the hush money, a substantial portion of which is sent abroad, giving rise to hawala transactions and fuelling a parallel economy.

When I took up the fight against the powerful and the corrupt, I found enough dedicated personnel in the CBI, eagerly waiting only for the clarion call. The fair and fearless investigators of my team had the audacity to record the name of the ruling Prime Minister P.V. Narasimha Rao, in the statement of S.K. Jain (the main accused in the Hawala case). I pressed for investigating the role of the then PM in the scam, but was prevented from and punished for straying into the forbidden territories.

Both, my deputy and I, were removed from investigation of the Hawala case in a span of six weeks and that was the turning point in the investigation of the scam. It was a foregone conclusion in July 1995 that the scam would be scuttled. I wrote accordingly to Rama Rao, the Director, CBI, on 1.8.1995 (Annexure A).

Interestingly, the fight against corruption at high places has been carried out successfully in several other countries against the powerful persons. In his book, Chandan Mitra, Editor of the daily *The Pioneer* states[5] that nine out of fifteen Prime Ministers of Japan between 1955-93 were forced to resign on charges of corruption. He further states that in Italy trial of VIP cases is telecast, so that people could witness and assess for themselves in what hands they have placed their destiny. When it thus becomes a public spectacle, it acts as a deterrent for those in power. At one time four former Prime Ministers of Japan were in jail and similar was the fate of four former Executive Heads of Government of Italy. President Nixon was brought down on his knees and eased out for a cover up of corrupt electoral practices, but the feudal mindset in this country forbids any action against the higher ups.

This book is an attempt to show that while corruption has become all pervasive and is controlling our destiny in various fields, the agencies entrusted with the task of fighting it, shy away from performing their duties in a truthful and a transparent manner, especially when it comes to taking action against the people at the top. The mindset of the people, their attitudes towards this malady and also the mindset of various denominations of personnel meant to check corruption has been highlighted in this book. The book also analyses what factors shape this mindset.

I have tried to trace the consequences of the malady and gauge the magnitude of black money/black economy from many angles, but all lead to a single conclusion that the size of black economy is much larger than the size of white economy and evasion of taxes is at least three times as compared to their actual collection. But for this ever mounting corruption, India would have been a rich and a flourishing country.

The detailed analysis of the existing conditions and the problem leads to the conclusion that it is only the firm enforcement of the law that can put the country back on track, as is also borne out by the experience of other countries, who were deep in the mire of corruption, but have fought their way out successfully basically by strong enforcement. It is a crime born out of greed and it is only the punishment that can check it.

The canvas of any fight against corruption has to be wide, as the problem has engulfed almost all the fields. So, the combat strategies stretch to diverse fields like political, economic, legal, administrative and constitutional. There has to be an all out war against this epidemic. Stray efforts or plugging of one hole here and there, cannot succeed as the web of corruption is very well spread and intricately interwoven carefully by the wise people as depicted by some poet beautifully in an Urdu couplet:

Gair Mumkin Hai Ki Halat Ki Guthi Suljhe
Ahle Danish ne Bahut Soch Kar Uljhai Hai

(It is impossible to get out of this mire, we have fallen in; the wise men have created these conditions after careful consideration)

I am not a pessimist and nor do I agree that it is impossible to measure up with the problem. The situation is extremely difficult as the corruption is threatening to tear the very fabric of the nation itself. All the more reason that we have to rise and fight this decay successfully, though the failure of Hawala case has cast a gloom, giving an impression that the fight is unequal and impossible. The book proposes to remove such misconceptions that have crept in, as details of investigations of Hawala and such other cases have always remained shrouded in mystery, as no one who had any authentic information has ever opened up. Though these secrets of yesteryears are now matters in public domain, but very few people know that evidences were deliberately not collected, thereby scuttling the Hawala scam itself. In the CBI, those who did not agree with the operation scuttle were removed, and the members of the remaining team were too junior, who finding themselves leaderless had no option but to fall in line and reconcile to the 'cover up'. I feel hurt for all those down the line, who were tirelessly associated with straight investigations and also had to participate in the operations for dismantling the case, which they had built bit by bit with their sweat and blood.

References

1. Gandhiji's address to the Constructive Works Committee on 12th December 1947.
2. Govt. of India, Report on Public Administration by A.D. Gorwala, 1951, Chapter IV "Integrity" page 26.
3. Govt. of India, Report on Public Administration by A.D. Gorwala, 1951 Chapter IV "Integrity" page 27.
4. Govt. of India, Report on Public Administration, by A.D. Gorwala, 1951 Chapter IV "Integrity" page 27.
5. *"The Corrupt Society"* by Chandan Mitra (page.38).

2

How the 'Jain Hawala Case' was Scuttled

The notorious Jain Hawala Case was an offshoot of a terrorist funding case registered by Delhi Police. It started with the arrest of one Ashfak Hussain Lone, a link in the terrorists' chain, engaged in funding Kashmir terrorism. The preliminary interrogation revealed that they received money from abroad through a hawala dealer Shambhu Dayal Sharma located in Delhi, from whom they collected it as per arrangements made by their principals and the hawala kingpins abroad. From Delhi, the members of terrorist organisation remitted the same to the valley. On finding terrorist and Hawala links, the case was transferred to CBI, which conducted raids on the said Hawala dealer and discovered some names, including that of J.K. Jain, who was getting money through hawala channels regularly. Amongst others, a raid was organised on the house of J.K. Jain on 3rd May 1991, from where assets worth Rs. 58 lacs in Indian rupees, 2000 Pound Sterling, *Indira Vikas Patras* worth Rs. 10.50 lacs were recovered. In addition certain diaries were also taken into possession.

The diaries mentioned some abbreviations alongwith some figures against each of them. Subsequent interrogation revealed that J.K. Jain maintained the diaries on behalf of his employer S.K. Jain and these contained the abbreviated names of VIPs including the serving as also the former Ministers and bureaucrats. The figures against each name indicated the amount of money passesd on to them by S.K. Jain. The VVIP names caused a stir in the CBI as also in the Government. Initially, the investigators proposed to send the diaries to Enforcement Directorate (ED) as they felt it was basically a case under FERA, but the then Deputy Inspector General (DIG) in charge of the case did not agree and retained the file. Further complications were created when it was alleged that the DIG was blackmailing the Jains and extorting money from them under the threat of booking them also under TADA. He was allegedly caught redhanded taking a bribe of Rs. 10 lacs for not implicating them. The diaries were treated as case property in this case against the DIG and were sealed as part of this new case. The diaries were thought to be very hot and explosive substance, so the concerned officers heaved a sigh of relief when these were sealed.

However, subsequently the diaries were opened, copies were made and some of these came in circulation amongst the elite of the capital, particularly the persons whose names were supposed to figure in these diaries. When K Vijaya Rama Rao took over as director CBI in July 1993, the copies of diaries were already in circulation. Since no attention was paid to this case for full two years, the director took serious note. On seeing the big names, he transferred the investigation to AC HQ-Zone that basically dealt with the VIP cases. However, no separate case was registered at that time as only the hawala angle, which was an offence under FERA, was being looked into as part of Terrorist Funding case registered initially by the Delhi Police under TADA. The investigations were taken up inside the country as also abroad for the FERA aspect. However, the basic questions remained unaddressed that (i) whose money it was that the Jains were distributing (ii) wherefrom and how did it originate and (iii) what channels did it follow.

Meanwhile, two journalists namely Vineet Narayan and Rajinder Puri filed petitions under Public Interest Litigation (PIL) in the Supreme Court alleging that, since big names including union ministers and also a former prime minister were involved, so the CBI had not investigated the diaries fully during the last two years.

When I landed in the CBI at the end of April 1994, investigations abroad in Hawala case, as part of the TADA case, were in full swing as the DIG was already on a visit abroad and returned towards the end of May. He established the channels of movement of money up to the hawala bankers in the UK and also traced the mechanism how the hawala money moved into India. He could not proceed any further as the hawala bankers did not cooperate and did not give full details or particulars of transactions/remittances, though they promised to provide some more information sometime later after their mutual consultations. However, it became clear that in the UK, sending money through private bankers was not an offence. Such bankers in the UK accepted money and remitted it to Dubai through normal banking channels. In Dubai, this money entered the empires of various Mafia Dons through these lawful banking channels. They took this money, purchased gold, smuggled the same into India, and the sale proceeds were utilised for paying the persons for whom the money was intended by various hawala bankers stationed in the UK or in other countries and dealing with India. We waited for more information to come from the UK, but nothing was received in the next few months that followed. However, the channel through which the money flowed, was identified.

By September 1994, the Supreme Court was taking CBI to task, which compelled us to go deep into the other two questions. After delving deep, it was revealed that Hawala, an offence under FERA, served only as a mechanism to channelise and remit the hush money to India. The investigations revealed that the Jain brothers had official dealings with various departments of the government and in particular the public sector undertakings mainly of the power and steel. There were reasons to suspect that the money was being passed on account of kickbacks, arising out of the favours shown in various projects or economic deals by the officials and the politicians holding high offices. We could now see a whole river of corruption flowing underneath the apparent thin cover of Hawala. Towards the end of 1994, perception of the case in the CBI underwent a sea change and the corruption aspect appeared more glaring and important.

Our conviction that the diary entries were true was strengthened by examination of some of those whose names appeared in them as all the persons whose names occurred in the diaries were examined by CBI teams in September-December, 1994, under orders of the Supreme Court. Some of them admitted having received money from Jains, though some like Sharad Yadav tried to mislead the CBI. His name appeared in Jain's Diaries as a recipient of Rs. 5 lacs. While admitting receipt, he introduced a number of variations. First of all, that the amount received by him was Rs. 3 lacs and not Rs. 5 lacs. Secondly, he stated that one R.L. Jain accompanied by Chiman Bhai Patel, one time Chief Minister of Gujarat had given him that money. Though Sharad Yadav made lots of publicity about the transaction, but at the same time planted material contradictions. R.L. Jain was not traceable in the establishment or among the friends and relations of S.K. Jain during the last few decades and Chiman Bhai Patel had died by the time Sharad Yadav was making the statement. Second, whereas the diaries disclosed an amount of Rs. 5 lacs, he had stated to have received only Rs. 3 lacs. Under these circumstances the so-called admission or confession led us nowhere. It remained a usual cock and bull story normally given out by any ordinary criminal as an alibi at first instance that breaks during interrogation. However it did create the public perception that Sharad Yadav had admitted receiving the money and that he dared the CBI, but still the CBI did nothing. Arvind Netam, in particular, was absolutely true to his word, who right from the beginning admitted that he received Rs. 50,000 for fighting elections, which according to him every politician did. I was personally aware that he was advised by his advocates not to make such a statement, but to my knowledge he remained steadfast till the end that he would not state anything, which was untrue. His statement, apart from some other corroborative evidence, determined our thinking that the diary entries were true and were decoded correctly, by and large. A large number of politicians did not deny the receipt of money while informally chatting with the CBI teams. They, in routine, advanced a justification for collecting such money for their election and other political expenses. Though they justified the same as legitimate activity, but at the time of formal recording of their statements, they either resiled or twisted the facts, as was narrated by the teams sent for recording the statements of those whose names occurred in the diaries. Some of them showed signs of great nervousness but that could not constitute evidence.

The public sector undertakings of the power and the steel sectors were asked for the details of projects/works allotted to or executed by the Jains. The records of all such projects, in which it was known that Jains had participated, were called for. The record of Kawas Power Project became available immediately. While looking into this project, motives could be seen and attributed to the allotment process. As the date for our appearance in Supreme Court was drawing closer, I proposed registration of a P.E. (Preliminary Enquiry) under the Prevention of Corruption Act. Since we had still not zeroed in on any individual, the proposal was to register a general P.E. against all the persons whose names figured in the diaries, so that the enquiry could be converted into a Registered Case (RC) in respect of the person against whom evidence could be uncovered. But Rama Rao was not in favour of an omnibus P.E. He wanted a P.E. or even a First Information Report (FIR, also referred to as R.C.) to be registered against certain officials only, in order to satisfy the Supreme Court, leaving out the politicians even though they also fell in the category of public servants, whom he did not want to touch. Apart from discrimination, right from the beginning, it appeared to be a strategy to sweep the case under the carpet instead of embarrassing the VIPs.

This led to a stalemate which continued till early January as no consensus could be arrived at in the various meetings held in this context. As the day of appearance in the Supreme Court was approaching fast, the director agreed for registration of a PE against all, whose names were mentioned in the diaries. This was a departure for the director from his earlier stand a few weeks back when I had proposed action under PC Act. He had remarked, "Lall, do not add more complications, the case is already complicated." But now there was no way out. Utimately, the CBI registered a preliminary enquiry on 13th January, 1995, to look into the corruption aspect. Since enquiries had revealed no terrorist angle in the dealings of Jains, as such the terrorist part was dropped and preliminary enquiry concentrated on corruption aspects basically.

After attending the Supreme Court on 16th January, we plunged straight into the records to find out and collect evidence. Very little time was available as the Supreme Court had fixed the next review on 6th March. They were told that massive records had to be examined for which the allotted time of seven weeks was not enough, but the court did not budge.

The records were yet to be collected from various units and ministries. Collecting records is a long and a laborious process, as each page has to be marked, counted and receipted, whereas we had to receive files running into lacs of pages. All the same, the records started pouring in. During examination of the record, we could readily locate bungling in one project i.e. Kawas. The available manpower was working day and night. Repeated requests for more hands were turned down on grounds of general shortages, though the director promised more Investigating Officers (IOs) as soon as he could manage. But the fact remains that not even one extra IO was provided for such an important and a high profile case. Per force the examination of record had to be slow as compared to the immensity as well as the urgency of the task.

As March drew closer, the director became restive, so was I, but one cannot take or propose action without the requisite evidence. The director revived his earlier suggestion to convert the PE into a registered case against a few officials and thereby close the PE. I realised why director was not providing any extra staff, though it was a fair routine in CBI for all the major and the important cases, whereas Hawala Case was both. It was obvious that he did not want detailed enquiries and investigations, but I vehemently opposed catching the small fries alone. Moreover I wanted conversion with some solid grounds in hand; otherwise the Supreme Court and the Press would tear us asunder. Further if a case had to be registered without full verification, it had to be against all, like the PE. Technically, the court could still question us why we did not register the case at first instance itself. Since the director did not want to name any public servant from amongst the politicians in the registered case, he suggested an alternative that the conversion of the PE into RC could wait, but the Jains could be arrested in the meantime, to satisfy the Supreme Court. I again brought to his notice that in the FERA case we had reached a dead end. Further, since the Jains had joined investigations whenever called for in that case, arrest under FERA was not possible.

Moreover that was a closed chapter. For corruption, in PE no one could be arrested. So his arrest or that of anyone else had to wait till conversion of the PE into an RC.

The month of March had set in. My team and I were literally working round the clock, chasing an unrealistic target. We could now clearly see through corruption, but that did not amount to evidence. We had some evidence only in the Kawas project. This was a cause of worry for all of us. The director summoned me on the evening of 4th March to his residence. It was a holiday, but I had just returned from the office. Immediately I made for his residence where N N Singh, Special Director CBI, was also present. We all agreed that the direction of the case had to be finalised that very day, as the Supreme Court would convene for this case on 6th March and before that we had to take some action. The director again suggested registration of a case against officials as the only way out, but I put forth my reservations and insisted that we had to be equitable to all, and that like the PE, should register case against all. Though the ideal course of action was to register cases as and when the evidence was found against anyone, but the Supreme Court was breathing fire for inaction since 1991, failing that the CBI could not explain. As such, showing action was CBI's compulsion, but discriminatory treatment with any category was unacceptable to me under any circumstance. Ultimately the director reconciled for an omnibus case against all and asked me to draft an FIR and show the same to him.

Now that the decks were clear for registration of a criminal case under Prevention of Corruption Act. Amod Kanth, the DIG, and M P Singh, the SP, were in their office in Lok Nayak Bhawan as they had been asked to remain available. I rushed there, took them into confidence and impressed upon them that this was the only way out. After initial reservations on principle to register a case prematurely, they agreed when told that nobody was being left out. I asked Amod to dictate the FIR and after vetting it, I took it to Rama Rao who approved the same. Since the preliminary enquiry was converted into a general registered case against all the 115 accused persons, the FIR so registered could not be specific. It could not be called a good FIR, but we were helpless and had to register the same in the present form, which was a little premature and also too general. However, it cleared all the hurdles for arrest of Jains. We had enough material to commence their questioning as *prima facie* links had been established in some projects in public sector and suspected kickbacks. Further their searches were expected to throw up more material to confront them.

Out of the 115 names in the diaries, some were of the members of the family of S K Jain, but most of the names as recorded were those of the ministers, the MPs, and the officials from the Government as also from the Public Sector Undertakings (PSUs). Some of the names looked insignificant. Further, *prima facie* it was clear that (a) it would not be possible to collect evidence against all; (b) the charge of corruption would not stand against those who were not public servants; (c) the FERA aspect had already been looked into the details and we had reached a dead end.

Following the registration of the FIR late in the evening of 4th March, we proceeded to arrest Jains. S K Jain was not in Delhi. We learnt that he would return the next day. Since he had been cooperating in investigations whenever summoned, a message was left at his place to get in touch immediately on his arrival. However, on his arrival on March 5th from Bombay (Mumbai), he was picked up from Delhi airport itself. J K Jain was also arrested at that very time. We had already prepared detailed plans for searches at his premises, which were put into operation immediately after the arrest of Jains'.

The interrogation of both S K Jain and J K Jain started immediately, but intense questioning could commence only from 8th March. Though they were remanded to police custody on the 6th March, we could be free from appearance in the Supreme Court hearing and the extensive searches on the 7th March only. The Jains were not communicative to begin with, till the bail petition filed on their behalf was dismissed. However, they started opening up from the 10th March and became communicative on 11th March and S K Jain broke down finally on 12th when confronted with facts as against his responses and in particular the contradictions in his own statements. It was at this stage that he revealed facts about the big wigs and also told us about the mechanism and routine, how they were managing sanctions of various projects at inflated rates, getting kickbacks and then distributing money amongst various persons.

S K Jain disclosed that he, in collaboration with public servants and certain others including foreigners like Gerni, Quattrochi etc., worked out the arrangements. S K Jain was to look after the official side and the ministers and to get various projects cleared at official and ministerial level, and Quattrochi was to work at the highest political level i.e. the Prime Minister's Office (PMO) and the P.M. They collaborated for NHPC Power Projects at Dulhasti and Uri, NTPC Kawas project and a few more. Sanjay Kapoor reproduced statement of S K Jain made to CBI in his book *Bad Money, Bad Politics* as early as April 1996. For benefit of the reader the same appears at Annexure B.

During the course of his interrogation Jain also stated that after the seizure of diaries, he had passed on Rs. 3.55 crores to P V Narasimha Rao (PVNR), who took over as Congress President after Rajiv Gandhi's death on 21.5.1991 and subsequently as Prime Minister of India. Jain gave detailed description of how on the direction of PVNR, the money moved on his account, through Capt. Satish Sharma, Chandraswami, etc. He also narrated the details of how and where a small part of the money was placed in the cupboard in a room of his (PVNR) residence as directed by PVNR himself. Jain also described how Rajiv Gandhi was paid Rs. 10.5 crores as kickbacks out of the scheme for modernisation of Durgapur Steel Plant through Capt. Satish Sharma with instructions to show it in the name of Lalit Suri.

Though he had not included it in his formal statement, Jain confided otherwise that the foreign companies were quoting for the projects (particularly the power projects) with certain amount of premium that could extend even upto 100 per cent sometime. A total of ten per cent would be passed on as kickbacks. Jain revealed that he got three per cent and Quattrochi retained the remaining seven per cent in various power projects for which he and Quattrochi worked together. Out of his three per cent, he was to pay to various public servants, both ministers and officials. According to him, later on his share in Kawas project was however pegged at Rs. 10 crores only. Durgapur Steel Plant Modernisation Project remained separate for which he was to receive a fixed amount of Rs. 15 crores. He was to collect something like Rs. 85 crores through all these deals; he had collected a part of it and the rest was still to flow in. The projectwise kickbacks were something as follows:

Table: Projectwise Kickbacks

Sr. No.	Name of Project	Project cost Rs. in crores	Partners	Paid in India/ Abroad	Jain's share Rs. in crores
1.	Uri Hydro Power Project	1200 crores	Quattrochi	Abroad	36 crores
2.	Dulhasti Hydro Power Project	800 crores	Quattrochi	Abroad	24 crores
3.	Kawas Thermal Power Project	500 crores	Revvilon	Abroad	15 * crores
4.	Durgapur Steel Plant Modernisation Project			India	15 crores
	Total				90* crores

* The amount was subsequently pegged at Rs. 10 crores; the total amount due also fell to Rs. 85 crores.

As disclosed by Jain, the arrangements for payments to be received from abroad were worked out in details. Quattrochi had introduced Jain to one Amir Bhai, a Hawala kingpin of Bombay (Mumbai). Amir Bhai worked for Quattrochi and was assigned the task of transferring the amount, as and when asked for by Jain, from abroad through Hawala channel and deliver the same to Jain in Indian rupees. S K Jain put J K Jain in touch with Amir Bhai, who then managed the show. He would collect the money as per requirement and would distribute it as per orders and authorisation of S K Jain.

He also disclosed that apart from passing on the kickbacks out of the commission for various projects, sometimes he provided only the services to senior politicians and senior civil servants for transfer of their own funds from abroad. In such cases he worked only as a conduit and a cutout between the hawala agent Shambhu Dayal Sharma and the politicians or the civil servants, but he denied charging any commission for such transfers, as that was *infra-dig* for him. This sounded convincing as his ambitions were very high and he could not stoop so low as to act as a commission agent. He was only providing a service for their own money or distributing the kickbacks on a pre-agreed formula or was only obliging the politicians as also the senior bureaucrats. Some of the payments had some *quid pro quo* or some expectation for future, but some others were just given, which in lighter vein, he termed as tips to senior civil servants or to politicians that if they requested for a lakh or two, he did not say 'no' to anybody as it was just a peanut for him and sometime he did not even record the paltry amounts in the diary.

During his interrogation he was confronted with certain names, which did not fit into the facts of the case as the payments were heavy but there appeared to be no *prima facie quid pro quo* or reason or rationale for the same. These names were PSB, initially decoded as Prakash Singh Badal; PB as Pawan Bansal and V K as V K Jain or Vijay Karan. Both of them did not know anything about P S Badal and Pawan Bansal i.e. how the two appeared, where they lived in Chandigarh and Delhi or exact description of the place where the money was given to them. After sustained interrogation and when confronted with the contradictions, the Jains opened up and deciphered these afresh. Their new narration inspired our confidence as everything started falling into proper place. They confirmed that PSB stood for P S Bami, the then Chairman of NTPC; PB stood for Prakash Bhatia, the then General Manager of Durgapur Steel Plant, who with V Krishnamurthy and not Vijay Karan or V K Jain had awarded a contract for modernisation of the plant to Tiazapermo, a Russian firm, for the alleged consideration.

This made sense as the diaries had specific entries against VK with four payments, of which three of them had specific mention of 'Madras' 'Son' and 'Oberoi' against each. These respective payments had presumably been made there. V Krishnamurthy had link with Madras (now Chennai) and in Delhi, the office of his son used to be in hotel Oberoi, so it checked well *prima facie.* Bhatia was the General Manager of Durgapur Steel Plant and Krishnamurthy was the Chairman of Steel Authority of India Ltd. at that time when Durgapur Steel Plant was being modernised at huge costs that provided large potential for kickbacks. Jains received the instalment of Rs. 15 crores by way of kickbacks through a cheque from the Russian firm under the cover of payment for a consignment of some-cast iron equipment that was shipped from India and was to be shipped back in the form of components. The cost of the consignment was inflated on paper and as such the firm could send a cheque for Rs. 15 crores. Since it was a public sector undertaking of Russia, it could not make payments off the record, so this drama had to be enacted.

Jain's statement became clear only on March 12th. I asked for compilation of details of interrogation since the 10th March into a systematic statement so that it could be given to the director for his perusal. However, the director could not be informed at night. He was briefed early in the morning about the contents of Jain's statement. The director took exception on two grounds, first that he should have been informed the moment the PM's name occurred and second that the name of the ruling Prime Minister should not have been recorded at all. He was surprised how the name of the serving Prime Minister could be included as it was not a "done thing". Since we were dealing with allegations against the Prime Minister of the country, we subjected Jain to intense interrogation and tried to secure and scrutinise the veracity of the statement from all possible angles, but having done so and once we had satisfied ourselves, it did not even occur to me how could we leave out the PM's name as suggested by the director.

I repeatedly argued with the director that I had myself personally verified the names and the circumstances a number of times and felt convinced that *prima facie* the Jain was truthful. In any case, when an allegation was made and it was specific, it required verification. So there could be no question of excluding a name howsoever big it might be. I also offered that the director could himself interrogate the Jains on the morning of March 13th, as they could be produced in the court in the afternoon and we could also try for their remand to CBI custody for another day or two. The director chose not to talk himself, and asked me to re-verify. I interrogated them again and confirmed my earlier findings. Fortunately the Jains were remanded to CBI custody for another day and the director was informed that if he wanted, he could himself interrogate them and be sure, but he chose not to make first hand enquiries, probably because that will commit him, once the Jains made the same statement before him. He asked the Special director to speak to the accused.

Jains reiterated their earlier statement before the Special director N N Singh, but Rama Rao remained adamant commanding me to delete the PM's name from the statement of Jain. The director renewed the pressure everyday. He argued that like Harshad Mehta, Jain was also trying to use the big name as a shield, but I argued that as Investigators, my team and I were *prima facie* convinced of his statement and that Jain was not beating about the bush. Since he was so specific, the circumstances required thorough verification. His statement pertaining to Mathai, a representative of Alsthom, a foreign company collaborating with Jain, was completely verified and articles worth Rs. 26 lacs were fully recovered when his house was searched. Our conviction subsequently checked right as the time progressed and the records of projects were looked into. The director kept on pressing me, but there was no question of deleting the name of the PM as I was convinced that the basic problem of corruption was from the higher ups and also the problem was more serious when it concerned them for three reasons. First, the volume of transactions is too large with these people and second, it is not in our psyche and the mindset to check them for their wrong doings. "Implicating a serving PM is not a done thing", the director said, as if there is some sort of immunity to high ups or they enjoy some licence and that faithfully recording a big name amounted to implicating him. Third, they can exercise influence and scuttle any investigation or prosecution against themselves. Further, people believe that nobody would or can touch them. The director would not allow the case to proceed further despite the fact that Jains had given minute details of the rooms in PM's house as also of the cupboards in which money was placed by S K Jain on PM's bidding as per his statement.

Jain had further stated that he had visited the Prime Minister at his residence in the company of Chandraswami, half a dozen times and had gone to the house of the PM on his own three times. During one such visit, he had gone inside the rooms and placed money in a cupboard as directed by the PM himself.

Director's argument was that with these microscopic details on record, where was the question of any further verification. He posed a querry to me that if some evidence were found against the PM, did I propose to chargesheet him. He was dazed at my response that he will be investigated, searched if need be and chargesheeted if the evidence so warranted. He accused the investigating team of trapping the Prime Minister, thereby putting Rama Rao himself in an embarrasing position as he also belonged to Andhra and had served with the PM in that state when the latter was the State Chief Minister.

The stalemate had to be broken if the investigations were to proceed further. Ultimately a bargain was struck with the director that he would allow further investigations if the lines regarding details of the room and the cupboards along with the fact of Jain placing money in them were deleted from his statement. I consulted senior members of my team. There was unanimity that the valuable time was being wasted, causing irreparable damage to investigations as the very serious and significant disclosures made by Jains were not being followed immediately. We further concluded that the evidence was a fast evaporating commodity and the director was unrelenting. Under the circumstances, the only alternative to holding up the investigations was the deletion of these two or three lines, which at that stage would not make any substantial difference. One view was that this part could be added later on also in the supplementary statement of Jain. We had to prepare a report to be presented in the Supreme Court on the 27th March. The lines in dispute were deleted before going to Supreme Court, with the expectations that investigations would now be allowed. The director maintained a studied silence till 27th March 1995, but after that Rama Rao did a turnaround and did not allow even verification into the most verifiable facts against the PM.

I was back to square ONE, arguing again with the director that if verifiable facts like entry of Jain into PMO or PMH (Prime Minister's House) were not established in verification, obviously the allegations will lose their punch. In case it was verified that he entered the PMO or PMH that too alone as claimed by him thrice, the suspicion will be confirmed as he had no ostensible reason to be there. Again, certain other points, which were capable of verification, were discussed, but Rama Rao stonewalled all the efforts. He was too afraid of finding/recognizing any link between the PM and the Jains. He was very clear in his approach that PM was not to be investigated under any circumstance and that basically the name of the serving PM should not have been recorded in the statement.

The statement including the name of P V Narasimha Rao was put up before the Supreme Court on 27th March 1995, and the three Judges of the Court in the in-camera proceedings read the same. Immediately, the judges turned rather serious and tight-lipped. They commended the work done by the CBI and exhorted it to continue doing the same way. However, the mood of the court underwent a change a little later when it resumed open session and Anil Dewan, the counsel for petitioners, mentioned that N K Jain, brother of S K Jain, was still at large and had not been arrested. Without asking us any question or knowing our point of view, the court came down heavy on us for not arresting N K Jain and passed very scathing remarks pushing into the background all that we had achieved.

N K Jain had gone abroad prior to the registration of the present case. We had then fought against release of his passport, but the Sessions Court had rejected our request and allowed him to go, maintaining that no case was pending against him at that time. So, we could take the next step only after registration of this corruption case, but before that he left India. Under the law of the land, we could not restrain him in any manner. After registration of the case, despite being pressed for time, we still had deliberated on his case in our comprehensive discussions. We thought of a better alternate use that N K Jain had to us a little later. Police custody remand is for a limited period and the courts are rather miser in granting the same even in most pressing circumstances. Though results are demanded, but due facilities by way of remand etc., are seldom extended even as per barest requirements. In such a case like Hawala, with eyes of the world on us, the full remand for fourteen days was not granted. Police custody remand was given to us only for seven days when the accused were produced in the court of jurisdiction on March 6th. It is a fact that unless the accused person knows that he has to stay in custody for a little longer, he tries to bluff and thus while away the short time. In case of Jains, they were produced on the 6th March in the court, and were to be produced again on the 13th March, so there were six clear days for interrogation from the 7th to the 12th March. In between, their baii applications came up for which they had to be produced in the court, so another day was lost. As is usual, while in police custody, all VIPs and moneyed people feign illness and try to get admitted to hospitals. Jain was no exception. There were hardly three to four days when S K Jain was available and during that period also there was discontinuity.

In any meaningful investigations, time is of the utmost essence. The law needs to be so amended that during police remand, period spent in hospital or in illness, be excluded for the purposes of calculation of remand period. Only the actual period spent with police should be reckoned even if the so-called time of total custody extends beyond fourteen days. Secondly if the bail application is moved when the accused is in custody, let the advocates fight, the accused need not be produced in the court, though ideally once the custody has been granted, no bail applications should lie during the period so that meaningful investigations can be conducted.

Within the limited period available to us, we could not question the Jains on all the entries in the diaries. They were very reluctant to name any official as they thought that he would be vulnerable to the charges of corruption, the moment the reference to handling of money by him occurred, whereas the politicians were not considered open to such charges. It had taken a lot of time of the team and involved much effort and research to check up on each and every name. After painstaking interrogation we could get the names properly decoded in the Durgapur Steel Modernisation case as mentioned earlier. It was in this background that the payment of Rs. 10.5 crores to Lalit Suri could be explained and the whole affair of Russian firm Tyazapermo in Durgapur Steel Plant Modernisation was exposed. Quite a few names were still to be verified, but then the time of custodial remand expired. If only we had the Jains with us for another four to five days, which was permissible under the law, not only more and more names could have been clarified, but also the details of bungling in the Durgapur Steel Plant modernization and other issues would as well have been elaborated.

Imagine the contradiction in this case. Whereas the Supreme Court was breathing down our neck to produce results and was talking of all facilities being granted, the lower court by not allowing the full quota of remand as permitted under the law, exercised its discretion in the manner not conducive or helpful to investigation. Despite the interest evinced by the Supreme Court, the suspicion against this premier arm of Law, called CBI, was deep. However, during the interrogation of S K Jain and particularly when his remand to police custody was not extended, we had planned that let N K Jain return from abroad and we would arrest him later for eliciting authentic residue information when S K Jain or J K Jain could no longer be with us. The Solicitor General was informed of the position relating to N K Jain, in the court itself, but he would not argue on these lines. It was a terrible disadvantage to us as Solicitor General (SG) pleaded ignorance about the criminal law.

At that time, meetings with the Solicitor General (SG), Dipankar Gupta, were very frequent and were mostly held at his residence in the evening. One day, accompanied by Amod Kanth, DIG, and M P Singh, SP, I reached his residence early. The director and the Special director were also expected to join. Meanwhile preliminary discussions started and a request was made to him to argue as per our briefings and marshal all the facts that we told him. Amod entered into heated arguments with Dipankar Gupta, that if our point was not put forth before the court, we faced unnecessary censure despite working so hard and besides, the case would also suffer. I was watching their arguments with interest when Dipankar Gupta turned to me complaining about Amod and requested me to restrain him. But I also gently confirmed what Amod had said making it clear that if he did not know the criminal law, he should not have touched such a case even with a barge pole. When Dipankar Gupta was remonstrating with me that I was also taking the same line as Amod had taken, director and Special director CBI entered. Our arguments stopped, but after exchange of pleasantries when SG wanted to start discussions in the case, I pleaded to sort out the preliminaries first (that whether the case should continue with him or not). Gupta bulldozed and started the discussion. The issue got shelved there.

The N K Jain episode had very far-reaching effects on the investigation and the future course of action in this case, as after

March 27th all our energies were directed to fulfil court injunction for ensuring his presence in the court. S K Jain had disclosed the name of Bombay (Mumbai) based Amir Bhai as the Hawala kingpin and the direct agent of private bankers based abroad. It was he, who remitted money to Shambhu Dayal Sharma, the hawala sub-agent in Delhi. A DSP had been sent to Bombay (Mumbai) probably in the third week of March 1995 itself for immediate verification for nabbing Amir Bhai, but there the DSP learnt that Amir Bhai had died. However sources from Bombay (Mumbai) did not agree and informed that Amir Bhai was very much there the day the DSP had visited the city. The version of his death had been a plant.

Before March 27th, we could not concentrate much effort on Amir Bhai, as we were busy preparing a comprehensive report for the Supreme Court, which by itself was a long and laborious affair. We had planned to mount utmost efforts after 27th March to nab Amir Bhai who must have been complacent having misled the CBI. But on 27th March, once the Supreme Court dropped the bombshell with their scathing observations on N K Jain affair, we were shell-shocked and forgot about Amir Bhai and focused all our energy on N K Jain. In any case there was a terrible shortage of staff as not even one man had been added to the team (except for conducting searches) and I was trying to manage within the local resources of my zone. I functioned with scant staff in the whole of my zone and my DIG in charge of Hawala case was functioning in his range at below 50% of the investigative strength. Later, when the team was despatched, it drew blank. It was learnt that Amir Bhai had gone underground in the first week of April. He could not be traced for long thereafter. Had the team been dispatched on 28th of March, perhaps we could have found Amir Bhai and that would have explained lot of things at that stage. Somehow our expert opinion and the considered judgement of experienced investigators, all stood over-ruled because of the diffident Solicitor General and the CBI's reputation for inaction for long two years (for which my team was not responsible).

When the case was registered on the 4th March, the director had promised to provide more manpower and full support to me, but the position entirely changed after the 13th March when name of P V Narasimha Rao was included in the statement of Jain recorded under section 161 Criminal Procedure Code (CrPC), and subsequently I did not agree to delete the name of the serving Prime Minister from the statement. The director got terribly annoyed with me and deprived the investigations of the much-needed extra staff, which he had promised earlier.

The line of investigation was discussed with the director time and again and he put a complete block on any verification against the Prime Minister. When the point was pressed that it would amount to leaving out the biggest fish and would also draw adverse comments from the Supreme Court, he only advised to investigate others. He further advised to take up cases against those whose names appeared in the diary and who had accepted big amounts of money around a crore or so. I again raised the issue related to the three time recorded entry of Jain in the PM's house, when he is supposed to have gone there alone. If Jain was telling lies and no such entries existed, the PM could be given a clean chit and matter against him closed, but if further verifications/investigations appeared necessary, these should be taken up immediately as after a few months all efforts at that may become redundant as the evidence gets destroyed in due course in routine. Besides, the SPG and housekeepers of the PMH, in their false sense of loyalty, would destroy the papers, once they hear about investigations against the PM.

Unfortunately, that is the essence of loyalty in our country, even for government servants. Once they are posted with a VIP on his personal staff or security, they totally commit themselves to him to the extent that they start believing it to be their duty to hide his criminal deeds and even to share the pursuit of crime by the guarded VIP, which is beyond their brief. Even if some personnel may not associate with his criminal actions, they try to protect him by concealing all his faults as if it were part of their duty. Actually they should dissuade their subject from committing any crime, but still if he does indulge, they should report to the concerned authorities as their loyalty is to the State, to the country and to the department and not to this individual. Men and officers on duty with VIPs do not cease to be Police officers. They should report to the law whatever offence is committed in their view or to their knowledge by these protected persons; otherwise they are not doing their duty. They are responsible for guarding his person, his body and not his secrets especially when these have adverse bearing on the law of the land, or on nation's security.

Reverting to the main topic, I again argued that we could be accused of sparing the star VIP and that the PIL in the Supreme Court was for that very reason only. We should conduct complete investigations against all, in place of selective investigations, that too against a few at the lower levels.

I am not aware what subsequently happened after the Hawala case was taken away from me towards the end of July 1995 and whether any investigation was conducted against the PM or not, but even if some formal enquiries might have been made after six months or so at the PMO or the PMH, no evidence would have been available as could be foreseen by me as also the director or any other professional or even a layman of ordinary prudence. I could see through Rama Rao's clever move, but I was helpless though I knew that later on, evidence against the PM would never be found even if it had existed at that time.

During discussions on the line of investigation, it was amply clear that diary entries were only a starting point and did not constitute substantive evidence in law. Further evidence was required to be collected and linked, including *inter alia:*

(a) Evidence regarding payments of receipts,

(b) Evidence that the persons were public servants so that it could amount to an offence of bribery/corruption,

(c) It was realised that there could be no evidence of direct payment, so there should be some evidence regarding favours, motives, assets etc., so that case based on such circumstantial evidence, or of disproportionate assets could be made out for which searches of their business and residential premises as also bank lockers and accounts were necessary.

Further, I impressed upon the director that awarding work on projects and contracts was a daily routine. If there was a reason to suspect a person of accepting kickbacks or bribes in one deal, he could safely be presumed to be accepting such payments recurrently in others as well. Normally, whenever such money is received as a matter of routine repeatedly from various sources, it is converted into assets both movable and immovable, so there was a strong case for investigating their assets for locating disproportion.

In corruption cases it is rarely possible to have direct evidence of acceptance of money as Chankaya said, "Just as it is impossible to know when a fish swimming in water is drinking it, so it is impossible to find out when Government servants in charge of undertakings are misappropriating money." But at the same time if a fish overdrinks and gets too fat, it can be identified. Similarly the habitual takers can be identified through their fat assets, which become disproportionate to their ostensible earnings. So the only way to do justice was to look into the assets of the accused persons that too maintaining utmost surprise till such time the searches commenced, otherwise investigations would serve no purpose and all efforts would be futile.

The Branch moved a fresh part file in the last week of March 1995 seeking permission to call for the property and income tax returns from all the accused persons under section 91* of the Code of Criminal Procedure (CrPC). This provision empowers any court or an officer in-charge of a police station to command a person to produce such document as is in his custody. When the file duly endorsed by the DIG reached me, I felt that calling for such information at that stage would not serve any purpose, as they would all give details of their holdings that they had already declared for the Income Tax or some other purposes. Further, they would be cautioned and would remove all the moveable assets and destroy evidence about their holdings or of transactions

* **Section 91: Summons to produce document or other thing:** Whenever any Court or any officer in charge of police station considers that the production of any document or other thing is necessary or desirable for the purposes of any investigation, inquiry, trial or other proceeding under this Code by or before such Court or officer, such Court may issue a summon, or such officer a written order, to the person in whose possession or power such document or thing is believed to be, requiring him to attend and produce it, to produce it, at the time and place stated in the summons or order.

of all such *benami* or other tainted properties. To look into their assets effectively and without providing them the chance to conceal, surprise was absolutely necessary. As such I felt that we conduct searches at their premises under section 93** Cr PC after obtaining due permission of the competent court in place of calling documents under section 91 CrPC. I recorded over half a dozen reasons why it was necessary to conduct searches before asking for any document and how otherwise the advantage of surprise would be lost and the accused persons would get alerted. All the assets would disappear and evidence of all *benami* properties and transactions would evaporate. A notice of a few hours or a day is enough to do away with such evidence, but when it is a notice against which one can raise objections once or twice and gain time, all the evidence would have been removed. We would only draw a blank and it would amount to helping the accused.

In view of the above, I converted this file into a search file and recorded a long note in hand running into half a dozen pages examining legal and factual position and sought permission of the director for conducting searches. The permission was denied on the ground that we could not go in for searches without verification of their assets first.

I was firm on conducting complete investigations. Accordingly, I planned to collect evidence of massive assets, and come back soon with renewed request or even pressurize the director with the sheer weight of evidence. I put all the officers including all the four SsP from four branches under the charge of the concerned DIG to concentrate all their energies on the Hawala case at the cost of their other work. I formalized this arrangement in the first week of May 1995 by issuing formal orders. The director did not approve of this arrangement and conveyed his displeasure, but I knew that he could not stop me as that would expose him. The director's

** **Section 93: When search-warrant may be issued:** Where any Court has reason to believe that a person to whom a summons or order under section 91 or a requisition under sub-section (1) of section 92 has been, or might be, addressed, will not or would not produce the document or thing as required by such summons or requisition or it may issue a search-warrant; and the person to whom such warrant is directed, may search or inspect in accordance therewith and the provisions hereinafter contained.

stance was understandable, as he did not want to conduct any search that could lead to collection of incontrovertible evidence.

The officers started acting with a sense of responsibility. As expected, quick results started flowing in. On the basis of the information collected into the assets of various accused persons, I again sent the file recommending (as I recall) over a dozen names of higher ups for being subjected to searches. However, the request was again turned down, though this time there was no ostensible reason as *prima facie* the evidence was there. In bureaucratic circles it is defined as audacity if one refuses to understand the obvious hints. As a bureaucrat of ordinary prudence, I should have desisted from such persistent emphasis on evidence, legality, investigative practices and investigative ethics, when the boss had clearly given his mind ruling out the very idea of searches.

Besides the searches for unearthing Disproportionate Assets, I put officers from my other branches for detailed examination of certain projects wherefrom money for kickbacks had originated. The Kawas Power Project had already been examined. Projects like Uri and Dulhasti (in hydro power sector) and certain others like Auriya and Anta (in thermal power sector) were yet to be examined. Besides, we had detailed accounts of bunglings in Durgapur Steel Plant modernisation and the tie up with Russian firm in which the initial payment by way of kickbacks was received through a cheque for Rs. 15 crores.

In view of the mammoth task, that too of technical nature, I decided to constitute a committee of experts to examine all these projects in detail. CBI officers were to assist and facilitate such examination. Only the experts from the power sector could conduct in-depth examination of projects, locate the origins of kickbacks and exactly pinpoint where and how bungling had taken place, along with its mechanics and the extent. Further I intended to compare the costs and other details of projects being executed in India and abroad for which some preliminary information was available from published accounts. These could be fortified by requesting our mission's abroad or through the Interpol.

Incidentally, we had encountered the patent bungling in Kawas project in which one director of NTPC had pointed out at the time of processing, much before its allotment, that through the mechanism of malafide loadings, the country was being made to suffer a loss of Rs. 125 crores. Even when certain justifications were put before him, still an amount of Rs. 85 crores remained unexplained. An examination of projects would have exposed the extent to which the costs were hiked up. This possibly was the most important factor in escalating power rates, as fixed costs for generation of power for both hydro and thermal, skyrocketed artificially to the detriment of the country during the decades of eighties and nineties.

Basically there were three broad aspects to investigations: the first was to investigate the persons who were accused of having received the amounts and to establish their *quid pro quo* so that the cases of corruption could be looked into. This line of investigation would ultimately culminate in searches and lead to Disproportionate Assets as well. The second pertained to the inflated costs of projects, origin of funds for kickbacks and the related matters. The third aspect was to fix responsibility, both for omissions and commissions, so that in future such things would not recur and the nation would be saved from being bled so profusely.

There were basic differences in approach to the question of investigation. In order to achieve the above three-fold objectives, I wanted complete investigations, that too against all concerned including the higher ups as well, whereas the director wanted some nominal action against a few at the bottom. I wanted to conduct searches and to look into the Disproportionate Assets of the accused persons, but the director would not. I wanted to enquire into the allegations against the PM also, but with the director such talk was a taboo. The director circumscribed the scope of investigation to the diaries only, on the plea that the Supreme Court had assigned the investigation of only the diary entries to the CBI and the name of the PM did not figure in them. It was patently a wrong order, as whatever other issues may crop up during any investigation, are all looked into fully even if these are not related at all to the main issues. Later either separate chargesheets are filed or separate cases are registered.

The director ostensibly taking shelter behind the urgency necessitated by the Supreme Court pronouncements, pulling up the Bureau, wanted to put in a few chargesheets with or without any evidence. Initially he had wanted to file a few chargesheets against some junior officials as mentioned earlier, and hush up the case leaving out the big altogether, but that could not be done as I had resisted the same fiercely. At this stage I recalled that he had made the similar suggestion sometime in August 1994 when I was new to the CBI, for putting in a similar chargesheet against Krishnamurthy and close the case instead of pursuing detailed investigations in a dozen countries abroad. His ostensible reason for doing so was on the plea that the Government would never allow such investigations to continue and reach any final conclusion. Though I did not agree, nevertheless I recorded a note to this effect and asked the branch to examine it. The suggestion was examined on file in detail and was opposed by the branch, the SP, and the DIG. I endorsed the same and director had no option but to see and return the file. Similar was the suggestion this time too.

Subsequently, when the political circumstances underwent a change, he also changed his stance in the Hawala case and moved to a position of selective chargesheets and asked for chargesheeting six persons both from Congress and the opposition. Some names appeared to be cover up but others were of very prominent politicians led by L.K. Advani. His case was discussed in detail. I did not agree with chargesheeting him or any other at that stage as no evidence of corruption was on record as yet. Director asked me about my conviction if the money as mentioned in diaries was passed on to Advani. He tried to impress that if we were convinced that money was disbursed to him then we should file the chargesheet. In cases where there is a reason to believe that the crime was committed but evidence adequate for conviction cannot be collected, the cases are referred for final judicial adjudication as per the conviction of the I.O. In this case, no doubt, we were convinced of the veracity of dairy entries against all (including Advani) decoded by Jain during custodial interrogation, but till that stage, there was not an iota of evidence to link Advani with an offence under Prevention of Corruption Act. It appeared that Jain had arranged only the process of remittance for Advani and not tendered the money and much less for any *quid pro quo.* God knows what evidence could flow in the detailed investigations, but chargesheeting in anticipation at that stage might be anything else but was not legal and truthful.

Of course the names were of persons not in power then or who were even otherwise to be punished by the powers that be. The director thus laid the ground rules for investigations and propounded the following new principles opposed to the law, the rules, the procedures and the traditions governing the conduct of investigations. The selection of victims was finally to be made within these broad parameters:

(a) Confine investigations only to those names that were included in the Jain diaries. Inclusion of any fresh name in investigation, irrespective of any account or nature of evidence, was strictly prohibited.

(b) The diary entry be taken as substantive evidence.

(c) The so-called substantive evidence of diary entries be fortified with the evidence of knowing each other and if possible by proving that they were in contact.

The director wondered fondly, "What else is required to file a chargesheet?"

For collecting evidence on these lines he wanted the Personal Assistants (PAs), the drivers and the servants of the accused VIPs to be contacted and evidence of their masters knowing the Jains and meeting them was to be recorded to prove that they knew each other well. He ruled that once this evidence was collected, it would be enough for chargesheet. I put forward the following before the director for his consideration:

- That this line of reasoning was not correct as everyone whom the Jains had known or had been meeting, could not be chargesheeted as that by itself constituted neither any offence nor any evidence in a corruption case.
- That the evidence of the diary entries was inadmissible. It was only the starting point and that was all. Such diaries were not covered as ordinary books of accounts under the Evidence Act. This issue was examined in detail, time and again, by legal experts in the CBI, who had arrived at the same conclusion that the evidence of diaries could not be introduced under any of the sections of the Evidence Act. If on the above two counts any chargesheets were to be maintained, anyone can manage to show

familiarity with the targeted person in many ways. The technical advisor, dealing with accounts, had also conducted a detailed examination and as I recall, had held Jain diaries analogous to rough notes that did not constitute books of accounts. He had given this opinion in perhaps December 1994 or January 1995 and to my mind the same was included by the director in his progress report presented to the Supreme Court on 16th January 1995, but he changed his views later for tactical reasons suited to his game plan, patently against fair investigations.

- That, by leaving out those whose names were mentioned during interrogation, all principles of investigation were being flouted. All cases start from the tip, but in due course the iceberg is discovered, which has to be taken care of. It was argued before the director that the whole Hawala case itself was born during investigation of TADA case and all the offshoots of that case were being investigated, then how could revelations in these investigations be ignored. The director would entertain no such suggestions. Such pointless discussions, leading us nowhere, continued during April and May 1995, but no meaningful investigation or looking into Disproportionate Assets was allowed, though, I had written in my hand detailed lengthy notes in search files, bringing out clearly the legal position, making out a forceful case for searches, as also for unearthing hard evidence. The last such note was sent on 31st May 1995, when Amod Kanth put up the file just before laying down his office in the CBI.

Once during discussions, when the director was driven to a corner, he ruled that he was the director and the Supreme Court had charged him with the investigation and the case be investigated as he desired. As a last ditch effort I again requested him that whatever he wanted within the ambit of law and the facts of the case would be done, but first he should permit the collection of facts and not impose predetermined conclusions. That conclusion should follow the evidence and not the other way round, but the director was clear in his mind that once evidence was collected and was on record, option to hush up would more or less be closed. To overcome my insistence to stick to law and collect evidence apart from doing routine compilation of evidence and interrogation of aides, he allotted all those six names to my colleague Gopalachari for immediate chargesheet. The inadequacy of staff with me was the ostensible reason given by the director for shifting the investigations. He did not agree that the staff working with Gopalachari could have been transferred to me instead. Reasons were absolutely transparent. He had asked me to chargesheet them, but I had not agreed, as there was no evidence against them on record till then. Any conclusion or decision could be taken after investigation and I ruled out any investigation with predetermined conclusions.

After studying the case, Gopalachari came to me and confided that the director wanted immediate chargesheet in these cases, but there was no evidence. We exchanged notes and I told him not to bend under the pressure. I also narrated to him what had been going on between the director and me. He swore that he would not do anything wrong and not be a party to a chargesheet without proper evidence. A few days later he repeated that the director was pressing him very hard. Gopalachari was surprised that how could I resist director's adamant demeanour. After sometime, Gopalachari stopped coming to my room. I also realised that I was not welcome to his room either. So I guessed he was succumbing to the pressure.

The director gave me a rude shock by repatriating my able deputy Amod on 31st May 1995, the very day he completed his deputation period. In the CBI, the officers at that level are not normally repatriated immediately at the end of their tenure, as there is a provision for extension. When an officer is handling such an important and sensitive case, he is given any amount of extension in the CBI. Under such circumstances, as in this case, transfer or repatriation is indicative of malafide intensions on part of the seniors or of foul play on part of the officer. Amod was functioning as an absolutely straight and steadfast an officer. Three months before completion of his tenure, i.e. in early February my comments were asked whether I recommended his extension, which I did very strongly in February itself. Extension of tenure of officers recommended by a JD is a fair routine. But in this case when the file was still under process, came the 13th of March and director made up his mind as that was the day when the name of the PM was included in the statement of S.K. Jain. Further Krishnamurthy case re-enforced his resolve as would be seen in the next chapter. In order to break my team the director first repatriated Amod and then followed it up with easing me out of Hawala case four weeks later on 26th June 1995 when I was disassociated from the Hawala case.

As a shrewd operative, the director proceeded step by step. However, formally the charge of the case remained with me till the Supreme Court hearing on 18th July 1995. On the 19th he expressed his intention of relieving me of the charge and handing over AC-HQ Zone to Gopalachari. Director was always very cautious of press publicity and watched the reaction at every step i.e. after removing Amod, then after informally disassociating me from the Hawala case and then finally when I made no noise, he transferred me out of the HQ Zone dealing with Hawala investigations, making sure that it happened after the Supreme Court hearing the previous day.

The director attached more staff with Gopalachari and placed services of a full time DIG alongwith an SP, IOs and the supporting staff at his disposal, which was not done when I was handling the case, but now all the help was provided in order to expedite the bogus chargesheets as a part of the operation scuttle.

Reverting to the question of disassociating me from the Hawala case, the director on 26th June sidetracked both, the Special director and me. He asked the concerned SsP and the IOs to discuss and take orders from him direct. However SsP concerned after seeing the director, would come to me straight and report about their discussions with the director. On the morning of 28th June, the SP in charge of the Hawala case appeared to be visibly perturbed and shaken when he dropped in my office. He informed me that he and the IO of the case were summoned by the director to his office at 5.15 the previous evening and instructed them in detail for about three hours commanding them to prepare draft chargesheets by 10th of July i.e. in just two weeks. The SP was upset, as he was asked to frame chargesheets without any commensurate substantive evidence. He sought guidance from me. I was placed in a peculiar situation. No doubt, *de jure* I was still the supervisory officer of the case, but any instruction from me contrary to the command of director would have been infructuous as he was himself handling the case directly and giving instructions personally to my subordinates. Nevertheless, I felt it was worth reminding him of his commitment to truth and law and exhorted him not to deviate. I also impressed upon him that the director could not make many changes in the team and would have to bow to truth, if only he and others held their ground.

Special director N N Singh was getting disappointed and desperate with passage of every day. He was already bitter that instead of retiring on 30th April, Rama Rao got extension in service by an year, thereby depriving Singh of his rightful promotion as director. This was compounded when Rama Rao ignored him in the prestigious Hawala case. By May he started criticising the director and by June his tirade against Rama Rao turned bitter and abusive. He declared that he himself was against extension and would not accept any even if offered and on 1st January 1996, after his retirement on December 31, 1995, he would expose Rama Rao at a press conference and tell the country what wrongs CBI was committing under him. However, the director called N N Singh for discussion in the Hawala case one day sometime in second week of July. On return he told me how embarrassed he felt.

On 18th July 1995, the Hawala case was fixed for hearing. The director asked N N Singh and Gopalachari to accompany him. I was not asked. I was now expecting my removal any time from this seat. It came immediately after the Supreme Court hearing. Next morning the director called me and discussed the Hawala case. He discussed various possibilities in final disposal of the case and in particular the possibility of chargesheets. Again the same very issues and the arguments were repeated. I held my firm ground and emphasised that, if there was enough evidence for chargesheeting these accused persons, the searches were a must when their assets had even been verified to be disproportionate during the preliminary verifications. I was surprised why at all he was seeking my opinion at that late a stage when he had cast me aside for all purposes so far as the Hawala case was concerned. Perhaps, he was trying to know if the threat of impending transfer had softened me down or perhaps it was his own guilt that he was rationalising, knowing fully well that no justification could be possible.

During one such discussion earlier, I had raised the case of a cabinet minister whose name had occured in the Hawala case and his assets as per initial verifications were reported to be running into many crores of rupees, but still investigations into his assets were not being allowed. Rama Rao immediately pulled out a folder from his briefcase and ridiculed me that he also had the details of the minister's assets that were worth Rs. 200 crores. I was shocked. I asked him what prevented the chief of the premier institution of this nation from registering a formal case and proceeding with investigations? Rama Rao betrayed nervousness. In his excitement and to counter my point, he had inadvertently mentioned about the assets of the cabinet minister. Soon he shot back, "I am not so stupid as to destabilise the union government. I have to see various angles including the standing of the minister vis-a-vis the PM, relations of the minister with 10 Janpath as also with the PM and then caste and communal considerations". Unfortunately, there could not be any straight action, as he had to weigh various political and other fallouts of the same. I was intrigued, why then he had collected the information at all. Incidentally, as per press reports the minister concerned was showing teeth to the Prime Minister. Whatever be the considerations, compulsions or strategies, to my mind it all amounted to cheating the country, which had entrusted such an onerous responsibility to us.

Ultimately Rama Rao concluded that our differences were irreconcilable, so he had decided to transfer me out of the zone dealing with the Hawala investigations and the Krishnamurty case. He informed me that earlier he had thought of repatriating me back to my cadre, or sending me out of the CBI, but finally decided to post me as JD (North) in CBI itself. I accused him of not conducting complete investigations against all and of deliberately relying upon evidence of diary knowing fully well that the same could not be sustained in law. As it amounted to scuttling of the case that my team and I had built with our sweat and blood, I informed him that I would write to him and place the circumstances on record. The diplomat that he was Rama Rao profusely complimented my work and me saying "I respect you for your efficiency, honesty, straightforwardness and fearlessness, but if the director and the joint director disagree, the junior has to go." I was embarrassed and did not know how to respond, as in particular the first word is unusual in government service and that too for a junior. I somehow thanked him and left his office.

I wrote to Rama Rao on August 1st, 1995 (Annexure 'A') stating how he had scuttled the scam itself and betrayed the nation, ensuring that in future also no one will dare conduct fair and true investigations against the high and mighty of the land. I discussed the Hawala, the Krishnamurthy case and the Assam LoC scandal in particular and brought out how, not only in these cases but also in all big cases involving big people, complete and truthful investigations were avoided in the CBI. I also reminded the director that putting up the premature chargesheets in the Hawala case at that stage without evidence would be an exercise in futility as[1] :

"a) There was as yet no evidence regarding receipt of payments made to persons named in the Diary.

b) Evidence of motive was yet to come.

c) Evidence of favours shown and irregularities committed was coming in, which had to be developed and put in right perspective.

d) For unearthing further evidence and the assets, searches were also required, in particular, of the big fish as they were emerging the main culprits."

All this had no effect on Rama Rao, who later on filed chargesheets without fulfilling any of the above four conditions. It was a forgone conclusion that the chargesheets had to fall and these did fall ultimately.

To Rama Rao's suggestion of chargesheeting some small fries and closing the case, I conveyed to him[2] ".... this scandal originated from kickbacks which were created/forced on this country and were perpetuated by the big ones including the Ministers and the Prime Minister. Chargesheeting minor functionaries only, for receiving fringe benefits of the scam would amount to a cover up of the scam itself... I was searching for further evidence... regarding payments/receipts/motives/favours... establishing identity was a minor matter."

The massive potential of uncovering hard evidence was deliberately left untapped. I objected to the same[3] "....myself and Special director both were not prepared for pre-mature chargesheet and chargesheeting of small fish alone........"

The director laid down the following ground rules for chargesheets in this case in addition to similar rules prescribed for investigations as enumerated earlier:

a) Confine only to the names included in the diaries. It ensured that PVNR, the PM, whose name occurred in the statement of Jain and not in the diaries, would be left out without even the formality of conducting any verification. While investigating the case, even if there was massive evidence against a person whose name did not appear in the diaries, was not to be investigated. It was flagrant violation of prevalent law, legal processes and procedures.

b) Further, the director knew that if others were convicted at some stage, the PM would also have to be investigated as surely someone or the other would take up the matter in some court. So he re-oriented his strategy. At the first instance he had thought of chargesheeting a few minor functionaries, subsequently a few select persons and finally, to chargesheet all those whose names figured in the diary, irrespective of the evidence. In order to save the highest, he decided to file bogus, omnibus chargesheets bereft of any evidence against one and all knowing fully well that all these would be thrown out at the initial stage itself.

The Supreme Court order of 30th January 1996, introduced a further complication for the director, compelling him to chargesheet all in place of the strategy of selective chargesheets against the targeted individuals. The operative part of Supreme Court orders is reproduced[4].

> "However, if in respect of any such person the final report after full investigation is that no *prima-facie* case is made out to proceed further, so that the case must be closed against him, that report must be promptly submitted to this court for its satisfaction that the concerned authorities have not failed to perform their legal obligations and have reasonably come to such conclusion."

So, all the cases in which no chargesheet was to be filed, were to be put up for the review of the Apex Court, whereas the cases in which chargesheets were filed, would stand disposed, so far as Supreme Court was concerned[5].

> "In case of persons against whom a *prima-facie* case is made out and a chargesheet is filed in the competent court, it is that court which will then deal with that case on merits, in accordance with law."

If the Apex Court saw a report later, they would come to know the details of investigation and the standard of evidence. Besides, other considerations and compulsions, after January 1996, the strategy turned into a compulsion that in order to conceal the details of investigations, chargesheeting all the names in the diaries indiscriminately became a necessity. Only that could eliminate threat against PVNR from the law as also from his own party. This explains why mass chargesheets without any evidence had to be resorted to, as this only could ensure that the trial court leaves all and the case gets a natural unceremonious burial.

If the entire case were thrown out, there would be no question of raising finger at Narasimha Rao, his mentor, who had brought Rama Rao to the CBI and with whom he had served in his state of Andhra. Rama Rao would reiterate time and again that how could he investigate the PM who had brought him to the CBI? He would remind me again and again that he (Rama Rao) only was responsible for bringing me to the CBI. He was very right, but did it cast a bonafide duty on me to become a part of the gang and out of gratitude, not to question him even for unlawful commands? Did I show disloyalty by not obeying him? I kept pondering over these questions.

I knew that deputation to the Centre in general, a posting in Delhi, and that too in a prestigious organisation like the CBI, were all great privileges and big favours. I had bitter experiences earlier when I had failed to secure a berth in Delhi for six years between 1987-93, despite all my merits. I served in North East from 1984-89. The Government of India has framed a set of incentives to attract personnel for serving there, as the officers avoid posting in that area. Further all over the country, a job in a police-training institute is held at a discount. One of the incentives is that after two years in the North East, one can opt for the station of one's choice. Having served there in a training institute for three years, I opted for a Delhi posting. I waited and pursued for two more years, but could not get the same and ultimately reverted to my cadre. In Delhi, a number of posts were available during the six-year period, and a number of officers were posted directly from their cadres, whereas I was the only officer in whole of the country having the two-fold merits, but I was not heard despite the fact that I kept on harping on the merits of my case. After joining in my state, I continued my efforts, but failed to get justice despite bringing it to the notice of the mighty Home Secretaries like Madhav Godbole and N N Vohra. Incentives are written down for all, but as usual, are extended only to a select few.

I agreed with Rama Rao that it was because of him that I was in Delhi and, that too in the CBI, and heading the zone dealing with the VVIPs. He had also found me upto the mark and appreciated my work all through, till we were faced with cases concerning the top people including his own mentor. With the feudal mindset, he could not go against his mentor and the Chief Executive of the country, but I could not follow my mentor blindly. Rama Rao had not known me personally and had picked me up on the basis of the information obtained from my records and the reputation for being truthful, honest, apolitical and straightforward, and I did not disappoint him on any of these counts.

Straight dealings recognize no relation. On 24th May 1996, during one of our various discussions, I had to make it clear to him that our country was groaning under the ill-effects of nepotism, patronage and favours. A civil servant does not belong to either a political party or a gang of dacoits or a mafia that under all circumstances, he must follow his mentor. A civil servant particularly in such agencies as CBI should act as an umpire. There was no reason to express my gratitude to my mentor, by committing an illegality, an undue favour or by providing a cover up. Towards the end of his tenure, he was perturbed by my remarks in my letter of August 1st, 1995, that the CBI (headed by him) had betrayed the nation. I had noted[6], "The worst malady that ails our nation is the corruption and that too corruption at high places by high and mighty. Hawala case is a classic example where as per the accounts, we have so far, about Rs. 80 crores were generated through kickbacks in which big people right up to the Prime Minister were involved. If we now concentrate only on minor functionaries, are we not aiding and abetting corruption? Catching Jains is the starting point only. There is no confusion that corruption occurred because of these high functionaries, Jains are only the peddlers who could do nothing if the authorities did not conspire and abet. Since nation has reposed its destiny in their hands and entrusted investigation of betrayal by them to us, to my mind, we would be betraying our nation if we do not concentrate on big people. I strove for complete investigation into power sector."

Rama Rao had accused me of being "self-conceited" as I had called him a betrayer to the nation. As against a betrayer, a patriot is defined as one who protects the country basically in his work sphere, as *Karma* is *Dharma*. The job of the CBI is to fight against corruption, I contended that any member of CBI who does not perform his duties to that end, exposes the country to economic danger and forfeits his claim to patriotism. All the economic crimes, including corruption, destroy the nation. So, all the people who may themselves indulge into or may aid or abet such crime, forfeit their claim to patriotism. The discussion closed at that.

Unfortunately the mythology (or even the history) holds a very shady concept of loyalty. Loyalty to a person is idealized over loyalty to truth or God or even the nation. In Ramayan, Vibhishan stood for truth, as against absolute loyalty to his brother Ravan, but he is known as a spy inside the house, despite the fact that he sided with *Satya*, represented by God himself.

Similar is the position in Mahabharat. Bhisham had taken the vow to be loyal and faithful to the king of Hastinapur. Bhisham did not object to various wrong actions of the king and he himself committed many indiscretions because of this mistaken concept of loyalty. In his skewed sense of loyalty, Bhisham could witness helplessly, the wife of his grandsons' being disrobed in the open court. It is this sense of loyalty on his part, which plunged the whole Bharat into a war that destroyed it including Hastinapur completely. Bhisham buried his honesty, patriotism, even his

Dharma under the debris of the sense of personal loyalty, loyalty to a person who happened to be the king, rather than to the State or the nation. The results were devastating, but we learn no lessons, though we may offer the ritual obeisance to Mahabharat.

Personal loyalty behoves the members of gangs of dacoits or mafia and not to the executives of the State. Basically such loyalties destroy the nation. To my mind such people can safely be called traitors to the nation. The Britishers recognized this fact that in India the personal loyalty has always commanded a premium over loyalty to the nation. They purchased the personal loyalties of influential Indians, with whose help less than one lac Britishers, could rule over 37 crore of Indians. This throws up many questions and creates conflicting situations. I projected myself as a servant of the state, at the service of the law and truth as distinct from the government or the persons running the government; the system rejected and threw me out like a foreign body. No wonder I was removed from investigation of Hawala case. We are still clinging to the medieval concept of personal loyalty. The rise of concept of the state as distinct from the king or the persons in power has made no difference to our thinking.

I was in for a greater shock in my lessons on human behaviour as related to personal integrity. I realized at great pains that self-interest was the only factor shaping the behaviour pattern of most of the people and they keep on shifting and continuously adjusting their principles, philosophy, loyalty and arguments in line with that. Since 26th June 1995, when N N Singh and I were disassociated from Hawala case, Singh's tirade against Rama Rao, with me as the captive audience, became a regular feature. After my letter to the director on 11th August 1995, Singh called me and as I entered his room, he congratulated me saying that every word in the letter was arranged neatly and the vast material had been soundly compressed, "but why have you gone so soft on director in Krishnamurthy case where Rama Rao had thoroughly bungled". I explained that I had only passed certain comments, facts were known. The letter was meant only to make him realize what wrongs he was committing. The director did not discuss the letter with me. However, Singh later told me that the director had accused him of prompting me to write the letter. I promised that whenever I happened to be with the director, I would clarify, which I did.

Singh's tirade against Rama Rao continued for the next few days, but waned suddenly. By the end of September, he started taking offence, even at a word uttered against the director. The riddle was solved soon. I learnt from a reliable source that extension case of N N Singh was in the pipeline as the director had spoken to the PM. I asked Singh the straight question about his extension, but he flatly denied any such move. But the month of December saw him restive and expectant about extension forgetting the earlier hard line of denial. Ultimately the extension orders were received on the 1st of January. It was all intriguing and image shattering as here was a person who swore against the corrupt system but managed his own extension when it came to self, as if all moral hyperboles are only for others, and sense of justice, right and wrong, the truth, the purity everything stops at the threshold of self-interest. This was ironically the day and time, when he should have been exposing the CBI, its culture of feudal bias and also exposing Rama Rao, but the deep embedded self-interest had tilted the scales.

Facts later unfolded from a very knowledgeable and reliable source, that it was my D.O. letter of August 1st, 1995, on which the extension case was built. Initially Rama Rao accused N N Singh of prompting me to write the letter, but when he declined and I also confirmed it, he threw bait to N N Singh in his most affable style that why he was so annoyed, he could also get extension and become director CBI. A bargain was struck between the two that Singh would give adverse comments on my letter, which will enable Rama Rao to straighten his position on record and also enable him to counter my allegations. Singh furnished his comments based on patent wrong premises probably sometime in September and that paved the way for his extension case to be taken up. Thus they came closer again. Relations between Rama Rao and N N Singh kept changing according to the perception of their self-interests, converging sometime and diverging at the other, like railway lines in a railway yard which keep on coming closer or drifting away depending upon which train they are to facilitate.

When N N Singh was on his second extension and posted as Special Secretary (Home), I visited him in his office and asked him how could he be double-faced? Just for an extension he could turn volte-face. He could not reply to any of my observations. I also wrote to him demi-officially on September 2nd, 1996, stating the essence of what I had told him personally, but I never received any reply from him, though I did receive his reactions through R C Sharma, Special director, and P C Sharma, the Joint director. Singh had requested both of them to restrain me from taking such devastating actions.

Sometime in November-December 1995, it appeared in the press that in the Hawala case, the statement of S K Jain while under custodial interrogation, was not authentic, that it was planted to mislead the CBI as was done by Harshad Mehta, that he accused the Prime Minister for accepting Rs. 1 crore and went scot-free in that case. I went to N N Singh and told him that it was wrong. He had also interrogated Jain, but in any case I took full responsibility that I stood by every word of the statement that was recorded taking all the precautions that an IO can and that such press briefing by CBI was an unprofessional act. This statement was planted in the Press a number of times during those few months. The worst was that it appeared in the same words in all the papers/journals and incidentally had identical words in which Rama Rao had accused me personally in March/July 1995. I checked up with SM Khan, DPIO of CBI, thinking director might have asked him, but he denied point blank. This happened in January 1996 but again towards the end of January or early February statement using identical words and phrases, indicating its common origin, appeared in another section of the press. I wrote to the director on 27th February 1996 (Annexure-C) that it was something very wrong and a contradiction be published in the press. Since I had reasons to believe that the director had himself planted it, so I took this opportunity to reiterate that he only had blocked the complete investigation in Hawala case despite the fact that whatever part of Jain's statement was looked into, was verified to be correct. I wrote[7], "... but his statement in relation to the Prime Minister, the present and the past, Shri Rajiv Gandhi was not allowed to be verified by yourself. It was one of the major issues on which I was transferred from investigation of Hawala case."

On the 16th of January 1996, the director called all the JDs to his office and announced that he had decided to lay before the court some chargesheets in the Hawala case and that this news would be aired that night. He asked us all to educate the public on the right lines. It was possibly a slip of the tongue that he said, "Now I will take up the pay revision case of CBI officers". It was at the close of the meeting and most of the officers had started leaving, but I was still in a pensive mood wondering at the plan to scuttle the scam. The words woke me up from my reverie. I requested him to repeat what he had just said, but he was on guard and said that till then he had been too busy in Hawala case, now only he had some time and had asked P C Sharma, his staff officer, to bring up the genuine case of CBI, DSsP and SsP for pay revision which was to be sent that very day i.e. 16th January to the government. This case had been pending for perhaps over two decades. The officers had argued through two Pay Commissions and had also fought unsuccessfully civil suits right upto the Supreme Court. Though there was merit in their case, the court had left it to the Government and did not like to intervene in this administrative matter.

We had been emphatically requesting the director to use his personal influence with the PM to get them their due, but he did not oblige. Now the sudden announcement by the director made it appear as if it was a part of the *quid pro quo*, a sort of deal that if such chagesheets were filed in Hawala case, the officers will be allowed the new upgraded pay scale. There was absolutely no doubt that the chargesheets were lame duck, premature and would be thrown out. Lo and behold, on the 6th of February, the new pay scales were notified. What could not be achieved over a period of twenty years became a reality in just twenty days after the chargesheets were prepared or filed. This sent out the wrong signals giving impression, as if the officers of CBI had been bribed to prepare chargesheets and that it was all pre-arranged and was pre-agreed.

I thought over it for the next couple of days, met the director and conveyed to him that it all gave an impression that the revision of pay scales was part of a deal with the PM, which was demeaning for officers of an oraganisation like CBI. They had all the merits on their side and he could have taken up the same earlier as we had been requesting him. Perhaps the intentions of Rama Rao were to give the clear message, cooperate and gain.

I also took the opportunity to emphasise that without complete investigation, framing of chargesheets was wrong and when case is fought, there would be terrible repercussions for the CBI and may be for the CBI officers, but by then the director would have retired. Later on, when the charges were framed for the first time against one or two politicians in May 1996, Rama Rao summoned me to his office and gloated, "Look Lall, the Court has vindicated my position as charges have been framed". I retorted, "Sir, you know, I know and every professional conversant with the law and the facts of this case knows that the charges will fall in trial. If someone takes the issue to the High Court, these charges will be thrown away immediately. No charge in these cases can stand without searches and uncovering disproportionate assets." I tried to stir his conscience by repeating what I had said in my letter dated 1st August 1995. I posed a question to him that did it not amount to betraying the nation? After a long silence he reacted, "well there may be an error of judgement, but I will never betray the nation". He was taking protection under the cover of bonafide mistake. A well considered action about which he had been forewarned a number of times, couldn't constitute a bonafide mistake. Like me, he could also see the whole of Hawala case crumbling down. The ace investigator that he was, could never have missed the important point. He knew it better than anyone else that it was not the lack of evidence but fear of massive evidence that deterred him from permitting investigation and collecting evidence.

I was desperate to expose the operation scuttle, but did not know how to go about. Leaking it to the Press in anonymity was not my way as according to me it was unethical. As a staunch believer in the Gandhian principles of purity of ends and means, it did not behove me to match the power games that the director was playing. At one stage I decided to call a press conference and give out everything there, but somehow my well-wishers restrained me from doing so. In February 1996, I drafted an affidavit to be filed before the concerned Supreme Court bench, exposing the entire investigation process in this case as the basic value system of our society, polity, administration and even the judiciary were at stake. I took it personally to Supreme Court in early March (as in between I was toying with the idea of holding a press conference) and met the Additional Registrar General (Judicial), Mr. Bhadoo and showed him the affidavit. I briefed him about my mission about which I had only hinted over the telephone while fixing the appointment. He was shell-shocked. He did not react but took the affidavit along with its enclousers to his superior, the Registrar General. He returned after sometime; I was disappointed when he informed that the Hawala bench was receiving too many petitions, so the bench had ruled a day or two earlier that all petitions be handed over to Anil Dewan, the *emicus curie* appointed by the court in this case. I expressed my desire to see the Registrar General. Bhadoo contacted him but the latter was not willing. I then left a copy of complete affidavit with Bhadoo requesting him to persuade the Registrar General to bring it to the notice of the Hon'ble judges as a special case. I returned to him after a week but with no success. I took back the affidavit. I was not prepared to hand it over to Dewan as perhaps the policeman in me saw him in the adversarial role. Incidentally I was not happy with the way he was conducting the case. He appeared to be more interested in flogging the CBI rather than making it work. Also his off the cuff deposition about the non-arrest of N K Jain had done incalculable harm to the Hawala case, the CBI and the dedicated team of officers. The director got a handle to beat us with, because of the scathing remarks the Supreme Court had passed on an event of no consequence. Interestingly at around the same time the trial court was speaking in a language just opposite to that of the Supreme Court? If only we had been heard, there would have been no occasion for such remarks. But it left my team vulnerable at the hands of the director who could blackmail us by citing that observation time and again and used it as a convenient excuse to take over the field himself, free to manipulate.

Time proved how right I was, when from April 1997 the charges against various accused persons began to fall one after the other. It was in any case a foregone conclusion that the case had been scuttled much earlier during investigations. The very act of mass chargesheeting without evidence had decided the case as early as January 1996; now it was only being formalized. Sudheendra Kulkarni later wrote in *The Pioneer* of 15th April 1997, after the chargesheets started falling "......Not that this was not known to the CBI or its mentors in the South Block when Mr. Advani was chargesheeted on January 16th 1996. The legal untenableness of the case was known to anyone who had even an elementary understanding of the Evidence Act and other relevant aspects of law." Kulkarni is very right, but what he does not know is that the director had repeatedly been warned about it almost two years in advance. However, in the process many innocents suffered and the guilty got the undeserved reprieve.

Rama Rao had tried to finish me completely. Such efforts had started immediately after the receipt of my letter of 1st August 1995. By January-February 1996, I could sense the plans to spoil my ACR when he started pulling up my subordinates for their performance during the previous year as also during the current year even when they had done very well. As part of his plans, he had removed nearly half of the IOs from most of the branches under my charge. I could see through his game and requested him to lower the targets of my branches so as to make them proportionate to the availability of IOs, but he would not agree to either verbal or written requests. I had no option but to send a strong note. Instead, he made accusations, which I was only expecting. I then sent a detailed note showing how the director was unjustified, as I had achieved the targets in 1994 despite shortage of staff and the output per IO in my zone was the highest for both the years 1994 and 1995. I also mentioned how the Jabalpur experiment was a grand success in the field of trial disposal for which Judiciary and prosecution were not finding any way out, but under my scheme the disposal under trial rose manifold. I also pointed out how I had done away with the false cases being registered by CBI branches for statistical purposes. I had to write at the end, "I understand, it is because of the prejudice against me in Hawala and other more important cases where again I should say, CBI has not been truthful as I had raised my apprehension in my DO letter dated 1-8-95 and 27-2-96. By now ....it has been proved that my line of complete investigation including PM and others , as against selective investigation, was correct, but all this has prejudiced the director CBI". This was written on 25th March 1996, when the nation was euphoric over these fake chargesheets. I knew that before long, the people would be wringing their hands in complete disappointment and frustration.

In view of the massive evidence of the highest output per IO in my zone for both the years, the director had no option but to lower the targets. Despite the fact that he had conceded to my point that I had given the highest output both qualitywise and quantitywise, and I had also introduced innovative trial procedures, which were conducive to rich returns at Jabalpur, the Special director and the director awarded me two damaging reports. They had teamėd up to inflict punishment on me, ensuring thereby that I never got any further promotion in my career.

To facilitate appreciation by the percipient reader, I pause here to introduce the form of confidential report laid down by the Government of India for superior Police Officers. The form is very elaborate. It ensures comprehensively that nobody can be prejudiced as it provides enough space and questions to elicit information about assessment of his work from those reporting on him. The first part is titled 'self-assessment', in which the officer in question enumerates the work done by him. The mandatory instructions lay down in detail how the comments are to be recorded by the reporting and the reviewing officers. The instructions also lay down certain ways in which comments shall not be recorded. The instructions prohibit the reporting officer from summarizing in one word any particular trait or from the use of omnibus expression or writing in a casual and a superficial manner, whereas on me reports were casual, superficial and omnibus, based on one single word "average" used for the year 1994-95 and the word "good" for the year 1995-96 to describe all the attributes thereby, violating all the mandatory instructions laid down in the service rules and reproduced on every form. It is a different story that under orders from the Tribunal to review,. the government later on held both these reports as inoperative, but Rama Rao's vengeance was complete. He had achieved all his objectives, i.e. he had saved his mentor, scuttled the Hawala scam and had inflicted punishment on the dissent. I only kept crying from the rooftop what was the correct thing to do in Hawala and other cases[8] ".... I was proposing to investigate and present a clear picture irrespective of the fact that who comes in. Certainly, some members of Union Cabinet, both the present and the past, would come in and evidence against some of them was being uncovered.

It does not matter if the name of former PM or the present PM figured or figured in a big way. As a professional, charged with the duty of collection of facts, I would not hesitate even if a big name comes in. Once we chargesheet the small, even if we do not intend to close the case, we would be forced to close the same as happened in Dharmender Deo Mishra's case and as per my information efforts are afoot in Assam LoC scandal as the line has reached the Assam CM". Mishra was a well-connected senior IAS officer, whose cases had to be dropped despite the best opposition that the CBI could ever put up. It is described in details in a subsequent chapter.

Having been a witness to how a sound case was scuttled, I was disgusted about the whole episode. When I met Justice JS Verma (Former Chief Justice of India) in June 1998, and discussed how tamely had the Hawala case ended. I explained to him my part of the case that the Hawala case did not fall or fail, but was scuttled. Non-collection of evidence and mass chargesheeting without any evidence, favoured all those against whom there could be substantive evidence, but prejudiced those against whom there was no evidence. Justice Verma was positively unhappy over the events, but felt satisfied that he did whatever was possible within the boundaries, assigned by the Law and the constitution, to the Judiciary. He regretted that the CBI had failed to look into the assets of the accused persons, which should have been the primary direction the investigators should have followed. On my humble suggestion that the bench could also have given direction if CBI had failed, Justice Verma observed that no accused in Hawala case was acquitted, they were only discharged for lack of evidence and that nothing prevented the CBI from taking up investigations afresh against those who were suspected to have amassed assets disproportionate to their income.

However, it left me wondering whether the mighty judge of the Supreme Court was also helpless in this helpless nation. This kept bothering me for a long, long time.

In a nutshell, in order to protect the high and mighty, the following questions were never addressed, which would have uncovered a whole wealth of information. This is done in the CBI in other cases as a fair routine.

i. How, why and wherefrom did the kickbacks arise?
ii. What was the extent of the kickbacks?
iii. Who was responsible for generation of this surplus being distributed as kickbacks?
iv. What was the mode of payment of the kickbacks in each case?
v. Who were the conduits?
vi. Who were the recipients of the kickbacks?
vii. Who were the end users of this money?

For delving deep into all these questions, study of various projects, which were the source of such moneys, was necessary, and the following steps were required to be taken against those who were identified through the above process:

a. to investigate them thoroughly,
b. to look into the evidence of, receipts/payments/favours/motives, etc.,
c. to investigate their assets, and
d. to look into the projects, their costs, tendering process, examination of tenders and allotment.

For taking these steps effectively, searches were absolutely necessary and a pre-requisite. The director ensured that investigations were not taken to their logical end. He took the following pro-active steps to scuttle the case completely :

(i) verifications of allegations against the big names were stopped;
(ii) decision was taken to stick to diaries alone;
(iii) detailed and complete investigations were prohibited;
(iv) the director did not permit searches, and did not allow investigation into assets;
(v) the director stopped examination of projects;
(vi) the director rushed in deliberately for pre-mature chargesheets without looking into or collecting or appreciating the evidence; and
(vii) investigation into bungling (or their wealth) by those who were dead was stopped.

The system was so operated that once the involvement of the big names was foreseen, all steps towards that direction were avoided. An illustration from the working of the CBI at that time will bring home the point straight. I had collected some very reliable information pertaining to the artificial hiking up the costs of Chamera Power Project (in Himachal Pradesh) from Rs. 1500 crores to 3500 crores by National Hydro Power Corporation (NHPC). As a consequence the cost of producing power was on rise and the common man as also the industry were reeling under high costs. Economic deprivation of the country because of this deceit was thus thrust upon the nation. I reduced it into a Source Information Report and submitted it to the director on 29th May 1995, but even bare verification into that was avoided.

I proposed to examine the whole system of allotment of works that is based on artificially inflated rates and made the following observations that needed urgent and in-depth enquiries:

a) To check the going rates as a preventive measure, so that the country could be saved from this colossal loss;

b) Why shouldn't such projects be executed internally by our agencies like NHPC, the purpose for which the organisation was created? I found out later, that the excuse of foreign resources, as normally given out, was not fully tenable. Nearly 50 per cent of the resources that the foreign companies raise, was by borrowing from our financial institutions as they brought about 25 per cent of the invested amount/resources from abroad, whereas they would levy all financial charges like consultancy, profits, interest etc., on whole of the amount and perhaps would cart back an equivalent amount back home during the period of execution itself. If we execute the work ourselves and borrow only the requisite foreign component the project cost would be much less. We thus lose on the precious foreign exchange and pay more thereby mortgaging the future of the nation.

Towards the end of June or beginning of July 1996, when the director was preparing to leave the CBI, he discussed the entire gamut of investigations into the scams with me. He was justifying his position in investigations against the big names. I did not agree with him and pointed out that he did not order inquiry even into the specific report made by a Joint director. He denied knowledge of such a Source Report, but he had no answer when I showed him the evidence that the report was received in his personal section. He promised to order verification, but till date I have not been contacted by anyone. Incidentally I had later brought it to the notice of Joginder Singh when he was director CBI, but again drew a blank. Dignitaries were too high and were beyond his leap as well.

I approached S R Narsimhan, the new Chairman of NHPC, and narrated the story to him. He assured me that he would look into and if the facts were borne on his files, he would not allow allotment of the project at such high rates. Ultimately in 1998, the work was re-tendered. My conviction and stand were vindicated when as late as 1999, after full four years, the project was awarded at Rs. 1684 crores as against the huge amount of Rs. 3500 crores. With involvement of the higher ups and the evidence pointing towards the highest in the power sector, the helplessness of both the directors of the CBI was understandable.

It was precisely the essence of my differences with the director against this immunity being extended to the highest. This feudal trait, that the King and his friends can do no wrong, should have no place in a democratic society governed by the Rule of Law. Was the CBI meant for middle levels only, and not for fighting corruption at high places? This was brought out clearly in the DO letter dated 1.8.95 which reads,[9] "If we get bogged down for whatever reason, it does us discredit. While investigating the corruption in high places, our subjects normally have to be high-ranking politicians and officers; if we start bending the law for them or interpreting differently, my conscience does not accept it. Will nobody or no agency in this country look into the corruption by high and mighty." I got no answer from the two Directors of CBI with whom I served. I only got punished for the audacity of asking such stupid and irrelevant questions and for raising such superfluous problems and issues.

A thorough professional like Rama Rao was a changed person when faced with VIPs in power or in whom they were interested. Is it the mindset of a typical Indian official to which Rama Rao could not be an exception even when he was holding the sacrosanct charge of Chief investigator of the country?

The failure of Hawala case has undermined the confidence of the people in our criminal justice system. Even those who believe that there was no evidence, are dismayed that if there was no evidence why did the CBI file the chargesheets. This is a misconception that there was no evidence as has been amply clarified in the narrative. There were evidences, but their non-collection was a willful and a well-thought act to scuttle the case.

Besides there are certain other misconceptions about this star case that are clarified as follows:

That Jains were the main culprits. Basically the takers of the bribe or say the persons in authority who are in command of the situation are always the bigger culprits. A person in authority can pressurize and even blackmail the other to give bribe to him. If the other person falls in line and pays up, all is well, otherwise he has to suffer. Who were the main culprits, also finds mention in the judgement date 25.4.95 of the Special Judge V B Gupta of the CBI Court, an excerpt of which is reproduced,[10] "It is hoped that CBI, the Prime Investigation Agency of this country, will make all the sincere and concrete efforts to nab the real culprits who are main beneficiaries i.e. politicians and public servants who have been named in the various Diaries and against whom there is enough material on record to initiate action in accordance with the law of the land. It is further hoped that the present accused N K Jain who is simply an abettor will not be made a scapegoat in this case and the main beneficiaries of illegal gratification of huge amount of 65 crores may not go scot free." Earlier while granting bail to S K Jain and J K Jain, the vacation Judge Dinesh Dayal had also observed on 16th March 1995, "the allegations against the applicants are at best under section 12 of PC Act which relate to abetment of offences committed by Public servants under section 7 of PC Act. The Principal accused are yet to be arrested" ...Remarks of the Supreme Court on 27th March 1995, create an impression that Jain brothers were the main culprits. Apprehensions of the CBI judge have unfortunately come true and so also the assessment of '*The Economist*'[11] that had predicted as early as September 1995, the course the Hawala Case would take. Unfortunately the learned *amicus curiae* could not appreciate this point, which led the investigations to focus on the Jains at the cost of investigation against the substantive culprits.

The next misconception is very misleading that Jain Hawala Case had a terrorist angle, which was not investigated. There is no doubt that the Jain Hawala case was an offshoot of a TADA case, but the terrorist angle had been fully investigated in the original case registered under TADA. This full-fledged case was registered in 1991 and five accused persons were chargesheet; some of whom were declared proclaimed offenders, whereas the others stand convicted. S K Jain or all those with whom he had dealt with had no such links or designs. It is important to make it clear that no character in this case was a risk to national security *prima facie*. Nor were there any reasons visible or invisible, for such suspicion. Jains were dealing with a hawala agent, who functioned like a banker. The Jains and the terrorists were all like account holders with the bank, who did not know each other. Certain quarters perpetuated this myth thereby undermining the confidence of the people in their safety and security.

Another misconception was maliciously and deliberately created to discredit my team that the FERA angle was not investigated and that Amod Kanth had dumped the case. It is correct that for two years from 1991 to 1993 there were no investigations, but the case was not with Amod Kanth. The papers were filed with O P Sharma case. The first time the case came from the Anti-Terrorist division to Anti-corruption division (where Amod Kanth was serving) was in 1993 only. Amod cannot be held responsible for the period prior to that. During 1993 and 1994 he did whatever could be possible at that late stage. He traced the path of movement of funds abroad, but then came the dead end. In 1995 the Supreme Court transferred the case to Enforcement Directorate and they also returned the same findings.

The fourth misconception is that it was a very bold step to chargesheet so many Ministers and the other big politicians. This is totally incorrect. It was a defence mechanism and the only way to save the real accused, and in particular, to divert attention from the ruling Prime Minister, PV Narasimha Rao. It was a foregone conclusion at the time of filing chargesheets that all would get reprieve as such chargesheets, bereft of any substantive evidence, were surely going to ruin the entire case. Apparently, though, it was done in compliance with the Judicial orders, but in effect it was to negate the same as there could be no evidence or uniform evidence against all the accused. Preliminary investigations had revealed that payments of diary entries were on the following accounts:

a) Kickbacks being brought back and being paid to the public servants as part of the *quid pro quo*. Alternately, Jains offering bribe out of their own money, accounted for in the diaries;

b) Jains acting as only the conduits for getting black money of various persons from abroad to India and delivering the same to them;

c) Jains channelising money remitted (i) by some foreign-based organisations that could not come to the forefront for certain reasons, or (ii) the person wanted to avail higher rates of exchange offered by the Hawala dealers; and

d) Money paid by the Jains to certain people, just to oblige them, but with no *quid pro quo*.

Only the first category constituted an offence under Prevention of Corruption Act. In the next two, offences under FERA were committed, but not under Prevention of Corruption Act. The last category amounted to no offence. There was no rationale for filing chargesheets against all and sundry. Instead, complete investigations should have been focused against persons falling in category (a) above and taken to their logical conclusion including conducting searches and looking into their assets. It all was conveniently brushed aside by mass chagesheets, whereas the CBI should have separated the grain from the chaff and chargesheeted only those against whom there was evidence.

Still another misconception is that the Hawala was a scam of Rs.65 crores only. In reality, it was a scam of over Rs.1000 crores. S K Jain had bargained about Rs. 85 crores, as has been mentioned earlier. His share was only three per cent of the project costs with seven per cent going to Quatrrochi or others. Had complete and detailed investigation been conducted, the exact quantum would have been known, but in absence of that, the statement made by Jain has to be taken as authentic. Besides the Durgapur Steel Plant Modernisation project, for which Jain was to receive a fixed payment, Jain's share at three per cent in the other projects was Rs. 70 crores. So Quattrochi's share works out to Rs. 163 crores adding up to total kickbacks for these projects to Rs.233 crores. In other words the total cost of these projects would work out to the tune of Rs.2330 crores. Out of the work of modernization of Durgapur Steel Plant, Jain was to get fixed amount of Rs.15 crores initially. What were the overall implications of the contract and its terms, was to be found in further investigations, which could not happen during my tenure. Initially the cost was assessed at Rs. 1450 crores, but it kept on escalating in stages and ultimately it is alleged to have mounted to over Rs. 5000 crores. Taking the initial cost of Rs. 1450 crores, total cost of all these projects comes out to Rs. 3780 crores. The persons paying the kickbacks mark up the project costs by 40 to 100 per cent as was learnt during investigations, and the same also finds support in case of the Chamera-II project. Even if the upmarking of costs is taken at the minimum rate of forty per cent, the value of upmarking of the cost of these projects is at least Rs. 1080 crores. Rs. 65 crores was the amount of kickbacks actually distributed. Extent of scam is over Rs. 1000 crores i.e. the amount the country has probably lost on this account. Hawala was much bigger a scam than is usually believed.

The analysis above presents the story of only a few projects, whereas a large number of projects were to be examined and evaluated. Auriya and Anta were already on record. There was some apparent evidence of kickbacks in Auriya Thermal Power Project. It is high time when public needs to be educated that the extent of loss to the nation represents the magnitude of a scam and not the kickbacks that some Indians or foreigners might have received. Had the Hawala case been fully investigated, the magnitude of the scam might have gone beyond Rs.2000 crores even.

The Hawala case could have been a turning point on the Indian economic and political scene. There can be no disagreement that this case had the potential for cleansing the stables. The CBI could have also brought to light the dubious rationale of high costs in all projects in this country as also the rationale of allotting simple civil engineering works to foreign firms, that too without global tenders, on limited or short term quotations for projects running into hundreds or even thousands of crores. Besides, the CBI had a chance, a God sent opportunity to look into the huge assets of the accused persons as information had also become available about huge holding by some of them. More information and evidences were flowing in, but that would have enveloped the higher echelons of society, which perhaps could not be allowed in public interest as in the so-called civilised society, public interest is interpreted as the interest of its elite, ruling at particular time.

References

1. D.O. letter No. 79 dated 1.8.95, at Appendix A, from the author to Vijay Rama Rao, Director CBI, para 6
2. Cited above paras 7 and 8.
3. Cited above para 8.
4. Supreme Court Judgement dated 18.12.1997 in writ petition (criminal) Nos. 340-343 of 1996 in Vineet Narain & others Vs Union of India. More popularly known as Jain Hawala Case.
5. Supreme Court judgement dated 18.12.1997 cited above.
6. Para 14 of Annexure A cited above.
7. Para 1 of Annexure C.
8. Para 14 of Annexure A cited above.
9. Para 11 of Annexure A cited above.
10. Judgement date 25.4.1995 of V.B. Gupta, Special Judge, CBI cases Delhi, while deciding the bail application of N K Jain.
11. *The Economist* – 16th to 22nd September 1995 Page 35, titled India—Deadly Diaries.

3

Midnight Deplaning of a Giant

In the month of April 1995, when the Hawala case was at its peak, the case of V Krishnamurthy gathered heat. Krishnamurthy, as mentioned earlier, had held very high positions in the government as also in the Public Sector Undertakings (PSUs) and at one stage was known as India's informal Economic Ambassador to Japan. He continued to be very influential for a quarter century on the Indian industrial scene, both in the Government and the Public Sector. There were, however, four cases pending investigations against him with the CBI in 1995 and in one of these cases against him the allegations were that he had received crores of dollars by way of kickbacks in his dealing with the multinationals and particularly the Japanese. He was also accused of amassing enormous assets and huge bank balances abroad. The CBI, *prima facie*, had evidence of creating/purchasing a number of firms by him in India and abroad, in the USA, Europe, etc. The bank accounts of his son showed huge transactions in yen and the US dollars running into hundreds of crores in rupees. A copy of their bank accounts with the Union Bank of Switzerland, disclosing huge transactions, was on the records of the CBI. There were strong reasons to believe that the hush money received by Krishnamurthy was credited into the same and also used in creating/purchasing various firms.

The CBI had traced that funds were transferred from one country to another, a normal practice with those who deal with such slush, so that the origin and/or the end disposal of the funds gets confounded and they cannot be caught in any investigations. So the investigations were required in about a dozen places in various countries. The case was registered as early as November 1992 and initially the investigations progressed quite fast, but then it became necessary to conduct investigations abroad. As I recall certain foreign governments had confirmed the suspicious transactions through Interpol informally and were prepared to supply the documents formally, only when Letters Rogatory(LR) from India were provided to them. Letter Rogatory is a letter of request from the court of one country to the court of another, to extend help in investigation of a crime registered in the country of origin of the letter. It is supposed to be supported by an undertaking of reciprocity by the government of the requesting country. The courts issue an LR only when government gives such undertaking, though basically it is a matter between the SHO/IO and the court. However if an IO applies to the court and the court allows sending of such a letter, it is then embarrassing for the government if it intends not to issue the undertaking of reciprocity for tactical or diplomatic reasons. In fair functioning, barring the foreign policy angle, the government has no business to have any discretion in these judicial matters as only a court or an IO knows what steps have to be taken in the interest of investigations in a particular case. Around that time, the government modified the procedures by an executive order that CBI should apply to the court for the LR, only after obtaining the undertaking from the government, thereby the possibilities of investigation abroad against any influential person were virtually closed, as it could deny such undertaking or at least delay its issue indefinitely. The delay would also have the same effect as denial, as all evidence could vanish with time and nothing would come out later.

Requests were made to government in the Krishnamurthy case for issue of LR in May 1993 for some countries, but the Government of India did not issue the requisite undertaking of reciprocity till I held the charge of these cases or even till December 1996, the time I left the CBI. The instructions for issue of such letters were changed. It was learnt reliably that the change was ordered to protect Krishnamurthy.

Following these cases the CBI had impounded the passports of Krishnamurthy and his sons. Krishnamurthy applied for release of his passport in February 1995. The Supreme Court had earlier turned down a similar request made by his son as the CBI had contested that forcefully. Krishnamurthy now moved a petition in the Sessions Court. We filed an equally forceful response in the Court on 10th March 1995. The same night or perhaps on 9th March there was a call to director from Mrs. Margaret Alva, Minister Personnel, from Copenhagen, where she was attending some conference, enquiring why did CBI file such a strong affidavit? Why could Krishnamurthy not be allowed to go abroad? On his enquiry I informed the director that we had only included the facts on record in the affidavit. The Sessions Court agreed with us and rejected the petition on 1st April 1995, when it came up for hearing. Krishnamurthy moved a petition in the High Court and it was heard in the corridors that the Court would release his passport, as the government will pursue a very weak line. This surprised both my team and me as the affidavit was to be filed by the same SP who had filed it in Sessions Court. As JD, I was the final authority to vet it.

We prepared a very strong affidavit on the basis of the one that we had filed in the Session Court, fortified it with more facts and with greater details, thereby, imparting more punch to it. Normally affidavits do not go beyond JD, unless he feels that it is beyond him or if a case is of some fundamental importance. This case had neither of the two attributes, so there was no question of sending it to the director or the Special director. However, the director summoned me, along with the DIG, the SP and the IO with the proposed affidavit and the records. I took the team and the records to director, as desired. He saw the affidavit and started deleting everything of importance right from the beginning. I protested against his doing so, but the director would not agree. Amod Kanth, DIG, also joined me in protests, but it had no effect on the director. I told him that the lame duck affidavit would ensure that the passport was released to Krishnamurthy and if he went abroad, the chances of his return were very bleak. The director dryly commented that he was only 'deleting the trash' that had been included, but when we reiterated our arguments, he said, "You can file all the documents as enclosures, instead of burdening the body of the affidavit with all those unnecessary details". His attention was drawn to the routine fact that if a document was attached and not discussed in the body of the affidavit, the High Court normally would not take cognisance of the enclosures. But all these weighty arguments did not cut any ice with him and he continued wielding his scissors, dismantling all that we had so carefully built our case upon. He spent some four hours for vetting a ten-page affidavit that should not have taken more than 15 minutes at his stage. No doubt, we were also guilty, as we kept interrupting him time and again, but it was difficult to witness silently the brutal deletion of all the meaningful facts. Later, when I was removed from this seat dealing with the VIP cases, I wrote to Rama Rao on August 1st 1995[1] , "As DCBI is aware, his *(V. Krishnamurthy's)* influence and intervention did not stop at this (*denial of permission for issue of letters rogatory*). He could successfully dictate us through his contacts in Government to file a lame duck affidavit in the High Court where his application was heard on 18.4.95. It was on this point that we had arguments before filing the affidavit and again on 18.4.95, when his petition was allowed and he was permitted to go abroad".

The issue was taken up by the High Court on 18th April 1995. I along with the DIG and the SP, had personally briefed the Additional Legal Adviser(ALA) to argue the facts that had been deleted by the director and gave him a list of nearly two dozen points. He did put forward those arguments in the court, but the passport was released by the High Court attaching more importance to what was contained in the affidavit about which the director had been amply sounded at the time of vetting. The information reached the director's room where the Special director, myself, Amod Kanth and MP Singh, the SP, were present for discussion of Hawala case as the same was listed in the Supreme Court that very afternoon. As the information came, I spontaneously observed that it had to happen. After a few moments, the mention of High Court decision in Krishnamurthy case came up again. At this stage I came out bluntly "with that lame duck affidavit, we had ensured that the judge would leave him out. Release of Passport was a foregone conclusion." The director took offence at this and nearly shouted that I was accusing him. I confirmed that I was doing just that. Suddenly the tempers flared on both sides and we were in the midst of heated arguments. I was aware of the great pressure the director was working under, to let Krishnamurthy go abroad as he was to participate in a dinner hosted by the then US President Bill Clinton in honour of the Rajiv Gandhi Foundation. The chairperson Sonia Gandhi had already left and Krishnamurthy, as a Member, had to join her. Probably, he could not accompany her because his passport was lying with the CBI. Our heated arguments continued for 15-20 minutes, when ultimately he challenged me that if I felt so strongly, I could file an SLP in the Supreme Court and he would like to see what could I do. Though I knew there was no time left, I nonetheless accepted the challenge and sought his confirmation for getting Government permission to file the SLP. In a huff he replied in affirmative. It was now time to proceed to Supreme Court for the hearing of Hawala case. The director quickly finished his lunch and we left for the Supreme Court.

We were delayed in the evening in the court as hearing continued beyond the court hours. Till late in the evening it was not possible to attend to Krishnamurthy case, But still I utilized the transit time to discuss the line of action with DIG who was very enthusiastic, who assured me that after return from Supreme Court, he would prepare the file for the next day. The next morning when I entered my office, the file was at my table and I moved for filing the SLP. However, there was a technical snag, as the copy of the judgement had not been received till then. I had asked the DIG, who in turn had directed the SP to get a copy of the judgement the previous evening itself, but the same was not available even till the morning of 19th April 1995, as the judge had yet to sign it. I could not wait any more as Krishnamurthy could fly that very evening and the SLP would then become infructuous. In anticipation of the receipt of the copy of the judgement, the file was moved and it landed in the Ministry of Personnel, which is the normal channel, but the file got stuck there. The enquiries revealed that the instructions to ministry were that the file was not to move upwards till such time, the Minister Personnel or the PMO gave informal clearance for which director CBI had to talk to the Minister. It was already around noon. I requested the Special director to pursue it with the director, who wanted me to take it up with the latter. I impressed upon him that director was under pressure. Though, in the heat of the moment he had committed, but he was not in a mood to permit. If I were to talk to him, heated arguments may ensue again. Ultimately, I could successfully persuade N N Singh to remind the director. The director did speak to the concerned people and the file started moving. The Ministry of Personnel cleared it and the same was collected at 5.00 p.m. by my officers and taken to Law Ministry as the final clearance was to be accorded by them.

In the meantime, the judgement was issued by the High Court at 4.30 p.m. i.e. exactly the time when the Courts close. Krishnamurthy visited the CBI office around 4.45p.m. and collected his passport. It was thought that he would go away. We were preparing to submit papers to Supreme Court that evening so that the case could be heard in the morning of 20th April at least. On my personal request, the officers of the Law Ministry vetted the file the same evening and conveyed their concurrence informally at 7.30 p.m., but postponed the issue of the formal orders for the next morning. We were in a dilemma that if formal orders were issued the next morning, it would be listed for hearing on 21st, allowing Krishnamurthy enough time to fly to the US. I persuaded the concerned officers of the Law Ministry to ring up the Central Law Agency (CLA) to take up the case the same evening in anticipation of formal approval of Law Ministry the next morning. In the meantime, as decided, Amod Kanth, the DIG, was in touch with Central Law Agency, the Additional Registrar General of Supreme Court and Altaf Ahmed, the Additional Solicitor General. They soon moved to the residence of the Chief Justice of India. When they reached his residence at half past eight, they discovered that he had left for dinner. They came back disappointed. Amod informed me accordingly and also told that a call was received from Krishnamurthy's PA that he was not flying that day. We had consultations over the telephone, suspected his call to be a ruse, but were helpless and felt that we could do nothing more that evening.

At around ten the same evening, I received another call from Amod that Krishnamurthy was flying the same night i.e. at 00:30 hrs on the morning of 20th. That galvanized us once more and we decided to take it up once again immediately. We had just two and a half hours for the flight to take off. The party was reorganized and reached the residence of the Chief Justice at about 11.00 p.m. of 19th April 1995. The Chief Justice AH Ahmedi arrived and expressed his anger as why we did not wake up during the day, but when he was told that the copy of the High Court judgement was released only at 4.30 p.m. and without that the petition could not be filed, he agreed to hear the facts of the case. After hearing the facts of the case, he decided to convene the court then and there at his lawns. He requisitioned the services of another Judge. While waiting for him Amod called me from the residence of CJI and informed of the developments. It was 11.40 p.m. by then.

I informed the director about convening of the court. He was furious at once that why he was not kept in picture earlier. I told him that once he approved to file the SLP, it had to go to the Supreme Court and there was nothing worth reporting till such time the Chief Justice decided to convene the court. The director now wanted me to ring up the Airport, instruct my officers there and ensure that Krishnamurthy was not inconvenienced or manhandled there. I took exception at this and told that in my charge manhandling had never been allowed even in the state, whereas at that moment I was working in the CBI. When the director still insisted about ensuring his security, I told him that Krishnamurthy was only an accused for us and, moreover, he was not in our custody. The director was under great pressure and appeared to be getting unnerved. Unfortunately, once a civil servant gets into politicking, he can never come out of the rut. Krishnamurthy was an important person in his own right. The golden principle the CBI normally followed was not to cross the path of the current VIPs and Krishnamurthy had continued to be high on the list. However, I assured the director that either way the Supreme Court may order, there could be no occasion for any mishap. Either he would fly or surrender his passport depending upon the court orders. So there was no question of any handling at all, whereas manhandling was absolutely irrelevant.

As such, there was no need for me to speak to CBI team at the Airport, but the director still insisted that I made all the necessary arrangements for the safety of Krishnamurthy and rang up the Airport. I had no option but to ring up the Airport and convey to CBI representative at the Airport what director had said. But to the query by the officer that if Krishnamurthy turned violent, my instructions were clear, that he should make full use of his legal powers under the law and brook no weakness. The director rang me up again to confirm if I had passed on instructions to the Airport and also asked me to let him know immediately when the Court passed any orders.

I was waiting with my eyes glued to my watch. At 00.24 hrs. my telephone rang and Amod congratulated me from the other end. Fortunately, the Court accepted our SLP and stayed the High Court order and asked Krishnamurthy to surrender his passport. The order was passed at 00.20 a.m., whereas the flight was to take off at 00.30 a.m. The CJI also asked Amod to convey the order over the telephone and the fax to the Airport from his residence only. Krishnamurthy's passport was taken from him by the CBI officers present at the airport, the airline offloaded his baggage and the airport drama came to a close. I conveyed the message to the director, who began to question me, why did I file the SLP at all. I calmly reacted that the government through the director had permitted filing an SLP and only that order was taken to its logical conclusion. I put him a counter question that if permission to file SLP was given, the intention was to stop him and not to let him go and that was precisely what I and my team had done. He continued harping in the same strain, again and again, that why he was not told earlier? He kept recounting the great pressures under which he was working.

I kept on receiving one call after another till almost 02.30 hours in the morning. The director kept on moaning what a difficult situation I had created for and landed him in. He repeated again and again that P. Chidambaram (the then Union Finance Minister) was very angry with him. He added that the situation was further getting complicated as Chidambaram had sent a FAX message to Sonia Gandhi in the USA and it would be difficult for him and the Prime Minister to reply to her. He grieved that I should have informed him of such an action in advance so that he could prepare the ground. I was clear that I had done whatever was legally and factually correct. I had no regrets.

In the morning, I was prepared to face a lot of unpleasant time and also the problems as the permission of Law Ministry had not been received. It was anticipated that this would be the first question asked in the office that morning. I had taken care that a DSP was nominated the last evening to go to the Law Ministry on the morning of 20th to collect the file at 10.00 a.m., when it would be ready as had been promised. Amod came to my residence and we prepared a list of events of the previous day and night, in the chronological order that culminated into Supreme Court decision. By the time I reached the office, the director had already sent a message that he would like to see the file of permission when he would come to his CGO Complex office at 10.30 a.m. I also received a similar message from the Special director. The file arrived direct from Law Ministry at 10.30 a.m. I immediately got photocopies made, as I knew that the file would be in great demand and would be probed by many people the same day. I gave one copy to the Special director and sent the original to the director. I discussed the matter with Special director. The director summoned us a little later. As expected, the director enquired when the permission was received on 20th, how was the SLP filed on the 19th before the Supreme Court. I told him that if SLP had not been filed, all efforts would have been futile and meaningless, as Krishnamurthy would have left India by then and after that there was no fun in filing SLP at all. Secondly, that was not the only case where we had filed SLP in anticipation of the approval of the Law Ministry after informal consultations with them. Thirdly, had Krishnamurthy left and the SLP had not been filed by then, the Supreme Court would have taken us to task just like the N K Jain affair in Hawala case and our position would have been indefensible. The director had no reply. He started repeating about the pressures and the strains he was working under. In the days that followed, he would repeatedly mention that I had let him down completely, that "Government is not trusting the CBI. The Prime Minister and the minister are all annoyed. Even Chidambaram does not talk to me." It was a little later, when one day I asked him, "how did it matter if one individual, be it the most important Union Cabinet minister, did not speak to the director of the CBI, on account of one unfair request not being acceded to. Was it not a compliment for the chief of an organisation like the CBI?" But nothing appealed to the director on this score.

Incidentally it throws up a bigger question. Should the actions of the CBI swing this way or that way depending upon how various interest groups view the same, at a particular time? Should the process of collection of facts be determined by the interests or perceptions of any particular interest groups, who may be the political or the administrative masters? Has the law to play its role as umpire or act as an agent of certain individuals in power? The incident threw up the basic questions for a society claiming to the governed by the Rule of Law, and that too, where the highest investigating agency of the country was concerned. Events have come and gone, but the basic principles concerning the fundamentals of our constitution stare us hard in our face questioning that should an agency or an individual, at this position, charged with collection of facts in fighting corruption, be so deep into politics, changing and compromising with political moods, political upheavals and all that, drowning the facts, the truth, the sense of justice and fair play in the quagmire of muddy waters?

After my removal from the hot seat on 26th July, 1995, I had raised the question of principles with the director in my D.O. letter dated 1st August 1995,[2] "if it (*action against V.Krishnamurthy*) had any political fall out, that is not a circumstance which I will take into account. If some politicians in power or out of power or anybody else gets angry, that is a non issue so far as I am concerned as a professional who goes only by facts and truth. To me, any mixture even of tact in truth, deflects the truth from straightforwardness. You have given me a crime for investigation and I am a collector of facts. I collect facts in the rightful, legal and truthful way, to whomsoever it may hurt, is no concern or consideration with me." But all this stuff had no effect on him and his tirade against me continued and culminated a year later into spoiling my confidential reports, the weapon of hierarchical bureaucratic control, which is also the most potent weapon of bureaucratic tyranny and despotism.

It was a late night judgement, so the morning papers carried no news on 20th, but from 21st April onwards various versions started appearing in the Press, all reflecting the speculations that PMO had ordered the move. *The Economic Times* on 22nd reported, "It is said that a person holding a constitutional office played an important role in lobbying with Mr. Rao to prevent Mr. Krishnamurthy from traveling to Washington. This person who held a high office in the Rajiv Gandhi government, is supposed to be close to both Nehru Gandhi family as well as Rao. He also is said to be implacable opponent of Mr. Krishnamurthy".

The *Business Standard* reported on 25th, "A Deputy Inspector General in the CBI was reportedly in constant touch with a senior aide of the PM on Thursday last before moving the Supreme Court...... Many eyebrows were raised at the timing of the CBI's approaching the Chief Justice near midnight. There was enough time available for the CBI to challenge the High Court order allowing him to go to US. The fact that it chose to move literally at the eleventh hour has provided grit to the rumour mill that it was prodded to move".

The Statesman wrote on 28th, "The suspicion arose whether the CBI was guided to take the action by someone in the PM's office. As far as this newspaper is concerned, we have carried a clarification from CBI that there was no such guidance, but several stories speculative of course, have continued to appear in the Press. These may be unfair to CBI, but the totality of circumstances under which the Agency functions cannot be wished away".

In almost all the papers from Delhi, the PMO angle was common. How wrong all these papers were! Only the Supreme Court bench, the Additional Solicitor General and the Additional Registrar General, besides the CBI party headed by the author, knew till the Supreme Court Bench pronounced its verdict. Though the director and the Special director CBI and for that matter the Ministry of Personnel, all knew that they had permitted for filing, an SLP, but it was thought to be an impossible task as permission of Personnel Ministry was accorded late in the evening when the courts had closed and we still had to go to the Law Ministry, Even the copy of the judgment also came around the same time. There was practically no time for filing any SLP. The speculation in the

Press that there was ample time to file the SLP and that the CBI chose the night time with some motives, is far removed from reality. It should be amply clear from the above narrative that under no circumstance could the SLP be filed even a minute earlier. Further there was tremendous pressure on CBI not to file the SLP. Had it not filed the SLP, the Press would have pounced on the CBI, and would have taken it to task for letting Krishnamurthy go. Basically, no one could believe that CBI on its own, could take strong action, against anyone of substance. Even the most straight action of the CBI was also subjected to the microscopic scrutiny with a high-powered lens to find some traces of political dust. It is unfortunate that the CBI is not supposed to have its own soul. It is not believed or expected to act, according to its own conscience and the law. Secondly, the CBI did not clarify the circumstances to the Press. There was no harm in giving out the information, but it is not a done thing particularly when big names are involved. Feudal bias just does not leave Indian Administration and the CBI is no exception.

Is it only the Press that feels that the CBI cannot take correct and bold action on its own? Unfortunately its past record and the contemporary events bear testimony to the fact that it buckles down before the high and the mighty and if any of its officers takes cudgels for truth and right legal action, nobody believes him outside the CBI and the government, who internally do not tolerate him and throw him out at the earliest.

References

1. D.O. letter No. 79 dated 1.8.95 (at Annexure A) from the author. Para 10.

2. Cited above page 8 para 9.

4

LoC Scandal Rocks Assam

In the early nineties, Assam was rocked by a major scandal, which came to be known as The Assam LoC (Letter of Credit) scandal. There was a run on the treasuries, as the Government servants, the politicians, the businessmen – all had combined to loot. Mandatory formalities were brushed aside and the mechanism of loot progressively became simpler with every passing day, till ultimately, all the formalities and procedures became ridiculously non-existent, requiring only to prepare a bill in the prescribed form or even on just a plain paper, fill in any amount, attach a letter purported to be from Finance Department (FD), but could actually be prepared and signed by anybody on the roadside to indulge in the loot. The only limiting factor was that there had to be collusion between the treasury, the drawing department on whose account the bill was supposed to be drawn and the supplier/contractor.

Ordinarily, the drawl of any bill from a treasury is not a simple process, as the rules and the instructions laid down in the treasury manual are very rigorous. It is rather a cumbersome process, with a chain of formalities prescribed under the treasury rules. First of all, there has to be the budget allocation as made by the State Assembly and conveyed by the finance department to the administrative secretary and the head of the concerned department who distributes it amongst various units and advises the concerned treasury separately. Under no circumstance can the drawls exceed the budgeted amount. A copy of this distribution statement is also sent to the finance department, who ensures that only the allotted amount is distributed and not more. Secondly, there is a detailed procedure for sanction of the expenditure, about which detailed rules have been laid down. The Drawing and Disbursing Officer (DDO) has to certify that all those rules have been observed while preparing and presenting the bill. The Passing Officer in the treasury personally checks such certificates before passing a bill and also ensures that the flow of expenditure is even and that the department concerned does not exhaust its allotted budget in a short period. Thirdly, the DDO also has to ensure that the proper purchase procedures have been followed and all the concerned persons of the department have certified to that effect. Such certificates are finally supposed to be checked in the treasury. Fourthly, the Deputy Commissioner keeps a watch on the operations of the treasury as well as on various departments in his district. The treasury is supposed to report any irregularity or departure from procedures to DC, who is expected to inspect the treasury from time to time. In any case, regular returns are forwarded to him from the treasury so that he can keep a check. Fifthly, the FD is regularly informed of the expenditure booked by each treasury and each Department. The FD is supposed to monitor regularly the progress of expenditure. Last but not the least, there is still a final check that all the drawls are reported to the Accountant General (AG), who accounts for all these transactions and keeps a keen watch on all the above aspects.

For each of the above, there are detailed procedures and various checks have been prescribed. If followed, no treasury can suffer the virtual drain that the state of Assam underwent. Unfortunately, all the precautions and the procedures were thrown to winds as no proper bills were prepared, and entries in the registers were avoided. Drawl became a matter of tripartite arrangements between the colluding parties, leading to complete breakdown of the system of financial discipline and controls. The letters of credit and that too the fake ones, became the only critical input for making drawls from the treasury.

The letter of credit was a device designed as an additional check over all the others as narrated above. To understand and appreciate the mechanism, the need and the role of LoC, one has to look into the brief history of its evolution. Since 1972 Assam had been witnessing serious imbalances between resources and expenditure. The state found it difficult to arrange finances even upto the extent of its budget. To restrict the expenses further, the normal budgetary controls were considered inadequate and the letter of credit was introduced as an additional check. Letter of credit is a communication from the finance department authorizing to incur a particular expenditure and that too limited to a particular extent as prescribed in the letter, notwithstanding the fact that much more was available under the budget. However, if the budget was exhausted, no drawl was possible even if LoC was issued. Any drawl had to conform to the twofold conditions of the budget and the LoC. In the absence of such authority, the departments could not operate the budget beyond the salaries. In due course of time, the budget became redundant and bills started going through, only on the strength of the LoC. The original intention was that the LoC would not be a substitute for normal procedures, checks and the provisions, but would be in addition to all of them in order to further control/contain the expenditure. Incidentally the finance department, since 1972, never issued/reiterated explicit detailed instructions. That provided leverage to the departments, and other dishonest persons waiting in the wings to manoeuvre. They saw through the weaknesses and started drawing money on the basis of the LoC alone, which they got issued from the finance department for some consideration. Thus the LoC replaced the budget. The essential requirements of seeking sanctions were cast aside. In due course, in place of the LoC issued by FD, the fake letters started pouring in and the treasuries on the basis of the same allowed drawls. Huge amounts of money would be drawn at random and misappropriated.

When the CBI commenced investigations, its officers heard an interesting anecdote indicating the extent of the brazen loot. That during the heyday of the scam, a peon who had gone to collect payments amounting to a few crores of rupees from a sub-treasury in the sub-divisional or the Block level town, could not manage to pack all the bundles of notes in the gunny bags he had taken. He, on his own, is said to have gifted the overflow of a few lac rupees to the Bank staff. Whether it is true or not, is not important, but it definitely indicates the ground conditions that how the treasury had been turned into a medium of loot, so that anyone with requisite connections, the crookedness of mind, coupled with arrangements to share the booty, could get away with as much money as he was capable of managing.

Many departments like Animal Husbandry, Flood Control, Dairy Development and Revenue were suspected to be involved, but the most affected was the Animal Husbandry Department. It is interesting to note that in one of the sub-treasuries, the cash holding capacity was very low, but drawls of over Rs. 44 crores were allowed for construction activities against the annual budget allotment of about Rs. one lac only, for the whole of Animal Husbandry department.

The expenditure of Government of Assam exceeded the budgeted amount. Certain people started getting filthy rich overnight and that created a terror of affluence in the peaceful Assamese society. Assamese are basically peaceful and simple people who lead simple life with a few material requirements. Is it not surprising that a peon could carry money in gunny bags in a rickshaw without any escort? That could happen in Assam only. Subsequently, with intrusion of terrorism, conditions did change, but the basic love for peace, respect for law and simplicity in habits of the society, remained the same. Vulgar display of wealth came as a violent attack on Assamese sensitivities. Immediately, there were demands for looking into the matter, but it was after a long drawn struggle that K S Rao, the Additional Chief Secretary, Assam, was asked to look into the scandal. He found a bungling of Rs. 112 crores, in just 10 out of 30 treasuries by the Animal Husbandry Department alone. Within his given meager resources, the one-man committee could not be expected to go into whole details of all the departments, an impossible task within any reasonable time frame. Varying reports were circulating in the Press in 1994 putting the total loss in this scam between Rs. 200 to 700 crores. He could not probe the other departments as also the other treasuries.

Following the Rao Committee Report, the Assam Anti-Corruption Bureau registered 12 cases and started investigations, but the people of Assam suspected involvement of the Government of the day and the Chief Minister Hiteshwar Saikia himself. So, there was a demand for investigations by the CBI. After a long struggle they could succeed in pressurising the State Government as also the Central Government to hand over these cases to the CBI. I flew to Guwahati in May 1994 with a team to take charge of the investigations.

I met the Chief Secretary, who introduced me to K S Rao (the Additional Chief Secretary and the chairman of one-man enquiry committee). Rao handed over six huge boxes full of record which were seized after due deliberations. The team also took possession of the 12 cases with relevant records available with the Anti-Corruption Bureau, who had pioneered the initial investigations. However, the CBI team did not have a place to function from, nor were there any means of transport and communications. A request was made to the Chief Secretary for the same. He initially expressed his inability as Assam was facing serious financial crisis. But, faced with the prospects of this very report being placed on record and sent to the court, he summoned the home and the vigilance department officers and gave suitable instructions. Immediately, however, the boxes were airlifted to Delhi where all the records were to be examined and line of action for future investigations was to be determined.

Assam experiences heavy rains from June to August and passes through heavy floods, so no fieldwork could be possible immediately. From Delhi I kept tabs on the progress and again visited Guwahati in August, but the infrastructure was not ready. It could be a deliberate tactic to delay the investigations, or perhaps the usual bureaucratic delays or genuine financial problems, the net result was that investigations were getting delayed.

Rao had taken substantial records in possession, which gave the team a fair idea about the dimensions of the scam in the Animal Husbandry Department. As a one-man committee of enquiry he had done a commendable job.

The direction to be followed was set, but before taking any action, it required extensive field verifications, which were conducted by the staff during September and October. The visible phase of investigations commenced in November 1994 when wide-ranging simultaneous searches were conducted at 38 places all over Assam. Despite long delays, that were unavoidable in the circumstances, the searches yielded very useful information, indicating that tremendous results would have followed had these been conducted in time.

After appreciation of the record and the documents gathered from the people who were searched, one Rajan Bora emerged as the kingpin in the investigations. He was arrested, which evoked immense jubilation in the State. People had made utmost efforts and taken great pains to get these cases registered and also to get these transferred to the CBI. In May when the CBI team landed in Assam, there was visible satisfaction, though the people could not express the same publically, as the atmosphere was visibly surcharged with a sense of fear. Since I had served in the North East for five years till 1989, I had my roots in Guwahati. I tried to talk to the people of various denominations, but by and large, they were not willing to speak on the subject.

I called on one senior retired officer, whom I had known since my posting in North East. He welcomed me, but once he learnt that I was heading the CBI team, investigating the LoC scandal, the old man started perspiring and was annoyed, why of all persons I had chosen to visit him. He told me in no uncertain terms, "Mr Lall, in that case you should not have visited me, my life and life of my family may be in danger as Rajan Bora is a very dangerous person, he has lots of money, spies, agents and political patronage from the highest level. You should not expose me." I quickly finished the nice tea and snacks that his household had offered, walked out. In his nervousness he had given me lots of information by confirming the name of the kingpin, Rajan Bora.

I also visited some of the intellectuals and certain other persons in the town. I recall they were quite insistent that the case be investigated expeditiously and the criminals be brought to book. They were not afraid at all, but felt miserable at their helplessness. As responsible and enlightened citizens, they feared that if this case remained undetected, the entire administrative structure, the economy, the development, the social balance, all would tilt, fall and crumble. Though the scam was detected in 1991, why then the bunglings in bulk took place even in 1992-93? How this could continue with impunity? They posed this and such other similar questions and wanted answers. Further, they felt that the twelve cases were inadequate and touched only the tip of the iceberg; actual implications were much higher and should be worked out completely. They also expressed apprehensions whether the investigations would be allowed to reach their logical conclusion as the scam involved bureaucrats and political functionaries right upto the highest levels in the State. I assured them that the CBI would not leave any stone unturned and would not be cowed down by anybody howsoever high and mighty he could be. They raised another suspicion, that of my transfer. They were emphatic that if investigations really took off, soon CBI will start closing on Hiteshwar Saikia, the CM, who would see to it that the team was disintegrated. I assured them that the CBI was a professional, an impartial and a straight institution, so there was no question of anyone being transferred, but even if I or someone else were transferred, the investigations would continue. They heard me in general disbelief, but I was sure as I had just taken over in the CBI and did not visualize my transfer. I, of course, could not confide in them that I was planning to superannuate eight years hence from CBI only.

Rajan Bora alongwith certain other accused persons was arrested in November 1994, and interrogated. As he was thought to be above the law, there was initial disbelief, and then surprise followed by exultation. When I went to public places, I found the atmosphere entirely changed and relaxed. People had opened up and were talking frankly about the arrest of Rajan Bora. It dawned upon me how the fear of Mafia holds the society in thrall. The Dons weave and spread stories of invincibility around themselves and their cronies indulge in public display of muscle. They also drop the names of high state functionaries – both politicians and administrators – to drive home that nobody could touch them. Thus, they create an atmosphere of mental terror and basically survive on that. But once the arm of law performed its duty, tightened the noose, people felt assured that there was rule of law and the public confidence returned. They now talked about the involvement of the highest executive authorities of the state, both political and administrative, whereas just a few months back, they were afraid of hearing anything about Rajan Bora even. How important it is that the organs of the State should perform their duties well, without fear or favour, in a free, frank, legal and truthful manner. It gives an instant boost to the public morale. In this case once this man was arrested and interrogated, the entire magical fabric woven around him and his mentors was torn, the pal of terror disappeared in moments and people were breathing fresh air freely. Our task appeared to be easier as we expected people's active participation and the channels of intelligence and information to open.

V N Ojha, the deputy Legal Advisor, was flown to Guwahati as the court battles commenced immediately. Ojha conducted the court proceedings very well. The court used to be jampacked with huge crowds outside the premises, and would burst into slogans, hailing the investigations and cursing the culprits and their mentors.

The story unfolded that the bogus bills numbering hundereds of thousands were prepared, most of which were within the limit of rupees five hundred in order to avoid the formalities of sanctions at higher level. The task of the CBI was mammoth as every bungled crore of rupees could have bills to the tune of 20,000. So, for every Rs. 100 crores, there might be upto 20 lac letters of credit, which along with other records in the Secretariat, the departmental HQs., the drawing office, the treasury, the bank and with the AG, would have to be examined. In November-December the investigations proceeded very fast and the progress made was tremendous in all the twelve cases, but then there was a temporary lull as the teams were to return to their families in Delhi. By mid-February the investigations picked up again.

I instructed my officers to look into the scam in its totality, covering all the treasuries and all the departments, so that more cases could be registered and the conspiracy aspect could be probed thoroughly covering *inter alia* the following:

(a) What was the total volume of bungling of both types i.e. within the allotted budget and beyond the allotted budget?

(b) To assess the Animal Husbandry Department in the entire state and look into the affairs of all the thirty odd treasuries as Rao had examined only ten of them.

(c) To look into the drawls of all the other departments of Assam Government during the crucial period, but remaining particular about Dairy Development, Revenue and Flood Control Departments which were rather infamous.

(d) Who were the kingpins and masterminds?

(e) Also to trace in details, how the system started, picked up and was perfected, so that the preventive action for future could be laid down.

Some information about these macro variables had started flowing and the remaining was expected to follow. Part of it was already in the pipeline. By April-May 1995, the complicity of certain highly placed officials and politicians was established and the line had also reached the then Assam Chief Minister Hiteshwar Saikia. This was mentioned in the court at Guwahati, which the Press naturally reported. It alerted the powers that be. The Government of India sought the details immediately after appearance of some reports in the local press at Guwahati. As desired by the ministry, details were sent in May end of 1995 in a note containing facts stating clearly the possible involvement of the Chief Minister. There were rumours in Assam that he was in touch with Centre and had made all efforts to get me transferred. I received a couple of calls from Guwahati informing me to this effect. However, I was already deeply involved in other matters like Hawala and V Krishnamurthy cases, which had perhaps already decided my fate. After that the issues of complete investigation i.e. macro variables or exploring the genesis of the scam or the conspiracy angle were not pursued. If the JD was removed and punished for reaching out for the big names amongst others in LoC scandal, how could anyone else think of taking up the cudgels? The system had delivered the requisite message. Later, perhaps what to say of the records, even the data about other departments and other treasuries was never collected and whatever had already trickled in, was never utilised. Though it was very big scam, the mother scam to the Bihar AHD scandal, the investigations remained confined to twelve cases, to ten out of thirty treasuries and just one department out of about half a dozen identified as infected. The total implications for all the departments for the entire state remained unassessed. Its full extent will always remain shrouded in the dark.

The people of Assam linked my transfer to my role in investigation of LoC scandal, and the local Press did report so. They naturally believed that their apprehensions had come true. In July 1995, I had to leave the investigations into this scam finally without completing my task.

5

Jungle Raj in CBI

Change, they say, is always for the better. When in the last week of July 1996, Joginder Singh was posted as director CBI, I thought things might improve; there might be less of political interference, more transparency and truth might prevail in a larger measure. On 31st July, in the farewell party for the outgoing director Ramo Rao, Joginder Singh had expressed his determination to strive for fair play, truth, transparency and his resolve to fight corruption, particularly in high places. I informally interacted with him at length and was happy that now at least there would be some romance in the fight against corruption.

My joy, hope and expectations were short-lived. The dream was shattered in the first week of August. At the marriage function of a former Minister's daughter, Joginder Singh created quite a sensation when he sought lift in the car of the former Prime Minister P V Narasimha Rao, while the latter was departing after attending the wedding. Joginder Singh rushed to him and sought permission for lift in his car and travelled with him to his residence. He was alone with the former PM for about 15 minutes. The media picked it up, and for the next few days the trip received adverse coverage on the TV and in the Press. Joginder Singh made a reference to it in the meeting of Joint Directors. He decried 'all this media hype' and explained it as a courtesy call to seek guidance and blessings of a former PM. I pointed out that Mr Rao was now our accused, and the director should not have called on him. Joginder Singh retorted that till yesterday we used to be at attention for him and declared his resolve to call on all the former PMs and seek their guidance and blessings. It was clear that he was trying to cover up the indiscretion that he had committed and also that he did not like my role as self-appointed conscience keeper of the CBI. His hard looks indicated that the battle lines were drawn and I should expect trouble as vengeance showed immediately in his eyes, which the ever-present mechanical smile on his lips could not conceal.

I was wondering what sort of times we were passing through. While entering the CBI, Joginder Singh had promised complete transparency and truth, but on ground, he had fallen right at the beginning. It was reliably learnt that when he took lift in Rao's car, he was on a political mission, to hold assurances to the former PM that there was no cause for worry and that the CBI would take care of his interests. It was clear even to a naive that his political mission was on behalf of the then PM Deve Gowda, whose survival in office was dependent on the support of PV Narasimha Rao and his Congress party and the excuse of paying courtesy call and seeking blessings/guidance was only a cover up. Courtesy call is made in a decent and a graceful manner by seeking prior appointment and not running around, crossing SPG cordon in an embarrassing manner and taking lift in the car of a dignitary by surprise. Had the SPG men not accosted him, Singh might have gone unnoticed. Perhaps his mission was secret and so urgent that he could not wait. The Supreme Court admonished him for taking the controversial lift. He promised to behave in future and not to indulge in such conduct unbecoming of the CBI Chief.

I was extremely disturbed, as Joginder Singh appeared to be in much deeper political waters than even Rama Rao, his predecessor. The future course of events and his subsequent conduct in several cases showed the depth of his political involvement. In a Bombay (Mumbai) case he ordered chargesheet by month end, overruling the submissions of the concerned JD that the investigations had just begun and the case was still not mature for the chargesheet. When pressed hard, the JD took shelter behind the excuse that he did not have legal support ready at hand. The JD Bombay (Mumbai) and myself were sharing the same Additional Legal Advisor (ALA) who used to divide his time between Bombay (Mumbai) and Delhi. This was the time when he was supposed to be in Delhi, but he was asked to proceed to Bombay (Mumbai) immediately. The JD had, perhaps, raised the point as a pretext for extension of time, but could not succeed. The ALA spent two weeks in Bombay (Mumbai) and prepared the case for being chargesheeted. Within a few days of his return to Delhi, he was ordered to proceed to Bombay (Mumbai) again and dismantle the case. Obviously the director was following the political directions and oscillated accordingly. He could have commanded the JD to expedite investigations, but it was wrong to have asked him to chargesheet when investigations were yet to commence and evidence had yet to be collected and appreciated. The order for dismantling was the worst thing that could happen in an organisation dealing with law and collection of facts. Truth and transparency should have been the guiding force and not the expediency that too changing twice in one month. I am not aware what ultimately happened to the case, but one could witness every now and then how he kept on tinkering with the system, breaking it at will, regardless of facts, laws and truth.

He tried to undo all the efforts of U N Biswas, the JD handling the Animal Husbandry scam of Bihar, obviously following the political equations and possible political dictates. He issued transfer orders confining Biswas, only to Calcutta, i.e. taking away charge of Patna. When this met with severe criticism, he decided to confine Biswas only to Patna in order to harass and embarrass him. Meanwhile it was time to file the Status Papers in the High Court on 30th September 1996. Biswas had taken great pains to prepare the papers compiling meticulously the evidence that existed against various persons involved in the scam, including Laloo Prasad Yadav and concluded that evidence existed against him requiring detailed investigations. I saw the papers with Biswas. There appeared to be enough justification *prima facie* to include his (Laloo's) name in the report for conducting further investigations against him.

Biswas had a tough time, as director would not agree for even the mention of the name of Laloo Prasad Yadav in the report. A via media was found that the senior most officer of the CBI next to the director, was asked to prepare a report, which could be filed in the High Court. The report was to make a mention of the name of Laloo Yadav, but would not talk about the extent of his involvement at that stage of investigations. R C Sharma, the Special director, prepared the report accordingly. It was learnt that Joginder Singh threw this report into the dustbin, prepared another report deleting Laloo Yadav's name. He gave a copy of the same duly sealed to Biswas to be filed in Patna High Court. Biswas had seen and agreed to the report as edited by R C Sharma, but he was shocked when the report was read in the court.

Biswas, on enquiry, informed the court that it was not his report. The High Court at this stage asked Biswas to report directly to it, as obviously, the director could not be relied upon. Joginder Singh stood barred from looking into any papers related to AHD scam of Bihar. An extraordinary situation had been created. In an organisation like the CBI, political commitment can never be tolerated. The order might have tarnished the fair name and the honour of the CBI beyond redemption, but the High Court was perfectly justified in passing such an extraordinary order and for taking such an exceptional step, never meted out to any officer and much less the director in the history of CBI. Left to Joginder Singh, Biswas would have been thrown out of the CBI, but the Patna High Court at the same time ruled that no officer investigating AHD case would be transferred out without permission from the court. Biswas came under court protection and could conduct investigations undisturbed.

A similar situation arose in Jharkhand Mukti Morcha (JMM) case in which also the Delhi High Court suspected Singh's bona-fides. He had taken this case away from the SP, Arun Sinha, a straightforward officer determined to do the right. Sinha was deep into the case when Singh asked him to conclude the case in a particular way and to collect evidence accordingly. When Sinha refused to oblige, Joginder Singh transferred him from Delhi to Silchar branch and thus took away the case from him. The court restored the case to the same SP and asked the DIG and the SP to report directly to the court. It also ordered that no papers concerning the case should be shown to Joginder Singh, nor the case be discussed with him. The main accused in the JMM case was none other than P V Narasimha Rao, the Congress President on whom the Government of Deve Gowda was dependent for political support.

It was for the second time that a High court suspected the bonafides of the director CBI personally. Thus two different High Courts had barred director Joginder Singh from the scrutiny of the records of his own organisation. He also had the distinction of being reprimanded for unbecoming conduct by the Supreme Court. It is remarkable that the three courts independently identified similar aberrations in him in such a short time. His behaviour and conduct was deeply steeped in politicking, as perceived by CBI officers, that he had no regard for professional morality or ethics, that he did not follow or respect the basic tenets of investigations that the conclusions should always follow the evidence and not vice versa, that an investigator should begin with a clean slate rather than with predetermined notions. In the sensitive cases, Joginder Singh would dictate or at least indicate in advance how a particular case or a person was to be treated. IOs were expected to mould, tailor or create evidence accordingly, which basically should be foreign to the members of a fact finding organisation like the CBI.

After committing such patent indiscretions, he has the audacity to preach scriptures when in his book *'Inside CBI'* he writes[1]: "When I took over reins, I found CBI under a lot of pressure to safeguard the interest of former Prime Minister P V Narasimha Rao." If he had so realised, why did he call on Rao? Does it not show that Singh himself was under so much pressure that despite realising what he states, he had to call on the same person who was pressurising the CBI? Is it that there is no relationship in what he did and what he writes and what he says? How could such a director rise above politics or political pressures or exhort his juniors to rise above or protect them against the same? It was the other way round that I had to tell him not to buckle down under the pressures and that his conduct in calling on the former PM was unbecoming. The chain of events starting with calling on PVNR continued unbroken all through till such time his mentor required the help of Rao.

JMM case is the next link in the chain. Arun Sinha, the SP, confided in me later that Joginder Singh had asked him to change the case diary and a material statement and on his refusal to oblige, he was sent to Silchar from where he came back under court orders. He was so disillusioned with the premier investigation agency that he opted to go back to his cadre, as he could not fight Joginder Singh beyond the JMM case. Whereas in JMM case he came under court protection, but not so in other cases, and finally his report had to be written by Joginder Singh only who could have ruined his career.

Continuing the same way, Joginder Singh extended protection to the family members of Narasimha Rao in the Urea case. He ordered post-haste transfer of R M Singh, the DIG supervising the case, who was camping at Hyderabad and was likely to come heavy on the family members of the former PM.

Same story was repeated in Lakhubhai Pathak case. The prominent CBI counsel Gopal Subramaniam threatened to, and ultimately did resign, in sheer disgust. The Press was full of criticism of CBI. I checked up with my friend Anand Kumar, who was JD in charge of the case. He confided that Joginder Singh, for obvious reasons, had told him to convey to the counsel not to oppose the bail application of Rao in the Lukhubhai Pathak case. Anand told to have recorded on the file that the CBI had no reason or ground for taking such a plea in the court of Law. Joginder Singh did not agree and said that he would go to the Attorney General of the government and get orders from him not to oppose the bail. Late at night Joginder Singh rang up Anand over RAX (official hotline), and asked him to visit the Law Minister along with a stenographer. Singh informed that everything had been pre-arranged; the Law Minister would issue a letter, conveying that the bail was not to be opposed. Anand was further asked to convey the decision personally to Gopal Subramaniam. Anand agreed to send a junior functionary and sent an SP with a stenographer to the residence of the Law Minister. The SP returned at past midnight with a letter from the Law Minister conveying government decision not to oppose the bail. The letter also mentioned that it had the approval of Attorney General. On receiving this communication, Anand informed Joginder Singh who in turn asked the former to send it to Gopal Subramaniam to whom Anand spoke at around 1 o'clock at night. Gopal Subramaniam received the letter, promptly sent a negative reply and threatened to resign and walk out of the case. Anand briefed Joginder Singh early in the morning. Fearing adverse publicity, about which Joginder Singh was highly conscious, he tried to persuade Subramaniam not to resign. Subramaniam appeared in the court but did not oblige. He opposed the bail application and afterwards walked out of the case. The CBI had turned into a handmaid with a completely politicalised director. The press naturally carried stories derogatory about the CBI and its director, but all that was well deserved under its new Chief.

All these clearly reveal how deeply mired Joginder Singh was in politics, completely contrary to his claims.

Joginder Singh was in the habit of dropping the name of PM every now and then, even in context of the most insignificant matter. Once I had a count and discovered that he mentioned PM's name at least once in every three minutes. It is not a sign of strength, but basic internal weakness of a bully, a person who felt helpless without any crutches. Such a person tries to pose brave, and out of his nervousness tries to show himself as a go-getter and tends to show disrespect for law. Posing himself above all, he becomes intolerant of dissent and flaunts his super connections to silence the same.

Flaunting his proximity to powers that be, may speak of his clout with the PM, but this proximity by itself is indicative of what political pressures he will have to bear with. All clouts are at a cost, but such close clout of a director CBI would rightly be viewed with suspicion by all intelligent people and is counterproductive to the task and philosophy of the CBI.

It was obvious that he was quite fed up with my plain speaking. Sometime in September 1996, he spoke to me about shifting my HQ from Delhi to Lucknow. There could be no reason for such an unprecedented step. I represented that my jurisdiction extended from Kashmir to Bastar in Madhya Pradesh, so Lucknow would not be appropriate as my HQ; Delhi was central and well established and all the JDs, except the metropolitan ones, were in Delhi only. Till sometime back, Delhi DIG also used to be part of the North Zone only. If anything, Delhi could be brought back to the North Zone. But instead, on 7th of October, he took away the charge of Chandigarh region leaving only UP and MP with me so that he could transfer me out of Delhi and place me at Lucknow and get rid of my inconvenient presence at Delhi. He had ascertained my family circumstances and knew that I could not move out of Delhi as my children were studying there itself. Besides, my wife was working at Gurgaon with Haryana Government and could not be transferred to UP. He had checked all this a few days earlier from me only and planned a perfect move to harass me.

Incidentally another matter with serious consequences happened at that very time. A complaint was received regarding a big mining scandal. I insisted to look into this case of Madhya Pradesh involving the big people, which he did not like. He had rejected my proposal on 4th October, and gave me the jolt of detaching Chandigarh from my jurisdiction on Monday, the 7th October. May be it was a step to intimidate me so that I could leave the CBI on my own and opt back for repatriation or fall in line. Following the action of 7th, I wrote him a D.O. Letter No. 296 dated 18th October 1996 (Annexure-D), telling him that whereas he had promised transparency, but his transfer policy was a hush hush tool of oppression. He had also used the same instrument on R M Singh, Biswas, Arun Sinha and myself in various cases. He used transfer as the stick to beat with, but after my D.O. letter, he did not pursue the case of transfer of my headquarter to Lucknow. Undeterred, I had throughout kept up my plain speaking on truth and transparency in the meetings and on the official files. He instead waited for the opportune moment to ambush, and his chance came during the CBI conference in November 1996.

It was a three-day conference of CBI, Chiefs of Anti-Corruption Bureaux of the States and the Central PSUs. On the 20th November, it was a get-together of only the CBI officers from all over the country. The director posed us a question "Why CBI got adverse publicity despite good work leading to recovery of Rs. 4 crores in the Sukh Ram case?" Only I reacted saying that people did recognise the good work in individual cases, but overall credibility was lacking as the CBI had to do and also to appear to be absolutely truthful and transparent as these were the two-fold basic and fundamental expectations of the people from us. The director was not prepared to listen the words like truth and straight forwardness. He commented on transparency only that he was absolutely transparent as he was interacting with the Press regularly. My observation that it was publicity and not transparency, peeved him. The issue was left at that.

On the second day of the conference, I wanted to react to a paper on "Fighting Corruption at High Places" presented by an SP, but the director would not allow. When I insisted, an order was served on me in the Conference Hall at Vigyan Bhawan itself, commanding me to proceed to Lucknow immediately to supervise the Ayurveda Scam. This was, no doubt, a big scam in which the treasury had been drained like the great Bihar or the Assam scandals, but whatever was to be done, had already been done and I had just returned from Lucknow after thoroughly reviewing the case and he was aware of that. My presence at Lucknow would have been counterproductive for at least another ten days. Moreover, what I was to do there when both the SP and the DIG of Lucknow were present in the conference itself. I recorded accordingly on the file in the Conference Hall itself and sent the file to him through my Special director. The file returned to me after two days duly seen by director. Though I continued to attend the conference, but Singh put an absolute ban on my speech. The flash point came when he declared that he would close the conference at 12 o'clock. He ruled that only the gist of the papers would be read, and after that the conference would close for the day, so that 'delegates from outside Delhi could make official/social calls in Delhi', which in his view 'was also equally important'. He did not respond to the question of mutual interaction at the conference. I took strong exception and protested that the Government had spent Rs. 20-30 lacs and 280 participants had gathered with the sole purpose of interacting amongst themselves to pool together their collective wisdom and experience and also analyse the same from various angles. They had not come all the way to Delhi to socialize. Singh was furious. He could not control his rage and came out in his true colours. Showing utter disrespect to the house, he declared that there would be no discussions "as all discussions lead to confusion". The entire house was shell-shocked. At this stage, there were protests from all around the house against his remarks. He had no option but to continue the proceedings. I again requested him to allow me to participate. Heated arguments were going on between Singh and me around 2 p.m., when the then Union Home Secretary K Padmanabhiah reappeared at the scene and was shocked to see how the flow of thought process was being choked. He was particularly shocked that this very point was being argued in his presence when he left in the morning at around 11 a.m. It was only on the intervention of the Home Secretary that I finally got my chance to put forth my views.

In my speech, I clearly highlighted the fact that corruption was the biggest challenge the country was facing. Corruption had made its inroads into social, economic, academic, political, administrative and even cultural aspects of life and was causing havoc everywhere. I defined corruption as the conversion of political and administrative power into money. If an individual had more power, his potential for corruption was also higher. So it was much more serious a problem at higher places, where immense power lay.

I underscored the point that corruption affected the lowest segment of the society, the worst. So basically it was a problem to be fought at high places, whereas the administration and the investigating agencies stopped when they faced the big and mighty, because of the feudal bias and also out of the fear of reprisals from them in administrative spheres as their own control lies with these very people only. I observed that it was in this context that even in the CBI the officers when faced with VIPs and VIP cases, instead of taking straight action, kept on weighing the political fall out and how it may affect them. It was for this reason that teams deputed to investigate VIP cases invariably stopped in their tracks when line of investigation reached the high and mighty. I continued that so long as the Executive would exercise control over the CBI, the organisation would not be able to function impartially and truthfully. It was a statement of facts, but the director took it as personal affront, stopped me in between and argued that there were no political pressures on the CBI under him and that all this was a campaign to malign the CBI. At this stage the Home Secretary intervened again and observed that it was an academic exercise and that I should be allowed to express my views and that he personally found nothing objectionable or wrong in my deposition.

Still, the director did not permit me to elaborate the theme. He asked me to give my solution very briefly. I suggested that the CBI be placed under the charge of an Independent Board, so that it could function impartially and truthfully, independent of the executive (whom it was supposed to investigate). I further elaborated that the CBI Board should get constituted automatically, according to a well laid out drill, instead of anyone picking up or recommending a particular person, i.e. the system should throw up the members so that a member is not obliged to anyone for having recommended him or selected him. That this board should exercise all the powers which were vested in the government. The director would act under the directions of this board and also be its member Secretary. Incidentally I had written an article outlining similar views on CBI Board, which was published in *The Hindustan Times* on 1st March 1996 (Annexure - E).

On the evening of 21st, Joginder Singh picked up certain participants to speak on certain assigned topics when the Prime Minister was to attend the conference the next day. He also briefed them separately, probably on what they were supposed to speak. It was meant as a public relations exercise and a cover up move to project a rosy picture, show approval of the conference for various issues, irrespective of the fact whether these were deliberated and recommended or not.

The morning newspapers on 22nd November carried reports on proceedings of the previous day. *The Statesman* reported under the caption 'Ugly scenes at CBI meet', "sharp differences of opinion and ugly scenes rocked the confidential seminar on anti-corruption held during the annual general meeting of the CBI today when a senior Joint director of the Agency raised the issue of political pressures, prompting the CBI director Mr. Joginder Singh to jump to advance his defence ......" The joint director continued "......officers of the Agency were not being allowed a freehand in investigation. They are forced to consider the political fall out of cases rather than concentrate on investigation to bring them to a logical conclusion......that the agency is following a feudal system,... investigating officers are being forced to go soft on politicians...The CBI officers are gunning for the people of inconsequence when records and investigations point otherwise."

Other papers also made similar reports and brought out and discussed the struggle that went on in the CBI and commented adversely on the director who did not want such (so-called inconvenient) matters to be discussed at all. Some papers questioned 'what for the conference?' I felt that the reactions, betrayed by Joginder Singh, were only natural, as non-investigation of VIP cases, stopping investigations where it crossed their path, were more of a rule and I had been crying hoarse before the two Directors for the last over two years that the CBI was not conducting complete, impartial, truthful and transparent investigations against people in high places. The media termed it as an internal struggle in the CBI.

On the 22nd, Prime Minister Deve Gowda was to address the conference. Instead of a formal address, he chose to interact with the delegates. He asked the media persons to leave the conference venue. In his initial remarks, the PM made a mention of ongoing dissatisfaction in the CBI and referred to the proceedings of the previous day as reported in the Press. The indication obviously was towards me. I was not scheduled to speak, but I raised my hand to attract PM's attention. Fortunately it worked and the PM invited me to speak.

I first spoke on the need for housing for all the CBI cadres all over the country for ensuring integrity and for improving efficiency, morale and discipline. Bulk of the manpower of CBI was located in metropolitan cities, with very high rentals. The inspectors and DSPs, who constituted the cadres of investigators, could ill-afford the luxury of a hired house in any metropolis. No honest person will like to join on deputation from states under such conditions. All the world over, the anti-corruption agencies, take experienced cadres on deputation mostly on a fifty per cent basis. In the CBI, getting just 200 investigators from all the states put together was a perennial problem. I diagnosed the lack of accommodation as the basic cause. I continued that allurements were great in CBI even at the level of Inspectors. It was not worth testing the patience of investigators. Even the financial implications were just peanut at around Rs. 100 crores for making good the total shortfall of 3500 houses all over the country.

I then reverted to the basic question of fight against corruption at high places covering the ground similar to my deposition a day earlier. First, I brought the seriousness of the problem to the notice of the house that corruption had traveled to the highest of levels and no level had remained untouched. Here again I defined corruption as conversion/encashment of power, both political and administrative, into money. The more the power, the more the potential for corruption and very few persons were avoiding this option of encashment. I continued that corruption was eating into the vitals of our society by its adverse effects on all facets of life, culminating into a sort of mafia because of the growing nexus between the criminals, the corrupt officials and the unscrupulous politicians. Though corruption was always believed to be there at lower levels, where it still continued to exist, but the problem had been aggravated by corruption at high places and it was here that the real serious fight had to begin. The laws to fight corruption existed, but like all other laws, the laws pertaining to corruption were also being enforced selectively, making the fight meaningless. I further spoke on strengthening the institutions meant for fighting corruption and in particular the CBI, which though was well equipped with the skills and was doing very well so far as the small fries were concerned, but in case of the big, it behaved differently and extended them all its possible services in hushing up the matter by not bringing the evidence to the fore. The reason for such behaviour was simple that since the agency was subordinate to the same executive, whom it was supposed to investigate, the agency suffered a basic handicap and could not be effective against its own masters who controlled it. Further I presented an alternate model for supervision of CBI advocating an independent board, automatically constituted, which should have all the discretion, that the Government had exercised so far, i.e. all the administrative powers including those of concurrence under the single directive (if it were to continue) for investigation as also the power of prosecution sanction, should vest in this very Board and not in the concerned departments or the ministries, whose heads themselves were subject of investigation as of late corruption had become a cooperative, collaborative and collusive venture and appeared to have been corporatised. So the same or the connected people could not be trusted for the judgement.

My speech became the trendsetter and after me certain other speakers also spoke in the language different from one expected by Joginder Singh. But I was taken aback when the Prime Minister spoke. He decried all the institutions engaged in fight against corruption and posed a question to us "...now I would like to ask a question. Let me ask straight question; which country is free from corruption? Can anybody stand up and say before me? I have given freedom to you. There is no question of reservation from anybody, even if you were SPs and DIGs. Which country is free from corruption? Please tell me. Is Japan free from corruption? Is America free from corruption? Which country today is free from corruption?" While posing these questions, the Prime Minister had mentioned my name, (which however, does not appear in his speech as reproduced in the proceedings, a copy of which is placed at Annexure – F). Though he was addressing the entire audience, but basically it was a reaction to the inconvenient questions, which I had raised and certain other persons had re-enforced. Further, his mention of disagreement in the CBI referred to my altercation with Joginder Singh a day earlier, so I decided to react to the statement of the Prime Minister that 'which country is honest'.

At that time the indices of Transparency International were not available, but I was aware of the effective and stringent steps that had been taken or were in the process in various countries to combat corruption at high places. Not one, but many countries like Japan, Italy and South Korea had taken effective action and even put their erstwhile Chief Executives behind bars for corruption. These countries are very strict in enacting stringent laws and also in enforcing them. South Korea for instance had concluded that most bunglings were hatched at golf courses. So they banned public servants from visiting golf courses for playing golf. Police chief of a state violated and had to pay the price – he was sacked. Even though these countries were not entirely free from the evil, they had the will and have been waging a fight against corruption to keep it under control as the subsequent surveys of Transparency International have shown.

But when I stood up to say so, he silenced me saying, "Mr. Lall, I have heard you patiently. Will you not listen to me"? I sat down in helplessness. The speech of the Prime Minister as may be seen was devastating. It has not been reproduced verbatim, but even in the form it has been reproduced, it hits at all the honourable institutions engaged in fight against corruption. He came heavy on the judiciary. "Don't be under the impression that judiciary today has got an opportunity to improve the system. If anybody is under the impression that corruption is going to be removed by this activism, they are in fools' paradise". He further decried the institutions of Lokpal and Lokayukt. Making contemptuous reference to Lokpal bill at centre he described how miserably the institution had failed in Karnataka. "Is Karnataka free of corruption" he posed. He went on, "No politician appeared before this Lokayukt. They tried to dilute the institution. And today nobody bothers. Don't be under the impression that the Lokayukt brought a revolutionary change. When the bill was introduced in the Assembly, I was hearing that. I was just laughing. Here also this United Front Government will introduce the Lokpal Bill. Let the bill be passed. I will also live for another 10-15 years. Let me see how much corruption is going to be reduced in this country. You also will watch":

The Prime Minister accused the judiciary of seeking revenge against the politicians, which according to him was the crux of all judicial activism. He cited the example of a veteran politician who was in public life for fifty years and his integrity was never in doubt, but now it was suddenly being challenged. In a nutshell, the entire speech highlighted the futility of any effort to fight corruption, as a useless exercise bound to end in failure. The audience was stunned. Since fight against corruption was a fruitless exercise as stated by the Chief Executive of the great nation himself, the cries of lesser mortals like a Joint director of the CBI, could naturally have no place in the scheme of things under the prevalent ailing system.

Joginder Singh had taken upon himself the task of cleansing the system of truth, transparency, straightforwardness and silencing all dissent against his autocratic unprincipled functioning. Perhaps taking a cue from the speech of the PM, he accelerated the process of complete mental subjugation, which he had started immediately after taking over the CBI; so much so that his words would not be open even to discussion, as "All discussions lead to confusion". He had become such a terror that officers were afraid of him particularly because of his proximity (which he very skilfully flaunted) to the PM and the continuous threats of transfer, repatriation etc., that he held out. His clout with PM proved the clinching factor in holding everyone to ransom. When any officer checked up with his staff to see him, he was normally said to be either with the PM or with the Press. He would never miss a single chance of telling how close he was to PM and for the smallest case even, he will make a mention that he would discuss the same with the PM. He enjoyed flaunting his connections and creating mafia like atmosphere in his office for his subordinates as also his visitors. He used to have half a dozen rooms reserved for himself, meeting this man in one room and that man in the other, in an atmosphere permeated with fear and intimidation. To overawe them, he even crushed the constabulary serving in the CBI destroying some of the families in the process. Incidentally it was my last sin as I had consistently opposed their repatriation till a week before mine own.

He exercised his prerogative of transferring officers at will and at random, choosing deliberately the time and the station where the officer would be inconvenienced. The transfer was perfected into an art of inflicting punishment. By and large he had subdued the officers of CBI and only I was yet to be muzzled. Singh was not a person to miss hitting while the iron was hot. Stealthily, and in violation of all the rules and instructions, he managed my repatriation prematurely. How can such a person invoke these very values, which he had violated and decried all along in context of others? In his book *Inside CBI* on his own transfer he writes[2],

> "Transfers are ordered either as a, follow up to promotions or because of inconvenience caused to powers that be. In my case they heaped opprobrium before stealthily ordering my ouster from the organization."

How can Joginder Singh write so, when he himself had been transferring/repatriating/reverting people without any valid reason, just at his whims and also with devious intentions to pressurise and punish for getting wrong things done.

He goes on[3], "such was the hurry to get me out that I was not given the time to clear out the office of my paraphernalia. It brings into sharp focus the class of politicians at the helm of the government."

How could he forget that he only established this tradition in the CBI? He transferred and relieved Arun Sinha and R M Singh too suddenly, in a hurry without allowing any time, creating thereby circumstances worse than his own. Neither of them had gone on promotion. Same rules, as he invokes for himself, apply to them also. They were all inconvenient as they were fighting to ward off pressure from the director (which is much more difficult and worse than any political pressures) to fall in line with his political designs. It is Joginder Singh, the director, who had nearly scuttled the Bihar Animal Husbandary Department (AHD) scam. It is strange how could his conscience permit him to write, "the attempts at interference in the fodder scam were beginning to irritate me." It was he who held repeated threats of transfer to Biswas, that too, in the shabbiest manner. All these transfers involved even the change of station. I had written to him about this in October 1996.

The worst happened in my own case. Immediately after the CBI conference the process of repatriating me back to my state was commenced. I learnt about this only in the first week of December 1996 after my return from Hong Kong, where I had gone immediately after the conference. I called on the Secretary Personnel to know the facts. He heard whatever I said, but avoided making any comment except assuring me that he would personally look into the matter and ensure justice. However, the CBI was agog with rumours that the repatriation had been approved. I sought appointment with the Home Secretary, the Home Minister as also the Cabinet Secretary, Mr. T S R Subramaniam. The Home Minister heard me with rapt attention, but at the end only stated "Joginder had come with a small file, only stating that Lall had to be repatriated as desired by the Prime Minister, so I just signed". He agreed that my speech in the conference contained nothing objectionable and only raised points of principle. The Home Secretary denied any knowledge before he saw the orders of repatriation of 19th December. The file was not routed through him, nor was it examined in the Home Ministry. I checked up in the Ministry of Personnel and learnt that the issue was not examined in their office as well. I called on the Cabinet Secretary on 27th December 1996, and briefed him about the circumstances and the serious irregularities that were committed in my repatriation case as follows:

a) Cadre clearance of MHA, the cadre controlling authority, was not obtained though it was mandatory.

b) All the prescribed channels were evaded.

c) The case was not submitted for examination at any stage either in the MHA or in the Ministry of Personnel.

d) Mine was a mid-term repatriation as I had completed only half of the five-year tenure, for which special reasons are required to be cited, otherwise the repatriation could not be ordered.

e) That I had given the highest output for 1994 to 1996 and also given new directions in trial disposal raising the annual figure from 1½ to 35 cases (23 times) at Jabalpur branch and conviction rate had also improved along with the quantum of conviction.

His only reaction was that if the director says that he could not run the CBI, with Lall being around, he (Cabinet Secretary) is bound to recommend the JD's transfer. I tried to plead about the great injustice and its fall out on others and requested to be heard, so that the right could prevail, but he refused even to listen any more arguments or pleadings on any merits. I then made a personal request for adjustment in any other organisation of Government of India, for the remainder of my tenure, as systems of education of Delhi, Haryana and Chandigarh were altogether different and my children might have to lose upto two years each. Even at this he did not assure me a placement in Delhi. He only observed, that if a proposal came from the Home Ministry, he would not oppose it. It was a response from negative angle. What made it more serious was that the highest bureaucrat of the land had no concern for the truth and merit giving impression that these were mundane and outdated matters. Later when I narrated the response of the Cabinet Secretary to a very senior IAS officer, and observed how could the Cabinet Secretary have a reputation for straight dealings. This senior officer had a hearty laugh and said, "Lall you should have thought of the timings. It was 27th and his own case of extension was to be decided by 31st. Joginder Singh could have punctured his case and sabotaged it as he had PM's ears and could do anything to anyone. Should T S R (T S R

Subramaniam, the Cabinet Secretary) bother about his extension or your affairs"? He further added, "T S R could not have mustered courage to go against Joginder Singh even normally". It was obvious that the sense of justice, the fairness, is all conditioned by the sense of self-interest and security and Joginder Singh was in a position to undermine that in the context of any civil servant including the Cabinet Secretary, so it was all waste of time and energy putting forth any merits before him.

Even in serving the orders, efforts to humiliate me continued. I was relieved on 27th December in absentia when I was with the Cabinet Secretary. The order of transfer/repatriation is served and if someone refuses to hand over, then only as a last resort another order is issued that the officer will be deemed relieved. In this case, the first and the only order issued vide No.3/44/94-Ad.V dated 27.12.96 reads "Services of Shri BR Lall are placed at the disposal of Govt. of Haryana. Sh. BR Lall stands relieved from CBI w.e.f forenoon on 27.12.1996". To say the least, this was too arbitrary, autocratic, and hush-hush. I was kept in the dark and members of ACC misled and then it was used as a lever to humiliate.

On my removal from the CBI, *Hindustan Times* wrote on 28.12.96, "Mr. Lall....had categorically told the CBI director that Political interference at the highest level was making work conditions difficult for the investigators."

Economic Times carried lead editorial on 30.12.1996 under caption "Revoke Transfer Order."

"He dared to speak the truth and was shunted out of his job. The CBI Joint director BR Lall, at the annual meeting of the CBI and State Anti-corruption Officers held in November in New Delhi, merely pointed out what is a very common, and serious, problem faced by investigating agencies today. That politicians involved in corruption cases interfere with the work of investigating agencies, hampering their progress. A few days later he was transferred out of the CBI for raising this topic at a meeting, which was supposed to discuss precisely these issues......In fact the annual meeting of the CBI and state level anti-corruption officers would have been a farce if this important issue....were not discussed....If the transfer order is not revoked, no cop would dare act against politicians he finds guilty in the course of his investigations... Instead of nabbing the guilty, all he will do is to protect the politicians; because that is the only way he can protect his job." The paper further laments, "What is worse is that instead of taking action against politicians who interfere, Prime Minister H D Deve Gowda, reportedly asked him the reason for his discontent, as if there is need for another reason."

The Statesman wrote on 13.12.1996 under the heading 'CBI Chief prefers Yes men'.

"Moves are afoot to remove a senior officer of the Central Bureau of Investigation for candidly expressing his opinion, much to the discomfort and embarrasement of the director, Mr. Joginder Singh....The move to repatriate Mr. Lall to his parent cadre comes close on the heels of the unpleasant exchange between Mr. Lall and Mr. Singh in the recently held annual CBI conference. Mr. Lall reportedly made strong observations about the politicization of the CBI and the immediate need to stem the same. Though Mr. Lall had made these remarks in general, Mr. Singh jumped to his defence, and as some of the senior officers remarked 'Let the cat out of the bag unwittingly'. Known to be the man who sticks to narrow straight path, Mr. Lall is believed to have peeved the director for speaking out and sticking to his guns".

After his retirement, Joginder Singh is speaking the language that he despised while in service. Should one start reciting scriptures after retirement, having violated them, with impunity, for so long? It is understandable as upholding the value system during service period has many disadvantages as one has to forego the perks, the privileges, the status and also one runs the risk of being thrown out. It has become a fashion that, while in service do all wrongs except cultivate the right contacts and after retirement, preach what one did not follow while in position and of course never believed. Is it not simple and plain dishonesty? Further he makes derogatory reference to the conduct of the politicians, but his own conduct was the worst possible. In the CBI conference on 21st November 1996, I talked of pressures and of feudal bias in investigation of cases against the big people. Joginder Singh raised a big hue and cry and vehemently denied any pressure. Having so denied then, how can he invoke the same now? Is he trying to cover up his weaknesses? Perhaps he very well describes his own weak character while referring to 'political pressure' when he says[4], "no serving civil servant will ever admit to its existence". How can he forget that though he was not prepared to listen even, but still I had raised precisely this issue in the conference emphasising the fact that the political and the administrative pressures were rampant in CBI under him? It was on this very issue that I clashed with him in the conference in the presence of all the delegates and also the Home Secretary Padamanabhiah. I also tried to elaborate the ill-effects of such pressures and solicited discussion, but his ruling that 'All discussions lead to confusion', left me helpless.

The personal vendetta continued. I wanted to visit my office room on December 28th, to collect my personal papers, hand over official papers and to destroy certain other papers, which is a fair routine. I was allowed entry only in the presence of R N Sinha, a Joint director. The director asked Sinha not to leave the room so long as I was there. I collected some urgent papers and destroyed certain others, which took two hours. Sinha had some other urgent work. So I left my task in between and my personal papers continued lying in CBI office. I approached Joginder Singh again, but failed to get any positive response. I could ultimately collect my papers/articles/personal papers only after Singh's departure from the CBI a few months later. In absence of my personal papers, filing of my Income Tax Return was delayed, inflicting penalty on me, but more important was the humiliation. By humiliating me, Singh intended to drive home the message in the CBI that how ruthless he could be to the officers who refused to toe his line.

After a few days, I received a message from Joginder Singh through R C Sharma, the Special Director, that if I wanted a Delhi posting, I should request Joginder Singh, who would get me a job in any other organisation of my choice. During that period, he was scuttling all my efforts to get any position in any other Central Police Organisation. I chose to decline the offer. However, the MHA appreciated and took up my case actively. Of all the CPO Chiefs, only the Chief of BPR&D, Gurdial Pandher, agreed to take me. I was under tremendous mental strain, not because of the repatriation, as I saw it as the continuation of the same fight, but because everyone in the Ministry and CPOs talked of 'helping' me. The thought of being helpless was painful. I was carrying on the fight on behalf of the nation and was only seeking justice in my own right, where was the question of pity or help?

After the departure of Prime Minister Deve Gowda, Joginder Singh found his position untenable as he had drawn his entire sustenance from the former. His affiliation needs with the PM were very high. In May 1997 he tried to fix up weekly meetings with the new Prime Minister. He writes[5], "I told him that I would talk to him periodically at least once a week." The director CBI has no business to see the PM so often unless he obtained his orders or discussed casework with him. However this was a fair routine during the times of the earlier PM, when he used to meet him at least two to three times a week, if not more.

It is a matter of public knowledge that Deve Gowda and Laloo Prasad Yadav were initially together and finally broke on 31.3.1997. The Government of Deve Gowda fell eleven days later. It was now time for Joginder Singh to change his tracks. First he tried to know the views of the new PM by seeking interview with him immediately after he took over. When it could not be possible, Singh suddenly chargesheeted Laloo Yadav in the AHD case. The PM did not interfere in chargesheeting as Joginder Singh admits in his book. In such circumstances, Joginder Singh must have been searching for or creating issues for putting up confrontation and he did find one at the time of arrest of Laloo Yadav.

On 10th February 2000, Zee-news, a channel of Zee TV, had invited Joginder Singh, Vijay Rama Rao and me for their programme, Prime Time. The subject of discussion was corruption with special reference to Jain Hawala Case as the last accused person of the case was discharged at that time only. No doubt Rama Rao was the main actor so far as the Hawala case was concerned, but even Joginder Singh entering CBI on 1.8.1996 had lots of time to give correct direction to the case, as all the circumstances of the case were to his knowledge within first four to six weeks of taking over the CBI. However, Rama Rao did not take part in the programme. Joginder Singh appeared to be blank on Hawala case and could not answer when confronted with questions from the anchors and myself. More important in this context are the questions that I asked him during commercial breaks with anchors also participating in the process. His statement that Gujral as PM had tried to restrain him from proceeding against Laloo Prasad Yadav in AHD case was raised by Zee TV team, but then I took over and stated that he himself was furiously opposed to Biswas in order to protect Laloo. He had exercised all sorts of pressure on Biswas in order to frustrate investigations against Laloo Yadav. I reminded him that he had twice transferred Biswas so that AHD case against Laloo Yadav could be scuttled and that I had also mentioned it in my letter dated 18.10.1996 to him. He had no alternative but to admit that earlier he had consistently opposed Biswas, as he had not appreciated the evidence till then, and added that he realised the gravity of the offence only during his Calcutta visit between 24th and 25th April 1997, when Biswas showed the graphics. Since I was aware of the core evidence and the fact that it essentially had remained the same as on 30.9.1996 and that graphics were also prepared by Biswas much earlier, I further questioned him that why he could not appreciate the same evidence earlier which anyone of ordinary prudence and intelligence would have done. It was unbelievable that the chief of a premier investigating agency, took eight months to understand the basic evidence. Such a long time at such a crucial stage is a great boon to any accused to scuttle the evidence of Disproportionate Assets in particular. No professional worth his salt at that level could take so much time, unless he deliberately chooses not to understand and appreciate. In any case where was the need to harass Biswas by issuing his transfer orders not once but twice, if the intention was not to scuttle the case? He did not answer. I suggested that he was playing political games out of loyalty to his mentor, or for his own survival. That he continued to protect Laloo Yadav right from 1st August 1996, to 31st March 1997, and changed his stance only on 31st, when as per Press reports, the final political break occurred between Deve Gowda and Laloo Prasad Yadav. After 21st April when Gujral became PM, he sought interview with him to test the waters. The new PM did not oblige. Joginder Singh gave him a deadline for granting interview by 23rd. The PM had just taken over and could not give time till 23rd but on

26th the PS to PM summoned him and conveyed the PM's message that he would not interfere at all and the CBI was at liberty to file or not to file the chargesheet, as quoted by him in his book[6] ,"PM had no reason or desire to interfere in legal matters and the CBI could go ahead as deemed proper". Then where was the interference or pressure from the then PM? I also informed that I was quoting from his book *'Inside CBI'*. His answer was that Gujral did not interfere in April, but he did interfere in June. The next obvious question was that what meaning the pressure carried once chargesheet had been filed. In June he said, there was pressure in the context of arrest of Laloo Yadav. Pressures are a way of life and I hold no brief for anyone, but in this case twofold considerations prompted me. First, Joginder Singh had held throughout that no case was made out against Laloo Yadav, which was the bone of contention between him and Biswas. Since Biswas was at Calcutta, I had also taken up this issue with Joginder Singh, as is clear in my letter dated 18.10.1996[7] to him. My reason was simple and I had advocated the same in the meetings, conference etc., that let truth and transparency prevail. Second, when till chargesheet was filed, there was no pressure as mentioned by Joginder Singh in his book, then where was the pressure? For what was he arrogating martyrdom to himself? On return I read his book again. As per his own account, the arrest is not in question. The PM was bothered about handling the consequential violence that could arise on arrest of Laloo Yadav. Discussing the consequential violence is no interference. It is the responsibility of the PM, the Chief Executive of the nation, that peace is not disturbed unnecessarily when arrest from the house of a ruling Chief Minister is in question.

Arrest incidentally was never a big thing or a big question in the CBI. Before Joginder Singh took over, barring certain exceptions in certain peculiar circumstances, arrests were just not made in corruption cases; only the courts summoned the accused persons at appropriate time. He only started this new trend. It was something absolutely of no consequence as court would have summoned the accused and he would have appeared there. Arrest could have been justified earlier during investigation as from the position of power he was likely to tamper with the evidence, but at that stage even investigation process was a taboo for the director. At this stage, the question of maintenance of order was something altogether different and did not amount to interference in investigation or chargesheet. Besides, it constituted no pressure at all, as it did not concern with or subvert the substantive justice, but only with the mode and the mechanism of producing him in the court. Even if for arguments' sake, arrest were considered essential and unavoidable, the consequential law and order situation would have to be seen and appreciated particularly when state forces were in the hands of the person going to be arrested. If central forces were called, it would raise the larger issue of Federalism and the Centre-State relations, which nobody in his senses could ignore in a federal system. Joginder Singh has to be commended for his immense capacity to mislead and twist all situations to his advantage by publicity. Having done all wrongs, he cornered the glory for the AHD case. Unfortunately, the pressure exercised by the politicians is so axiomatically believed that no one questions. In this case he was believed, forgetting that earlier the Press had consistently castigated him for this very case, and the courts had censured him in this and various other cases on no less than three occasions. He himself had all through been an active conspirator for exerting political pressure and in this series he had thrown away so many dedicated officers, transferred them, compelled them and coerced them.

In his own context he writes,[8] "No official should be transferred, unless there is concrete evidence of corruption or connivance with the accused." He further goes on to say[9] "there are ways by which investigation can be subverted. One is to transfer those who stand up to government pressures or come in the way of powerful politicians."

Joginder Singh has very rightly described these principles that he himself violated while in position of power. He transferred all such officers who stood up against the pressure or came in the way of powerful people whom he was normally found protecting and obliging, to the extent of scuttling investigations. He transferred Arun Sinha from JMM case when the former refused to change a statement and a case diary on Singh's orders. Again when R M Singh was about to search the former PM's son, he was recalled to

Delhi post-haste and posted to Madras (Chennai), not allowing a gap of even twelve hours. It was he who transferred Biswas twice when the latter did not agree with him to spare Laloo Yadav. It was he who issued politically motivated contradictory orders in a Bombay (Mumbai) case. It was he who got mid-night orders from Law Minister for coercing Gopal Subramaniam in Lakhubhai Pathak case. In the CBI conference, my reference was to such cases only and he saw me out. He had perfected the transfer as a tool on which I commented[10], "such hush-hush transfers are becoming a tool of punishment to the so-called inconvenient who work and speak truthfully. The mechanism is also designed as a pressure device for others to fall in line."

Joginder Singh said the following about pressure in the Jain Hawala Case[11], "The Jain diaries Hawala payoffs scandal was a key event, with the Supreme Court literally forcing the pace of the investigation, impelling CBI to file a number of chargesheets against influential political figures. Subsequent events have shown that under the goad of judicial strictures, CBI was stampeded into a number of prosecutions that it has been unable to sustain.....Sh. Shanti Bhushan says "CBI should have hauled up everyone of them with suspiciously large assets. The Agency let them off lightly."

Shanti Bhushan does not know and cannot know the contents of the CBI files, but Joginder Singh should have known that, as Hawala was a live case when he took over. It was incumbent upon him to have waded through the entire case files, as this was the personal responsibility of the director as per Supreme Court orders. Incidentally I had, in brief, discussed and raised all these issues and circumstances in my letters of 1st August 1995 and 27th February 1996. I had sent a copy each of these letters to Joginder Singh along with my letter of 2nd September 1996, which I had addressed to NN Singh. He was fully aware of the facts from this letter, even if he did not read the Hawala case files. I had not only raised the question of looking into disproportionate assets, but also pressed it hard. That this accompanied with the question of admissibility of evidence of diary entries and the issue of complete investigation, were the reasons for my transfer out of the Hawala case. Further I had personally handed over a copy of the SIR about Chamera Project where the interests of country were allegedly being squandered and, at that stage, I had requested him for looking into the projects and particularly the Chamera Project. Since bigwigs were involved and politically it would not have suited his mentor, so the verification was never taken up. If he still did not see the Hawala file and he came to know from the magazine, it shows either he was under pressures, was not telling the truth or it was a part of some of his schemes, or it was his acute negligence and casual approach to the CBI work that he remained ignorant of the case, its seriousness and implications and required a journalist through a magazine to make him aware! I quote one small para from my D.O. letter No. 238 dated 2nd September 1996, where I had detailed all what Shanti Bhushan says.

"........The same statement when came to Narasimha Rao, Capt. Satish Sharma, Rajiv Gandhi and Quattrochi, the thorough scrutiny stopped, the new principles of sticking to original Diaries and ignoring new found facts in investigation were adopted. Scant investigation and a rush for chargesheeting was resorted to instead of a deeper probe." The letter dated 1st August 1995, that was enclosed with this letter, is replete with and lays repeated emphasis on looking into the assets of the accused persons. Did he still require a fresh revelation from the magazine *Asia Week* ? All this and much more was contained in his own office files if only he had the will to read and guts to follow up. It is absolutely incorrect that he was prepared to shoulder and fight political pressure. If so, why did he not look into the assets angle? Why did he not look into the Chamera Project? Why did he organise the late night operations in Lakhubhai Pathak case and tried to pressurise Gopal Subramaniam? Why did he pressurise Arun Sinha? Why did he compel R M Singh not to proceed with Urea case and complete that process which he was deep into at Hyderabad? Post-haste he was made to leave for Delhi and transferred out immediately. Joginder takes credit that R M Singh was in Delhi for a long time and only he could take action and transfer him out. Why this action had to be taken — only when R M Singh was going strong in Urea case. Heavens would not have fallen in another week or so, but this very week could not be allowed to R M Singh otherwise he would have set in motion this irreversible fatal step of searches from which there could then be no escape. R M Singh had stayed for long in Delhi, but not Arun Sinha. Sinha had joined CBI on deputation only a short time back, why he was transferred to Silchar? Joginder Singh spared no efforts at finishing the individuals who were straight and would not bend to his fads and illegal commands.

Joginder Singh did not respect even the basics by which an anti-corruption organisation should swear i.e. the 'integrity'. The event is basically rooted into the regime of Rama Rao, who wanted certain imported equipment, which Government would not allow to import, whereas the CBI needed it very badly. Fortunately for him at the end of the financial year, certain amount was left unspent in the Secret Service Fund. He drew it and kept it with his PA in the cash reserve. As it is the Secret Service Fund, it is not subject to that meticulous accounting/auditing as other expenditure of the government is. A certificate from the officer that he has spent it in bonafide discharge of his functions, is sufficient. It has also to be so and officers have to be relied upon. Rama Rao kept this money separately and scrupulously. His PA recorded all the relevant entries in the *Kacha* register that they were maintaining for the purpose. As Rama Rao got busy towards the end of his tenure and the equipment could not be available, so he left behind a sum said to be Rs. 38 lacs with his PA.

Immediately after taking over, Joginder Singh wanted a handsome chunk out of this money. The PA asked for the *Kacha* receipt or signature on the register as per procedure in vogue. Joginder Singh refused to do that, but when the PA stuck to his ground, the former asked P C Sharma, the JD, who supervised the fund, to make the money available. Sharma also returned with the same requirements. Joginder Singh got so angry with Sharma, that it became a flash point for his immediate repatriation. No doubt he had completed the tenure and there was no extension, but there was no need for the hurry with which his case for repatriation was pushed through. Joginder Singh came very heavy on the PA and even abused him, but the latter kept up his cool and did not budge. Joginder Singh transferred the charge of secret fund to the other PA, but he also took the identical stand. Ultimately, when he could not browbeat his PAs, he directly took charge of the chest and the book. The chest was shifted from PAs' room in North Block to his own office in the CGO (Central

Government Offices') complex. Director CBI with cash chest in his own office room turned cashier for the Secret Fund. It was a talk in the CBI to what depth was the director stooping.

However the worst was yet to come. It is well-known that Joginder Singh was suddenly removed from his post as director CBI when he was abroad and R C Sharma was asked to take over immediately. After taking over Sharma called a particular IG and asked him to surrender whatever funds Joginder Singh had parked with him and the IG immediately handed over Rs. 16.00 lacs. He then called a particular SP who also had Rs. 6 lacs to surrender similarly. R C Sharma himself narrated this after his retirement. Imagine, it was all known in the CBI. How demoralizing should such shady dealings be for an organization that swears by and also enforces integrity?

During the tenure of Joginder Singh, all laws, rules and great traditions of the CBI were thrown to winds undermining severely the great organisation. The systems, held sacrosanct in CBI, disappeared into the thick dark jungles of anarchy, expediency, whims and all that. He had landed the CBI into the Jungle Raj, the single cardinal principle of which is enunciated by Thomas Hobbs when he says, "Kill when you can and have what you can."

References

1. *'Inside CBI'* by Joginder Singh, page 246.
2. *'Inside CBI'* by Joginder Singh, page 5.
3. *'Inside CBI'* by Joginder Singh, page 29.
4. Cited above page 9.
5. Cited above page 245.
6. Cited above Page 230.
7. D.O. Letter No. 296 dated 18.10.1996 from the author to Joginder Singh, then Director CBI, Annexure D.
8. *'Inside CBI'* by Joginder Singh, page 189.
9. *'Inside CBI'* by Joginder Singh, page 259.
10. D.O. letter dated 18.10.1996, Annexure - D, Para 4.
11. *'Inside CBI'* by Joginder Singh pages 47 and 50.

6
Beyond the Laws

No democracy can survive for any length of time without the rule of law. In a democratic society all the citizens are equal before the watchful eyes of law. The judicial dictum "be you ever so high, the law is above you", is supposed to rule the roost and determine the administrative, the political, the social and the judicial (embracing the entire criminal justice system including judiciary, investigation and prosecution) culture of the society. Unfortunately in India the golden rule of equality continues to be a distant dream in all the systems viz administrative, social, political and more so in the criminal justice system. All work for and cater to the requirements of the elite. All laws that come their way are brushed aside. That in turn shapes and determine the mindset of the administrator, the investigator, the prosecutor, the judge, the politician in power and of others. Such a mindset is an essential requirement for sustenance of any colonial regime, but in India, unfortunately, despite six decades of freedom, the same legacy of the colonial era continues. Adoption of a constitution that upholds equality has not made much difference.

A D Gorwala noted in 1951[1] "....with a parliamentary majority behind them, at least a few are inclined to hold that there is no difference between their will and the Law." The conditions have since deteriorated further and respect for law has fallen steeply. About sixty years of democracy in India has thrown up a system where the dictum "King can do no wrong", has firmly entrenched itself. The laws are violated, as the essence of being big is the capacity to violate law and hold it in utmost contempt. The officials of law enforcement agencies are insulted, intimidated and persecuted if they insist on discharging their lawful duties against the privileged sections of society, but if they align with the latter and spare them from operations of laws, such officials are duly rewarded.

In practice, the rule of law does not apply to those who frame rules/laws and who enforce them. The elite thereby assert themselves like masters over slaves who are the commoners, in the continuing colonial traditions of pre-independence days. This is beautifully depicted in the words of Brahma Chellany,[2] "...after independence, it has been controlled by self serving, increasingly debased elites who embody the same style, demeanour and interests of the preceding imperial aristocracies." He goes on to depict the conditions where we have reached during the last fifty-six years of Independence,[3] "half a century after its tryst with destiny, India remains nominally free but psychologically enslaved. With its subaltern mindset, it is still shackled to its colonial past."

This frightening environ compels one to wonder if we are still living in a feudal state. The system might have disappeared from India formally, but its manifestations i.e. the temperament, the attitude of arrogance towards others, the feeling of being above law, that one's word is the unquestioned law, that the self-interest of the masters is the interest of the state and so on, still continue to rule the roost. These traits have not taken any effective beating till this day and are the biggest hurdles in our progress both social and economic, as these prevent creation of right and suitable mental as also the social infrastructure, which is essential for a live, kicking, progressive and self-respecting nation and society. As per Brahma Chellany,[4] "...the colonial mindset of its governing elites remains the main barrier to the making of an India that is confident, secure, prosperous and internationally respected."

It may sound unbelievable, but a statue of Lord Irwin installed outside the Parliament House in Parliament Street, stood defiantly in free India till the late sixties or early seventies, declaring proudly:

"I like my choice"

It summed up the typical temperament of a feudal master that he likes his choice and that has to prevail upon others. That all others under his charge have to acknowledge his choice, under all circumstances.

It is ironic that in front of the Parliament House of the biggest democracy of the world, the statue flaunting medieval feudalism continued for over two decades after Independence. The extent of our mindset can be gauged from the fact that I heard a very highly placed person regretting removal of Irwin's statue as destruction of History. Is it some psychological state of mind that we have developed a taste for sycophancy or that the slavery has gone too deep into our genes?

Instead of rule of law, absolute discretion without any control or accountability that too exercised through whims or fancies even for personal interests is considered to be the essence of exercise of power as against judicious discretion in public interest. The worst is that it is not on way to decay, but is getting stronger with every passing day and acquiring mafia like proportions in our administrative system and psyche.

The system is very well entrenched, despite the facade to show concern and generosity in pursuing programmes like poverty alleviation, etc. In essence a poor person is made to realise everyday that he is poor and deserves pity, but cannot be permitted to exercise his rights. The corruption hits him most severely, as it diverts his share in national development to others, a little of this loot is doled out for poverty alleviation and such programmes.

Some of such oppressed people take to violent ways, which most often, is the rationale of the inland terrorism. In every such case, the analysis of the causes of terrorism has returned uniform findings that unemployed youth is misguided and ultimately indulges in such activities. In the short run the terrorism may have to be contained through coercion by Police as part of fire fighting, but in the long run, the only way is to develop the economy, generate employment and allow fair share to all. But the immense resources required for that cannot be found in the face of exploitation and fast flowing stream of corruption. So long as corruption and exploitation continue as privileges of the elite, the country will be bled and its resources continue to be drained abroad. Consequently the employment potential will not go up substantially. The phenomenon has been worked out in detail in the next chapter titled 'Scourge of Black Economy'. Inland terrorism is the direct consequence of this mindset.

There can be no hesitation in concluding that till such time the system is governed and guided by this mindset, there would be no reprieve from poverty as also corruption, and violation of law by people at high places. The genuine persons will feel helpless and marginalised or eliminated like[5] 'bad money driving good money out of the market'.

The general feeling is that the agencies of the state administering laws do not give justice when any report against the high and the influential is made to them. It is unfortunate, but true, that the entire administrative system suffers from feudal bias and from the same mindset that higher-ups are not answerable for any of their actions. In the field of criminal justice system, it acquires a special significance as that finally erodes public confidence in the entire system.

The investigating officers are not supposed to cross the path of the elite. No wonder that during the last about sixty years, no action has ever been taken against any higher-up despite rampant corruption. If my team and I, in the CBI, had the audacity of recording the name of the serving PM, or took steps to prevent a mighty influential person from going abroad, my DIG and myself had to pay. If I insisted on the CBI to follow the twofold principles of truth and transparency, the elite felt threatened and I had to be thrown out. Under these circumstances, even the honest investigating officers keep weighing the political fall out and the political and the administrative consequences, rather than the merits of a case, before taking any action. More thought goes in balancing their own position instead of collection of facts. Honesty of an individual public servant is not condemned or deprecated and is rather appreciated generally, but if it hurts the persons in authority, such individuals are expected to modify the definition itself well in time. In the process the IOs develop a typical mindset, subservient to feudal values of protecting the high ups. In fight against corruption in high places an IO develops the following mindset:

a) Condone the corruption of the high and mighty. It is hara-kiri to think of any action against this category of persons unless they have fallen foul of the powers that be.

b) Condone the corruption by their family, relatives and friends, but if sometime the worst circumstances are created, then at least take a lenient view and give them enough time and information to defend themselves. Slowly, the IO starts believing that any action of persons at 'A' and 'B' constitute no offence.

c) Against the above background, the IO feels paralytic and diffident, tries to play safe and takes no risk. If some misadventurer were to try otherwise, the system so carefully moulded, takes care of him by either jettisoning him or by conspiring against him to make him stand in the dock.

d) Statements are normally recorded in such a way as does not embarrass the high up, i.e. avoid recording his name and also those of the members of his family as far as possible. Even when under certain circumstances it becomes necessary to proceed against him, the golden rule is that leave out the escape routes so that it is possible to save him at a later stage.

e) Searches normally are not conducted into the cases involving the influential people. However, in absolutely unavoidable cases, the conduct of searches is delayed as far as possible so that the suspect could dispose of the assets or remove evidence against him. The investigations conducted even into the most serious cases by any agency during the last five decades bear testimony to this. Even when chargesheeting them became a compulsion, searches were still scrupulously avoided. Corruption cases can be viewed and investigated from two angles. First, it is episodal in character in which there is direct evidence of demanding and/or accepting money, which would be the rarest of the rare event in case of the bigwigs. The second is the culmination of a chain of such episodes of corruption and bribery resulting into assets of the subject beyond his lawful sources of income. Looking into the assets pre-supposes searches. Search, as such, is considered to be a highly dreaded weapon as searches throw up solid incontrovertible evidence that is difficult to dispute even. Had searches been conducted, a wealth of information would have been culled out regarding disproportionate assets possessed by the high and mighty during the last few decades and the 1990s in particular. But the sanctity of these unwritten feudal laws cannot be violated by the poor ordinary common law of the land.

f) Prosecution sanction is another big issue. It was perhaps provided as a safeguard in British India so that whosoever worked in the interest of the empire, could be protected for his loyalty if in the process he committed some misconduct not affecting the empire. Ostensibly, it was to have a check against non-appreciation of departmental procedures by an investigating agency or the court. So the department was given the discretion. At that time the senior officers were mostly the British, but even if Indians, they were thought to be honest personally and work for the Crown with single-minded devotion. But now colonial rule is no more, loyalty to rulers is not a requirement and the departmental procedures, actually are being analysed by courts threadbare. Besides, corruption has touched the highest levels. So there is no ostensible reason for such a provision to continue on the Statute Book. The rationale of Prosecution sanction has disappeared in our free society supposed to be governed by the rule of law. Since the crime of corruption (except the traps) does not have an eyewitness, so even in the most patent cases, Prosecution sanction can be denied. The influential can manage its denial and frustrate all the efforts of investigators, the complainant, the witnesses and finally the expectations of the common people. The denial of Prosecution sanction re-enforces the mindset that investigating bigwigs is practically a wasteful effort, which one should avoid right from the start.

g) Arrest is scrupulously avoided in case of the influential, even if necessary as the custodial interrogation leads to uncover not only so many facts, but also the entire mysteries which otherwise would remain shrouded in the dark recesses and pass into oblivion. Even the CBI records bear testimony to the fact that in identical circumstances commoners were arrested, but the big fish was spared. They could also use court processes to avoid arrest. If in certain cases the arrest becomes inevitable under public pressure, it is tailored to suit the convenience of such accused himself.

h) In the worst of the scenario, if a chargesheet has to be filed, still it is ensured that it has many holes through which all the substantive evidence, can escape, and only that evidence which can be challenged successfully by the defence counsel in court of law is retained. The points containing the real punch are not included or are watered down so that the evidence is not adequate to frame charges in the court of law. If, in some stray exceptional case, the charges are framed, weak evidence can take care during trial and the accused may emerge as a bigger hero.

i) Despite all this, the so-called hon'ble suspect still reserves the right to get the corruption case withdrawn when things cool down. Arguments of public interest can always be coined. A dispassionate observer will be dismayed as if corruption is being continued in public interest or for the existence of public order or survival of this great nation, which by implication cannot survive without these corrupt and dishonest elements and without their corruption and dishonesty.

It is a beautiful arrangement that persons in authority commit the crime of corruption, and they only decide whether to investigate or not to investigate; if investigations are conducted, they only direct the collection of facts, they only decide on prosecution and finally on withdrawal. Whatever serves them gets defined as public interest. In all this so called public good, the country is looted, bled, drained and deprived.

The privileged treatment accorded to one Dharmendra Deo Mishra is a classical case and constitutes a very interesting case study material as it exactly fits into the above stated module and hardly appears to be a real case investigated and buried in the

CBI. Mishra is a very senior IAS officer of 1969 batch of UP cadre. Two corruption cases against him existed in the CBI in 1994 when I joined. Both these were in the branches under my charge. My officers told me that he was a very influential person, highly connected politically and it was with great ups and downs that his cases could be investigated. The high point came when a communication was received from government of India to close both the cases. We expressed our inability. Then a demi official (DO) communication was received from Cabinet Secretary Zafar Saifullah commanding the CBI to close both the cases. He was informed that one case stood chargesheeted and the other had been referred for Prosecution sanction. So nothing could be done. Again came another demi official letter from Zafar Saifullah to director CBI mentioning in such big words as Sh. PV Narasimha Rao, Prime Minister of India, had personally desired that the first case be withdrawn from the court and in the second closure report be sent. The worst feature was the last sentence commanding that no more communications be sent on the subject and matter be treated as closed.

In the system all this is nothing but the privileges of the honourable accused. As per the classical mould, if nothing could be done in between, the honourable accused managed to get the case withdrawn at the end and the only ground advanced in such cases for withdrawal is "the public interest".

The above analysis and the privileged case of Mishra make it amply clear as why, despite a plethora of scams, no action could ever fructify against any influential persons involved in them, though during this period of over five decades since Independence, we might have hit a century of serious scams at the national level, at least half of which were very serious. Besides, the scams also occurred at the state level.

It is because of lack of action against all these people that the message has gone home that anything else could happen, but no big corrupt person could be punished. This psyche has gone deep and has played havoc. Recent scams and various other cases in recent times bear testimony that investigating agencies, with CBI in the lead, get jittery when they come face to face with the powerful and the influential. The feudal bias restrains the concerned officers from taking lawful action against them.

It is proposed to analyse critically a few of such cases, the facts of which have been narrated in earlier chapters. The endeavour now would be to trace the discrimination practised by the CBI by favouring the big in the Hawala, the Krishnamurthy and the Bihar AHD cases. *Prima facie* it appears that even the Supreme Court did not remain immune to this mindset. Efforts will also be to bring home the rationale, why no case reached any logical conclusion.

The Jain Hawala Case

a) The CBI did not look into the allegations against the highest authority, despite patent reasons *prima facie*. When the name of the then PM, Narasimha Rao, occurred in Jain's statement, all out efforts were mounted by none other than the director CBI himself to ensure that this part of the statement was not brought on record at all. However, when efforts of the director failed, the team itself was broken and the leaders were removed from the scene, thereby ensuring that investigations could not verify the unwanted facts.

   Jain had linked the tendering process of various projects and kickbacks in them to the Hawala scam. Examination of these projects, as such, was of utmost importance as only that could provide evidence into the rationale of bunglings, but the same was abandoned on the ground that this aspect was not a part of Jain Diaries, which the CBI was investigating. It was conveniently ignored that bungling in projects was the rationale of all the kickbacks and it is these kickbacks, which generated the largesse the Jains distributed. Thus, the investigators were restrained from tracing the origin of slush funds, the distribution of which the CBI was investigating. It is never done in any investigation unless the intention is to scuttle it. A reading of the chargesheets itself would give that impression to anyone conversant with law or investigations. All this was done as big names right upto the Prime Ministers were involved.

b) No big persons were interrogated, arrested or searched in the main corruption case. Besides Jains, some officials and politicians out of power were the only ones who were interrogated, searched or arrested. It is a basic principle that interrogation is the beginning of the investigation and chargesheet is laid only if there is evidence at the end. Since chargesheets were laid, it can safely be presumed that the evidence for bribery and corruption did exist. If it were so, interrogation and searches should have been conducted, but it was not done except in case of smaller persons or politicians out of power. The big shots were spared all these legal steps that were likely to adduce evidence. It is for different reasons that later on, all those whose names occurred in the diaries had to be chargesheeted, but they were spared from being searched. If the evidence was enough for chargesheets, it was more than sufficient to carry out searches. But evidence that would have flowed from searches, would have been damning and unsparing, whereas the general chargesheet, bereft of evidence, was the most gentle treatment and a real big favour that could be done to any accused person as that would defuse the situation immediately, and later during court trial, the hon'ble accused would get acquittal for lack of evidence. It is unfortunate for them that the court only discharged and did not order acquittal. The stigma of a chargesheet will always remain as Justice Verma inferred in 1998, that further investigation and trial could be resumed at any time in future, if some fresh evidence ever surfaced.

c) Custodial interrogation is a very effective instrument, but the same was scrupulously avoided. If custodial interrogation was necessary in case of Jains and other smaller fries, it was needed much more against whom there were allegations of accepting bribes. The responsibility of a public servant whether a politician or an official is much higher than the middlemen, which the Jains were.

d) Whenever there is reason to believe that the accused is ordinarily a taker of bribes, it is necessary and is routine to look into his assets. When chargesheets in Hawala case were being laid, it was clear that as per CBI, there was enough evidence against them for having accepted bribe. The assets of some of them had also been verified to be disproportionate *prima facie* in secret enquiries, but the honourable suspects were still given the most favoured dignitary treatment by sparing them from being investigated for the DA (Disproportionate Assets).

e) In the JMM case, the bribe takers were interrogated, arrested and searched. In the Hawala case, on the other hand, only the bribe givers met with similar treatment. This was bound to happen, as the bribe giver was a smaller fry as compared to the takers in the Hawala case, whereas the giver was the elite, the big, and the top, in the JMM case. The eternal feudal principle is to save the master, the big, the elite and in both the cases the mandate of unwritten elitist laws was carried out.

At the time of the trial in the JMM case, however, the judiciary on technical grounds spared the bribe takers, the smaller people, but that was with regard to immunity for conduct inside the legislature. The judge presiding over the trial court has rightly charged those MPs for possession of disproportionate assets, which was scrupulously avoided in the Hawala case, but this again, only proves the rule of feudal bias.

Whenever the name of a serving PM occurred in CBI investigations in the past, the investigations came to a halt. It was only in Hawala case that the team had the courage to record his name and suggest investigations against the PM. In a number of countries, their Chief Executives have been investigated and are also being investigated, as there is nothing special in crime committed by them. Unlike India, no regard is shown in corruption cases even for the special services rendered by the corrupt.

Incidentally foreign media observed and came to same conclusions even without that inside knowledge. *The Economist*[6] anticipated the shape of things to come as early as 1995 and strange enough the time has proved the forecast made by the magazine absolutely correct. The following paragraphs from the article titled "Deadly Diaries" are worth quoting:

> "In any other country it would have been a sensational exposure. In India it barely creates ripples. In 1991 the Police arrested two people suspected of operating a ring for illegal

> foreign exchange transactions. The diaries kept by the couple listed payments to numerous prominent politicians, including the late Rajiv Gandhi, together with several top bureaucrats.
>
> This was confirmation for most Indians for what they had long suspected that politicians of all stripes had their hands in the till. However nothing further happened for sometime. There was no outcry in the Parliament, and no arrests. In 1993 two journalists Vineet Narain and Rajinder Puri brought the matter to the notice of the Supreme Court............
>
> In 1994 the Supreme Court ordered the Police to take purposive action. The Police have finally stirred themselves, and have questioned one businessman and one minor politician, Arif Mohamed Khan. Mr. Khan was a Govt. Minister in 1989-90, but later went into political wilderness. He is an obvious choice for sacrificial goat, although because of laws delays in India, nothing is likely to happen to him for years, if ever. His reaction to police attention has been 'why only me'.
>
> Some Indians think that the stellar names in the diaries may be raided close to the next general elections. Such talk typifies the public attitude that police action has nothing to do with the guilt of the individuals, but a lot to do with political expediency. In public perception politicians are above the law... The police follows instructions from their political masters."

It is astonishing and intriguing how correctly the magazine could depict the conditions in India and how correctly did it predict and conclude:

a) That as suspected by Indians, politicians of all hues had their hands in corruption, bunglings, etc.

b) That there would be no action ultimately.

c) That whatever action was being taken apparently, was eyewash in reality.

d) That only some small fish will be proceeded against and nothing will happen to anyone big as they are above the laws.

e) That whatever action the Police (CBI) was taking, was not in pursuit of investigation of crime, but in accordance with the political expediency.

   The reader will bear it out that the expediency had been followed right from the beginning in the CBI, though at one stage there was stiff internal resistance from within. That resistance was removed in June-July 1995 and after that there was no investigation as all played to the set tunes as visualised by the magazine in advance as early as September 1995.

f) That the police follow the instructions of the political masters, is a severe indictment of our system of collection of facts, i.e. investigation.

g) That in India, because of delays in laws, nothing will happen is a sad reflection on entire criminal justice system of which judiciary is the leader.

The Economist was very true in anticipating that the action will follow around elections. Process of chargesheeting against politicians commenced in January 1996 and continued thereafter when elections were round the corner in May 1996.

The brilliant analysis reaches the same conclusions that nobody can touch the category that is beyond the operation of laws.

The infection of feudal bias did not spare the Hon'ble Supreme Court even. To my knowledge, the Supreme Court never checked what CBI was doing against the big shots particularly the PM, but they had enough time to ask about insignificant people like Abi. Abi is a diary entry in the column for those who paid money to the Jains. S K Jain identified him as a contractor who owed him money on account of purchase of scrap from them and as such the amount occurred on receipt side. Jain deliberately did not include this amount in his regular account books. When the diaries were produced in the Supreme Court, initially it caught the judges' eye and one of them asked pointed questions about Abi. On being told that the entry in question was on receipt side and that it was for a minor amount, so the CBI did not propose to make any further inquiries, the judge asked us to check if Abi might be an IAS officer of Commissioner's rank from Madhya Pradesh cadre who could possibly have connection with the Jains. It was not a one-time affair. At the next hearing again similar queries were made about Abi. By then the CBI had verified and confirmed its earlier findings and informed the court that it did not propose to investigate this name any further. Nonetheless, a number of times that we went to the court, the same judge would call the IO or the SP near the podium and make identical inquiries.

Similar was the case of a legal advisor in CBI on deputation from Law Ministry. He initially belonged to subordinate judicial service of the state in which this very Hon'ble Judge was on the High Court and did not have a good impression about the former. The judge came down heavily on the Legal Advisor in 1994-95 while criticising the CBI for the delays. Even when it was told that he had come to the CBI after the diaries had been sealed and that he had not given any advice at that stage, the judge persisted in his attack on two three continuous dates. The scathing criticism stopped only after his transfer back to the Law Ministry. I sometime think what would have happened to the poor man if he did not have a place to return to the Ministry.

From time to time progress of investigations was being reported to the Supreme Court and the Press also carried the stories of day-to-day happenings. Somehow there was no specific direction from the court in case of any big name, except the general refrain that CBI take action against the mighty as well. As such, the Hon'ble Judges knew that no big fish was arrested or searched. Jains were only peddlers and starting point for investigation. The major portion of the blame lay at the doors of the ministers, the Prime Ministers and the officers, as they were responsible persons and also the persons in authority. The bribe giver may have some compulsion, but the taker cannot have any. Giver has much less or no responsibility once the bribe has been accepted. If the CBI was shirking its responsibility, was it not upto the Hon'ble court to take the CBI to task and point out specifically the names of such individuals? If it could point out the Jains, Abi, or the Legal advisor, why could it not nail the PM and the Ministers. The mindset perhaps overtakes all of us in this country.

In 1998, I called on Justice Verma, the presiding officer of the bench that had heard, monitored and guided the proceedings in the petition of Vineet Narain, etc. I explained to him my position that how I stood for complete investigation against all the big names including the PM and how I was thrown out. I also told him that I wanted to look into their assets, as in my view the assets were in the nature of stock, fossilized form of amounts taken as bribes. Basically both were the same and in such a wide investigation when action for corruption was being taken, looking into the assets was a must. He fully endorsed my views and categorically stated that he also intended to look into the assets, but felt that he could not have ordered such action specifically. He took shelter behind the judicial restraint that judiciary has its own *Maryada* (limits), which he could not violate. I was left wondering if the limits could be crossed for Abi, Jains and the Legal Advisor, why not in the case of PM and other highly placed accused persons. I, ultimately, rationalised that the feudalism was a brain infection, which in this country had infected everybody as a class, including the whole criminal justice system and had become a part of our mindset.

V Krishanamurthy Case

The government did not allow letters rogatory against Krishnamurthy, so there could be no investigations abroad, though he with his sons, was accused of receiving kickbacks, keeping huge balances in banks abroad and acquiring a number of firms, in India and abroad. So much so, that power to apply for letter rogatory, vested in the police under the Code of Criminal Procedure, was withdrawn from the CBI and concentrated in Government of India and that too in the PMO, so that nothing were left to chance. Though the papers were pending with Union Government for years, but still this fact could not be made public by the CBI, as that would amount to censure of the Government, which the CBI could not afford.

Ultimately the cases ended in closure. If investigations are not allowed, it has to happen. I am not aware if ultimately letters rogatory were issued or not, but even if these were issued with delays extending to years, not much purpose would have been served. Krishnamurthy in *Sunday Express* of July 21st, 2002, posed as a martyr of CBI atrocities, a wronged man against whom there was nothing and he was unnecessarily harassed. His case falls into the classical mould of investigations and other processes as per convenience of the VIP so that he emerges unscathed and a bigger hero. If someone can manage the powers that be and thereby subvert the law, all the punch in the investigations is taken away, the case is naturally finished. Giving the final assent then is a matter of time only.

The main narrative shows how in the great tradition of facilitating the big fish to benefit, a clean arrangement was worked out and the case presented in a way that the High Court had to allow him to go abroad. However, Krishnamurthy could still be prevented from going abroad by the mid-night orders from the Apex Court on persistent pursuit by a determined team of investigators. It was nothing but a favour, if not a conspiracy, to facilitate release of his passport. I am glad that my team and I could successfully challenge the feudal order upto the highest levels. The empire struck back and my DIG and I were thrown out. The system had conveyed the lesson for others, that don't try to reach those who are beyond the laws and attempts at overreaching would be punished and frustrated.

Lakhubhai Pathak Case

When Lakhubhai Pathak made complaint initially it included the name of P.V. Narasimha Rao but since he and his party were in power, the case was not registered. It is a matter of common knowledge that the case was registered a few years later. When the circumstances went beyond the control of the CBI and registering a criminal case became a compulsion, a special Officer was deputed from Delhi to U.K. to obtain a fresh application from Lakhubhai Pathak which did not contain the name of P.V. Narasimha Rao. The case was registered on the basis of such amended application. Factual statement of Lakhubhai Pathak in the trial court about presence of PVNR posed a material contradiction that was more than enough to break prosecution story and the case ended in acquittal. This is a very clear example how the deliberate scuttling of VIP cases goes on in the agency.

Indian Bank Scam

It is interesting though unfortunate to see how the officers think and act while under pressure even if the nation suffers tremendously. One of my branches was looking into a case of Indian Bank where the bungled amount with other consequential losses had risen to almost 100 crores. Another branch of CBI was also investigating almost a similar amount for the same bank. In both these cases it is the Chairman of the bank who had committed the indiscretion by asking and coercing his officers to advance loans where it was patently know that these would be unrecoverable. Also there were reasons to believe that the staff down the line had pointed out in no uncertain terms. Our verifications established that informal understanding was that these monies advanced by way of loans will not be returned at all. When these cases were under investigation, we received papers about extension case of Gopalakrishnan, the CMD of the bank. I fully opposed extension and drafted a detailed note clearly pointing out that he should not be allowed any extension and that if extension was allowed, we will be investigating many times more the value after the end of two years extended term. One day after a few weeks while we were in a meeting with the Director, he received a call. We heard the Director responding "no Sir, who can call you behind." After finishing the call, Director asked me if I wrote to the Finance Secretary, Mr. Montek Ahluwalia that he was blind. I was surprised as there was no occasion to my mind, as I had never met him. Director then told that the Finance Secretary was referring to some Indian Bank case of extension to CMD. I could not recall what it was all about. I called for the file there and then. I had mentioned that even a blind man can see the whole range of bunglings indulged into by Gopalakrishnan and if he is allowed another two years it will cause havoc. I showed that to the Director and told that it was metaphorical and not that the Finance Secretary was physically blind. At the same time in a lighter vein I quipped that if still Gopalakrishnan is granted extension, the Finance Secretary and the Government of India deserved to be termed as blind. At the same time in a lighter vein I quipped that if still Gopalkrishnan is granted extension, the Finance Secretary and the Government of India deserved to be termed as blind. Sure enough the extension was granted.

The question that arises is why the Finance Ministry that granted extension despite the obvious, should not be held responsible and made to pay the entire amount sanctioned during extended period that turned bad.

Bihar AHD case

This case passed through many phases, many controversies and witnessed numerous vicissitudes, but still managed to survive through the muck. So long as the party of the main accused was in power at the centre, there were efforts to extend due perquisites of the feudal order to him. It is the judicial activism, judicial protection to the investigators and the conviction and dedication of the investigators that the case could not be scuttled and chargesheets could be filed.

Initially the party in power at the centre and the state were the same. The reader may recall how in the process there were powerful moves to disassociate the chief investigator UN Biswas, the Joint Director, from investigations. The efforts had started to destabilize Biswas in order to scuttle the case immediately after Joginder Singh joined. I had been rather vocal in deprecating Singh's attitude about which I made a mention in my D.O. letter dated 18th October 1996, "I have been commenting freely on certain decisions which to my mind have been against the CBI culture of truthfulness and have been affecting vitally the organisation and its reputation........Similar is the impression that has gone down in the CBI with two time transfers of Shri U N Biswas confining him to Patna only and stranding his family or taking him off from Patna altogether". In the first week of October 1996, the Patna High Court was constrained to disassociate the director himself from the case. Though the accused person remained the same, the evidence remained the same — but when his party went out of power at the centre in April 1997, the same director did not bat an eyelid in chargesheeting the same person as he had ceased to be a person in authority.

Two points are worth noting that people cling to a person or to a view for their self-interest and it is purely out of fear that they bow to the feudal lord and that loyalty is out of fear and the perpetuation of self-interest. Either way the concept of right or wrong, facts, or fiction, moral or immoral, legal or illegal has no place. All these variables, in fact, remained unchanged in the instant case. What changed were the master and the direction of self-interest, which kept on defining the persons who were beyond the laws at any particular time.

The feudal bias is no more a static, but a dynamic concept.

References

1. Government of India Report on Public Administration by A D Gorwala 1951, Chapter IV page 16.
2. *Pioneer* dated 13.8.1997 article titled "World's largest soft state turns 50" by Brahma Chellany.
3. Ibid
4. Ibid
5. An axiomatic economic principle.
6. *The Economist* - 16th to 22nd September 1995, Page 35 titled India—Deadly Diaries.

7

Scourge of Black Economy

At the dawn of Independence in 1947, India was on very solid grounds in comparison with other world economies, for it was saved from the destruction of Second World War. Besides, during the war, the British had raised public debt in India and owed us Rs.1713 crores equivalent of Pound Sterling on this account. This amount came to be known as Sterling Balances. It was a big sum, which if put to development, could have led to tremendous progress as those were the days of low costs all over the world and more so in India as immediately after Independence, the costs of constructing hydro-electric projects perhaps might have been @ Rs 4 lacs per mw only. Since labour constituted the major component in a hydel projects, as per the technology prevalent at that time, the capital cost might have been around rupees 1.5 lacs per mw. Even if it is presumed that all the material and equipment had to be imported, an amount of Rs.1200 crores or two-thirds of the Sterling Balances alone would have been adequate to harness the entire known Hydro potential of around 80,000 mw at that time, whereas till today, we have developed a capacity of 24,000 mw only. The raw material costs are nil in case of hydropower. Had we developed it, there would have been no need to pay exorbitant power rates under which the country is groaning today. The story is similar in other fields of development as well.

Basically we did not visualise future requirements even for a couple of decades ahead, not only in the power sector, but in all the other essential fields as well. Other countries did plan for the future. They initially conceived steel plants of 5 to 10 million-ton capacity, whereas India was gloating over having just three plants of one million tons capacity each. In 2002, as per International Iron and Steel Institute[1], the per-capita steel consumption of India was just 24 kg. as against the world average consumption of 153 kg. and China 131 kg. Except Africa, every other conceivable country is ahead of India. India has remained poor both amongst capitalist as also the socialist nations.

India was very fortunate to have tremendous physical resources and potential for growth. We had identified hydroelectric resources for producing over 80,000 mw electricity, we had iron-ore, coal and all other ores and raw materials required for industrial progress. Arable land in this primarily agricultural economy at 0.53 hectare per head was one of the highest in the world at that time, far better than China. Above all, the people in fifties were highly enthusiastic; their will and resolve to build a new India carried a patriotic fervour and was all pervasive as symbolised by our school song *"Nav Bharat! Nirman Karenge Hum Apne Balidanon Se, Bharat Mata Jholi Bhar Do Tum Apne Vardanon Se."* (We will build a new India by our sacrifices, Bharat Mata you bless us with your benedictions.) Even with a little sincere lead, the nation could have achieved remarkable results, as all the ingredients to build economic infrastructure were readily available, only the vision in planning and the honesty in execution were required. Unfortunately we lacked vision, and the abounding corruption made honest execution impossible. An illustration below depicts the conditions existing at that time.

Our neighbour in the village installed a *"Rehat"* (persian wheel) by raising a Rs.300 loan under a special scheme called "Takavi" from the tehsil office in 1952. Unfortunately he had to bribe his way with a handsome portion of the loan amount, but since the terms of return were very soft and also it was interest free, so it was a preferred source over the money-lender. Needless to add that the very first crop was bumper and the family became prosperous. If only there were no corruption, many more would certainly have come forward and the country could have attained self-sufficiency in foodgrains in fifties itself i.e. three decades in advance. Free of this basic problem we could have moved on to the fast track of economic growth forty years earlier. It is not that I am stating in hindsight, the common people at the grassroots level did visualise and were amply clear as by 1956 the song which used to enthuse us in the school in early fifties was replaced by a different tune" *Desh Mera Behal Para, Ao Iska Karen Sudhar Re, Bharat Maan Ke ladle,* (oh dear children of Mother India, the country is lying in shatters, let us get together and reform it.) As the song progressed, amongst others the need to provide water and to banish corruption echoed its central theme. What a change, unthinkable steep degradation and demoralisation was overtaking us.

The Turning Point

Colonial powers have a one-point programme, i.e. to exploit the colony to their best advantage, but the Independence of a country is seen as a turning point that affords an opportunity to develop. Unfortunately, in India it was seen as a licence for its privileged section(s) to exploit for their personal gains, following the model of erstwhile masters. Contrast with Singapore that immediately on winning its freedom in 1959, took a resolve and laid down the ground rules to regulate the economy, the conduct of its ministers, civil servants and the people and enforced the same with an iron hand. Even the Chief Executive of the nation was no exception. Against this, we slackened in work culture, on moral codes and ethics and on the contrary indulged in the vulgar display of wealth, wasteful expenditure, etc. The abuse of office for personal ends became a sort of perk and norm. Corruption became universal and rampant, almost a way of life. The administration became non-responsive. So much so that as early as in 1951, a Committee on Public Administration under AD Gorwala had to be set up to suggest ways to improve Public Administration so that there could be speedy execution. Its report included a special chapter on integrity. The findings of the committee hold true even to this day. It aptly summarises that the lack of integrity takes many shapes like[2] "Corruption, patronage (based on communalism, sectarianism, nepotism and favouritism) and influence. Whatever the form, there can be no doubt that it vitiates policy, weakens administration and undermines confidence." Patronage has now virtually degenerated into naked corruption. If the timings of this report were not mentioned, one would think that it relates to the present day crisis. It is intriguing that the country had degenerated to that extent in just four years after Independence. The report laments the lack of transparency and the tendency not to take any action against the higher ups and also to keep the reports concerning corruption as secret.[3] .....occasionally their reports have been made public, but often they have remained secret...In any case, no action has been taken. It is not surprising that when grave allegations by responsible parties are made against people holding positions of high authority and they continue to remain in power without being cleared of the accusations, the public generally feel that anybody really influential can get away with anything..."

India is at the same stage even now, as in most of the cases, no note is taken of corruption by those in power and particularly those in high places. If at all enquiries are held, these are not thorough and impartial. People in any case are kept in the dark in the so-called public interest, as if continuation of corruption were in public interest. The lament of Gorwala was very genuine, but the worst is that till this day, impartial and fair enquiries against the big fish are still a mirage. The failure of Hawala case, despite having been monitored by the Supreme Court itself, has rightly re-enforced the impression.

The elite generally do not pay taxes and nor do they return bank loans. Gorwala observed[4] ...."while small men are often troubled quite unnecessarily; tax-evaders, whose assessment should run into lakhs, seem to escape. The failure of the Income Tax Investigation Commission to produce any real results and the ease with which the most blatant tax evaders seem to be able to manage their affairs undisturbed has caused a very wide-spread belief in the impotence of the government when pitted against the really influential and wealthy people." Sixty years later, only billions have replaced the lacs of that time.

The great turning point that normally comes to the nations along with their independence, failed to visit India and those who could have turned the events in favour of the country, went the other way, arrogated all the liberty and the licence for whatever served their personal selfish ends, satisfied their egos, earned them money material etc., and brought all the good things in life (as per their perception) including the foreign jaunts and the imported stuff at that time when the country had imposed very severe import restrictions (perhaps for commoners). It destroyed the integrity of the Customs Department. Similarly non-payment of Income tax by the influential destroyed the integrity and the efficacy of the Income Tax Department. Presently, these departments may actually collect no more than twenty to twenty-five per cent of the tax amount due, which forms the rationale of all financial, fiscal, economic and social problems that the country faces.

The Consequences

The economy picked up some momentum immediately after the independence, but it slowed down in mid-sixties after probably we had exhausted the Sterling Balances by 1964-65. The artificial support was no more available, whereas the bleeding and the draining of the country through tax evasion, smuggling, black marketing, pilferage of government sector, corruption, manipulations through the mechanism of over invoicing and under invoicing in external trade, creating assets abroad by carting money through Hawala, and such-like other malpractices continued unabated giving rise to a class of parasitic exploiters in the economic field.

As if all this was not enough, big scams kept on occurring at regular intervals after the jeep import scandal of 1948, which was the first scandal of independent India. Immediately after that occurred the steel plate scandal. Both these were in the defence sector, and V K Krishna Menon was the person responsible for both the scams and he rose to be the Defence Minister of the country. That perhaps mitigated the sense of guilt in others and there was a spate of scams thereafter, the extent of loss or bungling in most of them is not known. A list of a few major scams is attached as *Annexure 'G'*. Some of the scams were so neat that neither their extent could be gauged, nor could anyone be held responsible for them. The urea and the sugar scams are the outstanding recent instances.

Urea was the simplest of all the scams in which the payment was made full in advance, but the urea never landed. Since it was said to be a fake transaction managed by the family of the ruling Prime Minister, it was a classical case of the privilege of the big, so nothing could be done. What if the nation lost just a paltry sum of Rs. 133 crores?

In the Sugar scam of 1994, one afternoon, suddenly the sugar prices soared from Rs. 8 to Rs. 16-17 per kg. After great hue and cry, the price settled back at Rs. 14-15 per kg. The facts unfolded that some nominal shortage of sugar was expected; so one shipload was imported at a high rate of Rs. 16 per kg. around May, when 70 lac tons of sugar was in stock in our godowns. Since sugar production season was complete by April, all the costing had been completed and the issue price was also fixed. Subsequently when sugar was imported at such a high cost, the inland prices of stocks were made to jump to the same level. At least an additional sum of Rs. 6 per kg. was added on a stock of 70 lac tons which worked out to a neat amount of Rs. 4200 crores. A number of questions arise. First, when sugar required for next 7-8 months was already available, why there was indecent hurry to pay such a high price by importing sugar? Second, when sugar was a controlled commodity and its release was under government control, why the prices of Indian sugar were allowed to rise? Third, who pocketed this large surplus? Fourth, was this surplus accounted for? Such like many questions remained unanswered. The customary political game of mud slinging ensued and as usual the real issue, who pocketed Rs.4200 crores, was muddled, diluted and buried.

Who paid for it? The lower sections of society mostly consume sugar. Further, in the well to do households it makes no difference. Even an average government servant did not suffer as his dearness allowance went up. The senior officers gained. In my own household, the extra increase in the dearness allowance on our two salaries, primarily because of rise in sugar prices, was of the order of Rs. 40 per month, whereas on our 2-3 kg. of monthly sugar consumption, we paid Rs. 15-18 extra. We were gainer by Rs. 20-25. As usual people down the line lost.

In all corruption apparently anyone may pay, but the actual loser is the lowest at the end. The buck is passed but the lowest 60 to 70 per cent cannot do so any further. It is for this reason that no scam has ever been worked out. Consequences of this loot are very deep that the resources are diverted leading to (a) lack of infrastructural development, (b) lack of educational, health, hygiene, sanitation and such like other services and facilities, (c) lack of growth of employment opportunities, (d) increased pressure on land, (e) pressure on land leads to Naxalism and (f) as a consequence the country is forced to spend on gun in place of development. The circle has been going on and on and because of our dishonesty, all of us have been suffering and the country has not been able to develop to its full and continues to be backward despite our immense resources. This destroyed the nation's morale so painstakingly built by the sacrifices of the freedom fighters. It was basically the greed, which is not satiable as Gandhiji said, "there is enough in this world to meet every single individual's need, but there could never be enough to meet even a single individual's greed." Such extremely greedy people with unsatiable lust for pelf and power, enjoyed life with this boundless ill-gotten wealth, whereas, the poor, the impoverished and the exploited teeming millions toiled, day in and day out, but only managed to survive at just the subsistence level. This has created a great economic divide in the country.

The Economic Divide and Black Economy

As per the World Development Report of the World Bank, the lowest 10% of the population shares only 3.5% and the highest 10 % takes away 33.5% of the national cake in India. The ratio of national income or consumption between the poorest 10% and the richest 10% is 1:10. Further the black income, which is concentrated in the hands of the rich only, augments their share, and that of the lowest witnesses steep decline because the black economy tilts the scales against the bottom and creates a class that finds it difficult to arrange its subsistence and is perpetually doomed to languish for its survival. It is in this context that the problem of economic divide carries the seeds of unending class struggle, threatens the society with explosive consequences and as such assumes great significance.

Besides, the black money has a tendency to flow into the unproductive channels and also takes flight abroad. Thus, the small top not only corners the productive resources, but also turns them into idle, unproductive or stagnant assets and even carts them abroad. Among other ill-effects, the country is also deprived of the large employment potential that again adversely affects the lowest.

Before proceeding any further a few lines about the mechanism of the black economy may interest the reader. At a social gathering in 1995, I came across a practical instance of how the resources of the country were being drained away and how costs of production were being pushed up, making ours a high cost economy uncompetitive in world markets. On my being ushered into the party, a person working as General Manager of a urea plant was introduced to me, but the host missed introducing me to him. The man appeared to be on his second or third drink and was absolutely frank and truthful. I learnt from him that his firm had three-four units producing fertilizers. Urea was in news those days and the scandals in its import were being talked about. It was only the next year that the great Urea scandal, in which the whole amount was paid in advance and disappeared, as against certain percentage as kickbacks in other cases, became public. I enquired why our industry was so irresponsible that it produced urea at double the prevalent international prices. The gentleman in him felt challenged and confided in me that the roots of the high costs lay deep in the industrial houses and the government. He narrated that a few years back, he was asked to prepare a scheme for a new plant designed for a particular capacity. He prepared a proposal for Rs.350 crores. The management asked him to raise it to Rs. 700 crores in a way that Rs. 300 crores could be kept aside abroad, of which Rs. 100 crores would go to the authorities in central government as hush money and the remaining will constitute deposits for the industrial house abroad. The balance Rs. 50 crores would create the necessary cushion for use within the country i.e. it would be black money within. In the government, they ultimately would not agree for less than Rs. 200 crores, which the industrial enterprise was not prepared to part with. So there was a stalemate for a few years before the exercise was resumed.

In the meantime the fair estimates rose to Rs. 700 crores. This time the industrialist had prior discussion and the share of those in government was pegged at Rs. 400 crores. The house planned its own deposits abroad amounting to Rs.400 crores and kept another Rs. 100 crores aside for any exigency and hiked the project cost to Rs. 1600 crores. If fixed costs are hiked from Rs. 350 to 1600 crores, the costs of production have to go up. He blamed the corruption in the government for all this. When I asked him how about his masters, he was very candid that if only people in government were clean, they could have prevented his masters. Very proudly he declared that their old plant that had come up in the good old days, was producing urea at the rate of Rs. 3000 per ton as against Rs. 8000 per ton of this new plant. There was subsidy of Rs. 4000 per ton and they sold their entire produce at Rs. 4000 per ton in the market and that his factory as also other factories of the group were making huge profits. In any case, the industrial house had recovered its entire investment by withdrawal of its own funds even before the factory commenced its operations.

Similar are the findings of a study, in the sphere of external trade, conducted by professors of Florida International University, Miami, USA, in 1995, titled 'Capital Flight from India to the United States through Abnormal Pricing in International Trade', published in *Finance India,* December 1996. The study concludes that through overinvoicing and underinvoicing the country lost Rs. 50,000 crores annually in 1993-94, in its trade with the USA. It confirms the unbelievable fact that our friend from the Urea sector had categorically stated. There was an overwhelming similar testimony in Chamera II project, in which, as stated earlier, the negotiations were being conducted at more than double the rates. Power projects were allotted during eighties and ninties at much higher costs. *The Economic Times*[5] dealt with the point when it discovered the electric tariff of a captive plant set by 'Ignifluid Boilers' India Ltd. (IBIL) to supply electricity to Sanghi Industries was @ Rs. 1.60 per unit against a rate of Rs. 2.10 to Rs. 3.15 being signed all over the country at the same time. The paper finds the reason saying, "The IBIL plant will cost only Rs. 1.33 crores per mw, against more than Rs. 4 crores per mw for 'public sector projects'.

The detailed account as given by our friend from Urea sector and corroborated by other sources, raises certain questions and answers certain others as also rationalises certain other situations.

First, a project of Rs. 350 crores is hiked to Rs. 1600 crores, but still everyone is satisfied and this passes through various checks and finally the subsidy settles everything else. The country stands to lose at least in five ways directly, (i) foreign exchange to the extent of Rs. 800 crores, (ii) drain of resources to that extent, (iii) subsidy has to be given, (iv) production turns high cost and cannot compete in world market that threatens the very survival of our industries and even agriculture and (v) production loss of urea and utimately of agricultural produce during the period of stalemate.

Second, the high prices of agricultural produce, directly affect all poor sections of the society and also raise the wage rate, which affects costing in all the other sectors including the industry.

Third, there are kickbacks and people talk about the same gleefully as if it is a venture completed successfully. They steal like the ordinary thieves and forget the concept of right or wrong. They commit further crime in carting it abroad. In due course, the crime becomes essential to their operations necessitating the nexus between industry/business and the mafia for international transactions. To cover up their crimes they sometime physically eliminate all opposition that comes their way. Apart from draining the country, there is violence, which undermines the very confidence of the people in themselves as also in the system.

Fourth, there is massive tax evasion on all those transactions, which remain outside the domain of accounted economy. As per World Development Report 2000-2001 in economies with comparable rates of taxation, collection of central taxes was much higher. India at 8.6% of GDP was one of the lowest against the world average of over 20%, though our business and industry will like us to believe that our rates of taxes are much higher. It is argued that in India the incomes get divided into a broad based poor section of society who cannot contribute anything by way of Income tax. Incidentally the distribution of incomes in the USA and India is similar that the top 10% of population net as high as 33.5% of the GDP and the bottom 10% get only 3.5%. Moreover the other poorer countries placed like us are also collecting far higher a share of GNP as central taxes as compared to us. So the argument holds no water. At the world average rate, the Union Government in the year 2004-05, should have collected RS.5.64 lac crores out of India's accounted GNP of Rs.28.20 lac crores, whereas it collected just Rs. 2.25 lac crores. Collections should have been at Rs.18 lac crores if unrecorded income were also included. No doubt there must be some evasion of taxes in other countries as well, but much less when compared to India. Moreover in recent past they have made continuous efforts and backward economics like Ghana, Philippines, Peru and Bolivia have raised their collections from as low as 4% to a high of upto 16% in just one decade. There are no means to compare the data with any standard work for the states, but the same proportion can be assumed for the states also.

Besides the evasion of taxes, some of the other accompanying tools available to black economy that cause a heavy drain on the nation are as follows:

a. Pilferages from State sector, like that of electricity which merge in the black money stream.
b. The money squandered by the government in its acquisitions by way of awarding contracts/making purchases at higher rates, which the contractor accounts for by presenting false and fictitious bills.
c. Kickbacks originating from the higher rates that are limitless as discussed in the narrative elsewhere.
d. By entering in the books of accounts losses/expenses which the firm has not suffered/incurred.
e. The money lost in over-invoicing/underinvoicing of imports/ exports or vice-versa as may be advantageous to the trade or industry at a particular time.

As touched upon earlier, a study was conducted by professor John Zdanowicz and others of Florida International University, Miami, for the year 1993-94. The *Hindustan Times* [6] reporting on the study mentioned, "India charged 200 times less for selling its exercise cycles to the US . The similar concession for industrial miners diamonds was 100 times less, for unworked diamonds nearly 120 times less, storage batteries 40 per cent less and regulators were found underpriced to the extent of 30 times." On the other hand, the picture was just the opposite in case of exports from the USA to India, "if in a unit-form US sold tetracyclines at 11.74 per gram to other countries, the rate was 1102.50 per gram for India... for video cassette recording India paid 40 times higher, for chlorine India paid over 22 times higher." Alarming indeed!

The study repeated for 1994 and 1995, reported in the *Times of India*[7] disclosed similar facts and estimated maximum and minimum losses that might have been caused to the economy through the dual processes placing the capital flight i.e. losses caused to India at a minimum of twenty per cent on imports and forty per cent on exports. The USA is among cleaner countries in the field of international trade as compared to others. Even if the same percentage is extended to trade with other countries, India thus lost more than its annual balance of trade deficit on this score. Extending the same rates for the year 2004-05 as per RBI for the Indian exports of $79, 247 million and imports of $ 1,07,066 million, the losses at the above scale, will amount to $31,691 million and $ 21,413 million. In total, the country might have lost $53,111 million or Rs. 2,38,999 crores against a balance of trade deficit of Rs. 1,24,995 crores. The country, as per the study is cheated to the tune of Rs. 2.5 lac crores annually in the form of foreign exchange.

This ill-gotten money is used in extravagant or conspicuous consumption in India and abroad or in creating assets in the black sector inflicting an immediate corresponding loss on our economy as the resources are frozen, taken outside the economy, carted and spent or stored abroad giving fillip to economic activity in other countries to our detriment. Lavish spending both at home and abroad are beyond imagination.

Indian tourists are believed to be the best spenders the world over and enjoy the select luxuries like[9] "A serene evening at the Niagra Falls, a shopping spree at Marks and Spencer, playing with fortunes at Las Vegas casinos, romancing in the Swiss Alps, or putting across the lush Scottish greens......Indians have emerged as the largest group of international tourists ahead of Japanese and Americans." Indians are bracketed amongst the top three spenders. A survey conducted in Singapore revealed that the Indian tourists made three times the purchases as compared to their Chinese counterparts visiting the city-state. The Income tax returns that the Indians file do not permit that sort of spending which obviously is funded by the black economy.

Expenditure pattern of Indians inside the country also weaves the same story. If only an account could be drawn of the conspicuous consumption, regal style of life and festivities of the elite, it would throw light on the extent of daily expenditure of these people which would bear no relation with their declared incomes. Marriages are getting more and more costly in celebrations. Lavish expenditure at marriages and diversion of state funds has been alleged during past also quite often. There can be innumerable instances, but a few prominent cases can be recounted to illustrate the point at this stage. The marriage of the daughter of Dinesh Singh, the then External Affairs Minister, the marriage of Madhav Rao Scindia's daughter, the then Railways Minister, the marriage of Jaylalita's foster son, all were commented adversely for the unbelievable pomp and show, misappropriation of state resources and the spate of gifts, that all was beyond imagination or the affordable limits of the accounted income as an individual. Even the birthday bashes at Mumbai are said to cost to the tune of Rs. 5 crores. This happens either by misappropriating the Public Funds that amounts to corruption under Prevention of Corruption Act or it is the black money, which also is raised through means that are definitely dubious and culpable.

The money thus cornered becomes a separate entity by itself in the economy. A part of it is then drained out abroad, which, again is partially brought back into the country, but still the bulk remains abroad. The following flow chart illustrates the mechanism:

i) The country turns poorer by that amount directly.

ii) Incomes and employment by this investment accrue abroad and India stands to lose.

iii) India loses by way of loss of economic activity within the country.

FLOW CHART

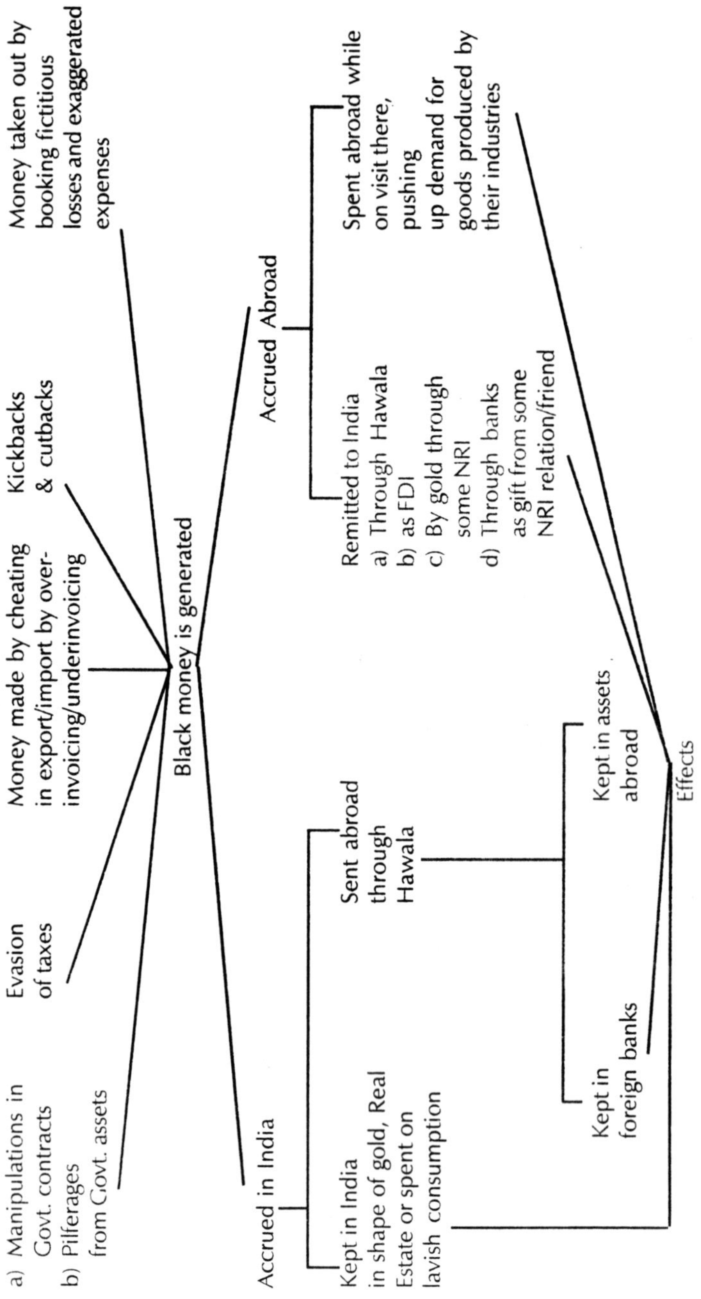
a) Manipulations in Govt. contracts
b) Pilferages from Govt. assets
Evasion of taxes
Money made by cheating in export/import by over-invoicing/underinvoicing
Kickbacks & cutbacks
Money taken out by booking fictitious losses and exaggerated expenses
Black money is generated
Accrued in India
Accrued Abroad
Kept in India in shape of gold, Real Estate or spent on lavish consumption
Sent abroad through Hawala
Remitted to India
a) Through Hawala
b) as FDI
c) By gold through some NRI
d) Through banks as gift from some NRI relation/friend
Spent abroad while on visit there, pushing up demand for goods produced by their industries
Kept in foreign banks
Kept in assets abroad
Effects

iv) Losses are not only direct but also on account of non-accural of benefits by operation of multiplier and accelerator effects.

v) Conspicuous wasteful expenditure to flaunt one's riches leading to demonstration effect and various consequential vices.

It is clear enough that losses are beyond any imagination, and have crippled the economy of this country and brought all-round misery for the masses and also the country as a whole.

The Great Uninterrupted Drain

There is nothing new to this drain of the economy of the country. In the nineteenth century, the Indian nationalist economists led by Dadabhai Naoroji had forcefully opposed the drain of national resources. Drain theories of Dadabhai Naoroji supplemented by carefully worked out minutest details are very well-known. Dhires Bhattacharya states,[(10)]"Dadabhai himself believed that in the forty-year period between 1788-89 to 1828-29 the amount of resources transferred to Britain from India was no less than 1500 million pounds,"that was quite heavy at the price levels and the size of the economy at that time. That was the loot of the economy by the masters who plundered and carted away Indian wealth abroad, but still the process was transparent, recorded and definitive, whereas today in free India, the loot is by the Indians themselves in the most clandestine way and there is no check and no effective opposition to it. The worst aspect is that the politicians, the bureaucrats, the business and industry alongwith mafia, all are deeply entrenched in it.

The extent of dizzy heights that the drain has attained during last few decades is mind-boggling and unimaginable. Olga Tellis, with reference to a statement of some Swiss Bank official, states[11] that holdings of Indian money in Swiss bank accounts was around 2550 billion dollars or Rs. 119 lac crores that was equivalent to 40 years budgets of the government of India at that time. The law of the land does not authorise anyone to keep money in a foreign bank abroad. It is all black money drained out of this country. Such holdings by now must have doubled to at least to $5 trillion. Much noise is made about our outstanding external debt of $100 billions, which is peanut when compared to these huge big holdings that by itself can settle our external debt many times over. This huge amount represents part of the drain over the years from free India.

Further since it is black money, it is stored secretly in the Swiss Banks and such like other banking chains. The account can be operated on the strength of the password which is known only to the account holder. Normally the password is not shared with anyone. If this account holder passes away, the money lapses to the bank ultimately and Swiss banks are known to have such accounts in plenty. Since Indians keep their accounts of bank money in complete secrecy, the incidence of lapsing is also equally high.

Extent of Black Money

Often it is said that black economy runs parallel or is bigger than the accounted economy. Various estimates of black money in the country have been made from time to time. Vinod Pavarala in his book[12] quotes D.R. Pendse who estimates black money generation at Rs.1 lac crores in 1990 (almost 25% of the GDP). Arun Kumar estimates[13] the growth of black income at 40% of the national income in 1995-96. By now it has safely mounted to at least 50% of the total income i.e. recorded plus the unrecorded or in other words the size of both in any year is now equal. The accumulation has of course continued during the last six decades and the cumulative amount has the capability to hijack the economy.

Such magnitudes sound impossible *prima facie*. No fool proof method or statistics are available either to prove or to disprove the staggering amounts supposed to have been stacked as black money or as black assets, but still some rough methods can be evolved to check whether the unaccounted economy statistically permits such a colossal drain as quoted by Oliga Tellis. This can be studied through various modules aided by making certain assumptions that could be as realistic as possible, but the results would only be indicative and not definitive.

In the table below the unaccounted income has been calculated at the rate of forty per cent of the total income, as if no income had been hidden. Basing our calculations on the declared income would be inaccurate and misleading as whatever goes into the unaccounted stream is to be reckoned as part of total income. Since the two are in the ratio of 60:40 or 3:2, the unaccounted income has been taken as 2/3rd of the accounted income as per the table

Table
Un-accounted Income

(amount in crores of rupees)

Year	GNP at market price	Percentage accounted	Percentage of un-accounted	Un-accounted
1995-96	1174528	60	40	782235
1996-97	1355127	60	40	902514
1997 -98	1509342	60	40	1005221
1998-99	1726017	60	40	1149527
1999-00	1921400	60	40	1279652
2000-01	2071391	60	40	1379546
2001-02	2256418	60	40	1502774
2002 -03	2450158	60	40	1631805
2003-04	2745947	60	40	1828800
2004-05	3087805	60	40	2056478
Total	20298133			13518552

The accumulation of black money is thus Rs.135.18 lac crores during a single decade. For the last few years in media the current rate has been mentioned at fifty per cent i.e. the size of both the accounted and unaccounted sections is the same i.e. 50% of the total income accrued in accounted and 50% in unaccounted sectors. In that case black money generated will be over Rs.200 lac crores during the decade. The money/resources thus diverted from the mainstream would also have grown further though continuing in the unaccounted sector. It can be anyone's guess how much black money has been generated during the five decades of independence. If black money accrued during last fifty-nine years since Independence is added, the results would be beyond imagination. In the light of the above, the figures of deposits in Swiss Banks at Rs. 119 lac crores in 1996 could also be probable.

All the black assets are not kept in Swiss banks alone. There are other banks, and also other forms such as real estate, investment in business, investment on children's education abroad, purchases, abroad while on visit, lavish spending abroad for which certain sections of Indians is well-known. India's black money abroad could be anybody's guess. Besides the black money and the real estate, assets are also held in various other forms like gold, diamond, other jewellery and business. When all are clubbed together, the extent would be astronomical, absolutely a frightening scenario!

In view of the unbelievable figures above, this very important issue needs to be analysed and looked into from other angles as well. Such an attempt has been made here.

This assessment of the size of the economy is based on the CII surveys of 1996 as quoted by Pawan Verma[15] that while assessing projections of aggregate demands in the economy, the CII survey "concluded that there are 180 million people in India with an annual income exceeding $3197 or Rs 1,20,000. By itself the total income of these 18 crore people alone will add upto Rs 21.60 lac crores annually as against our ostensible GNP figures of Rs 13.55 lac crores that year for the entire population of the country.

Following the classification as per the World Bank, the share of the highest 20% in national cake is 46.1 % and of the remaining 80% is 53.9%. Applying the same proportion, the remaining population has at least an income of Rs. 25.25 lac crores, adding up to a total of Rs. 46.85 lac crores.

Even this estimate suffers from under-estimation on three counts:

i) 18 crores formed 19% of the population in 1996, whereas the World Development Report places the share of top 20% of population at 46.1 %. The income of 1 % population is still to be added.

ii) The Report places income of highest 10% at 33.5% and next 10% at 12.6% of the national income. Since the CII surveys talk of the minimum of $3197 per head for the group, it appears that at least the top 10% of the population will have substantially higher incomes than the stipulated lower limit of $3197. Though very substantial, but anyway it is the guesswork. The fact remains actual national income will work out to much beyond Rs 46.85 lac crores.

Thus the GNP of India at Rs.46.85 lac crores exceeds the official figure of Rs.13.48 for 1996-97 by 33.37 lac crores. In other words the unrecorded income is 2.48 times the recorded income.

Basically it is nothing but bleeding the nation and draining this blood abroad. Our own blood is then transfused back by way of external aid. The secrecy of Swiss Bank(s), who store and channelise the funds to their advantage is nothing but the secrecy surrounding a criminal mafia or the receivers of stolen property. These banks are conspirators who aid and abet white-collar criminals from countries like India. Their black laws of secrecy are rather seductive and lure people towards the crime of draining and money laundering as they get services of their criminal' brethern (the bankers) who keep their loot in safe custody and get their own pound of flesh. No wonder the Swiss enjoyed a per capita GNP of $39,880 per annum as in 2003 which is only the second highest in the world, without any comparable ostensible economic activity except the banking. They were way ahead of the USA at $37,610. The so-called civilised people of Switzerland and other such European countries, under the garb of banking secrecy, suck the blood of poor nations. Such banks are no better than other white-collared criminals as without their association, collaboration and protection amounting to conspiracy, abetment and harbouring , these criminals would not be able to loot India and the such like other nations. They also reap the fruits of multiplier and accelerator effects, which rightly should have accrued to us and other such countries.

The Culmination

No doubt, primarily these are the Indians themselves who arrange the flight of lacs of crores of rupees through various ways. Bulk of money is from the black sector, as they do not pay taxes, and open the floodgates of hawala and drain money abroad. But all this becomes possible and defies any action by the state, as secure, well-laid and tempting infrastructure for such crimes is available to them. Unless these very countries relax banking secrecy, as they have already done in the context of money obtained from drugs, the poor nations would be helpless. Even the mighty US was helpless so long as the secrecy laws were in force and could achieve practically nothing in the field of drug control, whereas it has done very well after relaxation in secrecy laws in context of the drug money, but there is resistance against such change for slush born out of corruption as that is the problem of the third world. The drug is the problem of the mighty who can enforce laws as per their requirements, whereas the third world can only beg. Further, internally, the Indian elite will also oppose any such relaxation. Irony is that from Indian side, it is only the elite who can raise voice, which may be heard in the world community, but at the same time it is also equally true that they will actively oppose any such move.

After 9/11 the banking secrecy has become inconvenient in fight against terrorism for the USA. So the rules have instantaneously been relaxed. Corruption is no less a financial terror than physical terror. Physical terror is sporadic and intermittent whereas financial terror is continuous, though both have the same effect of killing the people, one instantly and the other slowly. What physical terror or drug terror is for the USA and such other countries, financial terrorism is at the same pedestal for countries like India.

The damage that corruption can cause cannot be questioned. No live or vibrant country can allow such a situation for any length of time. If it is not checked at the present stage, our country will be hijacked. So long only Indians have bled and drained our economy, but in future in the wake of liberalisation when foreigners are coming freely and participating in its economic life more and more, they naturally will not have any compunction. The drain would grow larger, steeper and faster as unscrupulous Indians will find more easily ready collaborators from abroad.

If only the taxes were collected and the drain reduced, the country should have no problem of resource crunch, but if resources keep on leaking how can the economy and the country be sustained? All the state governments are without money. If taxes are not collected, how can they have money for development works, for providing essential services like health, water, education, electricity and roads? Besides, it will not be able to pay well to its employees for running the administration itself. Employees need be paid well but any plea that the low wages turn them corrupt would be untenable as they cannot be paid more unless they collect more in taxes. Incidentally a similar plea was taken by most of the accused persons particularly the all-powerful politicians in the Hawala case, when they cited high electoral expenses for fighting electron as the justification for their corruption. At that stage it was adopted as a defence mechanism, but of late it is being argued openly with impunity that raising black money is a compulsion with the politicians, as they have no other option but to collect the tainted money. The sense of guilt that visited them sometimes during the Hawala days stands mitigated. They have also not evolved any alternative legal methods for funding of elections, as that will cut away their continuous source of unlimited easy money. The theme will be developed in the ensuing chapter, but suffice it to say at this stage that there is absolutely no justification for anyone including the politician, the civil servant, the businessman or the industrialist to be corrupt and even the excuse for fighting election and of election related expenses is as lame as the excuse of the civil servant or any other denominator.

There cannot be any escape from collecting taxes. Nonpayment of taxes is a theft, a very serious theft and purely a legal problem. There can be no moral restraints about it as even the most religious people are not immune from the bug of such crimes. The scourge has to be contained by the honest enforcement of laws backed by strong political and administrative will if fatal consequences that are staring us hard in our faces, are to be avoided.

References

1. Website of International Iron and Steal Institute.
2. Govt. of India, Report on Public Administration, by A D Gorwala, 1951, Chapter IV titled 'Integrity' page 14.
3. Ibid page 15.
4. Ibid page 18.

5. *Economic Times* dated 29th August 1995, editorial titled "How to Cheaper Power".
6. The *Hindustan Times* dated 16.10.1995 feature report titled "Exports to US under-priced, imports over-priced."
7. *The Times of India* dated 30.1.1997 front-page report titled "Study estimates $4-11 billion capital flight from India to US in 1994-95".
8. RBI Handbook of Statistics on Indian Economy 2004-05. Tables 196-197 pages 380-382.
9. *The Times of India* dated 28.3.2000. Article titled "Indian Tourists are big spenders" quoting from Manish Pandey, an expert on tourism.
10. Dhires Bhattacharya *"A Concise History of Indian Economy,"* page 16
11. *Observer of Business and Politics* dated 23.11.1999 Article titled "Empathy for the Guilty" by Olga Tellis.
12. *"Interpreting Corruption"* by Vinod Pavarala, Sage Publications 1996 page 156
13. *"The Black Economy in India"* by Arun Kumar, Penguin Books 1999.
14. RBI Handbook of Statistics on Indian Economy 2004-05 Table 1 page 6.
15. *"The Great Indian Middle Class"* by Pavan K Varma, Penguin Books 1998 page 171.

8

Corruption in Elections – A Case for Structural Reforms

India, the largest democracy in the world, is suffering from very serious threats from within. Justice, transparency, equality, rule of and respect for law, which are the basic hallmarks of any true democracy, are disappearing, yielding place to corruption and other accompanying aberrations. In the words of SS Gill,[1] "politics becomes a purely commercial transaction with maximisation of profits (or political power in our context) as its sole objective. Graft, patronage, spoils, violence, booth capturing, defections, manipulation of vote banks, double talk and false promises, and heavy reliance on publicity in place of performance, become the main props for gaining and retaining power." Ever since Gandhi and Patel departed from the national scene, personal integrity has been held at a discount. In 1963, the then Congress President D Sanjiviyya in the formal session of the party regretted that the "Congressmen who were paupers in 1947 are now millionaires and multi-millionaires. They own palatial buildings and factories... without having any ostensible source of such income," Such frank talk was intolerable even in the Nehru era and Sanjiviyya was punished for his audacity in attacking the hon'ble political dons and was soon eased out into anonymity. That was the beginning of organised mafia like actions in politics. This high handedness crept into the services also and in due course the dangerous unholy nexus developed. Lots of unemployed youth available in the wings, served as the musclemen for whoever could pay and some of them selected politics as a career, basically, to blackmail and make money. Though some of them held respectable positions, but all the same they polluted and subverted the system.

Unfortunately over the years, a justification has been built up that democratic elections are a costly affair and a politician cannot contest election and maintain himself later on within the meagre compensation that he gets from the State as an MLA, MP or as a Minister. That the compensation is only token, whereas he has to live, bring up his family, look after the long queue of guests that troop in, into his house everyday, and has also to find money for fighting the next election. This was the cover taken in informal chitchat by most of the politicians interrogated in the Jain Hawala Case. A number of them had initially admitted informally that they had accepted money, as per Jain diaries, for political expenses as a political necessity. In other words, it was an argument for continuation of graft, black money and the entire gamut of illegalities on grounds of political compulsion. Initially they were actually bewildered at the events that how action could be taken against them for their legitimate "political activities" for which such illegalities were the accepted norms ever since.

After Independence, we adopted democracy as the form of government that entrusts the country into the hands of the elected representatives. They only have the prerogative to lay down priorities, standards, ethics, laws, and the code of conduct for themselves and the nation. They have to devise ways and means of providing/containing political expenses for elections, conforming to legal and ethical standards. It was never difficult for the country to afford adequate compensation for the clean MLA/MP and Minister, obviating any need for corrupt or illegal means on their part. They chose to wear a facade of false idealism, false feudal dignity and selfless service. Though it was considered *infra dig* to accept appropriate salary, but in their perception, the respectability remained intact even if huge amounts were accepted through under-hand and high-handed methods; and in due course the inadequacy of compensation or say salary was used as a shield against allegations of corruption. Under no circumstances, in any enlightened society, can this be made a protective shield and cited as justification for corruption, loot, tax evasion, smuggling, blackmarketing, kickbacks, boot-legging, graft, violence, bunglings and such other illegal activities.

It is an axiomatic fact that our electoral system is suffering from very grave disorders and requires basic reforms. In our elections, votes are purchased, liquor flows like water, muscle power is used to intimidate the people and the black money is used freely. The caste and communal cards are stretched to utmost extent and at the final crunch, the booths are captured. Initially the criminals were inducted to scare the people, but slowly the criminals have themselves successfully entered the political arena thereby criminalizing the politics. Since politics is seen as a money churning business, the number of candidates applying for each seat has risen very high. The money power rules the roost and the impression has gained ground that those who do not have big money and musclemen at their command, cannot contest and much less win elections.

The motto of service, the vision about the country and patriotism, have all gone out of reckoning of the political and the administrative leadership. Corruption has, by and large, become the beginning and the end of all political and administrative activity. K Subramaniam beautifully depicts this phenomenon in the following words:[2] "The corruption driven political process, though democratic, brings to the top people who are corrupt and incompetent. Most of the incorruptible or the competent would have been sidelined and eliminated by the system as alien bodies before they reached the top."

This is a very dangerous situation, which if allowed to continue, will drown the poor further in the mire of poverty and deprivation, would mentally subjugate the entire population and keep the country perpetually weak and poor. Basically, the weak countries only break under their own weight as also under pressures from abroad. Electoral reforms as such constitute the cornerstone in fight against corruption and assume great significance. Only a government that has will to fight this menace can do so, but no government born out of corrupt electoral system can have such will.

The following paragraphs suggest some measures for cleansing the given system of elections or the electoral processes. Basically, it concerns enforcement of integrity and conduct of elections in a fair and the most economic manner. The objectives considered essential in this context are summarised below.

Objectives

The electoral system has to address itself to the following:

a) Everyone, who wants to vote, should be able to vote without any fear or without being under any undesirable influences i.e. there should be a free atmosphere for everybody to vote.

b) Only the right type of candidates should be fielded. The system should be so designed that it should be able to debar the criminals, members of mafias both physical and financial, as also, the corrupt from contesting elections.

c) The system should reduce the very requirement of funds for fighting an election. The emphasis is on evolving a system, which makes big money irrelevant in elections. It will have another advantage that if requirement of funds is not very high, it will allow and encourage an ordinary and a straight person also to participate as a candidate in the electoral process.

d) The number of candidates in a constituency should be within reasonable limits as a very large number is unmanageable by itself and leads to many other attendant problems.

e) The system should be able to prevent offences under the Representation of Peoples Act.

No doubt, it is easier said than done, but it is not impossible or very difficult to attain the above objectives. Apart from the suggestions, a model has been worked out, in an attempt to visualise an infrastructure, which can cut down expenses drastically.

The following measures are suggested:

1. Declaration of Assets

Every candidate under the law, along with his application form for candidature, should be required to declare all his assets, both movable and immovable in India and abroad, owned by himself, his wife, sons, daughters, daughters-in-law and sons-in-law. The returning officer in the initial scrutiny should reject applications not accompanied by such declarations. It should be clearly laid down in the law that in case of false declaration (a) all the undeclared assets whether moveable or immoveable will lapse to the state if discovered at any subsequent stage, irrespective of the fact that having once filed his nomination papers whether he contests the elections or not; (b) his membership of the house would stand automatically terminated in case the declaration is found to be false after the poll and he has been elected; (c) he should be debarred automatically from contesting any election to any political office in the country for next 10 years; (d) false declaration be defined as a corrupt practice which by itself should be enough to attract prosecution under Representation of Peoples Act and stringent punishment needs to be prescribed.

Since no member of a mafia gang, criminal or corrupt person can risk declaring his assets at the risk of above punishments being enforced they will automatically refrain from filing nominations. In one single stroke the quality of candidates will improve, and their number would also steeply decline.

2. Person Under Chargesheet Not to Contest Elections

Democracy is a very sensitive type of system in which the propriety should take precedence over the narrow legality. Unfortunately the current thinking is that unless one is convicted of a charge and the conviction is maintained by the final court of Appeal, he is not to be treated as guilty. Incidentally in the UK from where we draw our traditions, even a suspicion is enough to compel one to resign from the political office. Such offices are held in trust and suspicion is the antithesis of the trust. No wonder that a minister in the UK had to resign on just the mention in the media that he had links with Hindujas, who were appearing as accused persons before the CBI/courts in India, a different country. Moreover, vacating an office is no conviction. Why should people under suspicion rule us? There is no need for us also to tolerate the tainted persons in these sacrosanct offices, as we also require the fairest of the fair to lead us and not the pick of the scum who are under accusations. If he continues to be in power, first he will block the evidence and break or even eliminate the witnesses and ward off the conviction by misuse of his office. Second, this honourable criminal in high position would have wrought irreparable irreversible further damage before conviction, if at all that comes about.

The grievance that a case of corruption or economic crime takes twenty years before it is finally decided is genuine no doubt. For that we should evolve an efficient judicial system and procedures in order to ensure disposal of a case within a given time frame. Such time frame does exit for Police who have to expedite the chargesheet within 90 days. The same principle, though in a different context, can be extended to trials in courts. The court in such cases should frame charges within seven days of filing of the chargesheet and the trial could be completed in sixty days in such cases against the politicians. Once police and prosecution know that the case would come up for expeditious hearing, they too will not indulge in filing fake, premature and motivated chargesheets as they would run the risk of being exposed immediately. If in the Jain Hawala Case it were known that the chargesheet would be put to trial in next two or three or even in next six weeks, no officer of CBI would have dared to file such a chargesheet devoid of any substance. Once it is known that the system is so efficient that such underhand tactics cannot harm any innocent person, false complaints will automatically stop. Under any circumstance delays cannot be used as a justification for a tainted person to continue holding office. If all others suffer, let politician also suffer the judicial delays. Since he is the organiser of the whole show of governance, let him bring out a system for expeditious trials for advantage of all.

However, at the same time some statutory verification is a must to ward off against the false/motivated complaints. If the preliminary verifications return him guilty, he should be eased out of the office and also debarred from fighting elections before the detailed investigations are commenced. The court while looking into the disposal by the police should specially comment on the investigations and the investigator and any failings by the investigators should be viewed seriously.

3. Funding Election Expenses

The question of state funding of elections has engaged the attention of the Election Commission, the media, the political parties, the academicians, the financial experts and many others. All have deliberated on this issue, but none has reached any conclusive findings. Even if certain amount of money were given by the state to the individual contestant, there is no guarantee either that a candidate will spend it usefully for the purpose or that some other candidate will not spend more from his own resources. So, the problem will continue. Second, the state can contribute only a limited amount, which by itself may not be adequate or of substantive help for fighting an election for a fresh starter in the field and for the other it may be of no consequence. Third, many dummy candidates may be fielded to claim the amount and drain the exchequer. If not controlled in some way, even a number as high as 500 contestants per parliamentary constituency would not be an exaggeration. The implications of funds required have to be looked at before deciding on this issue. At the minimum, as the projections are appearing in the press, the candidates spend Rs.10 crores to fight a parliamentary election. Even if the state were to bear just Rs. 1 crore per candidate, it may require a huge sum of Rs. 500 crores for the 500 candidates for each of the parliamentary constituency making a total of some 2,70,000 candidates in the fray requiring as many crores, which is nearly 60% of the annual Union budget. State funding will have to be allowed for some 4500-assembly seats as well. Even if the scale of funding were at 10% of the parliamentary constituency, the implications would just be astronomical, which I dread to calculate even. State funding can be successful only where the number of political parties is limited and there is no provision for any independent candidates. It could be possible if the number of contestants could be limited to say just 5 per constituency. In our context even thinking of state funding in cash should be a sin, the burden of which the poor ordinary Indians will not be able to bear.

The state, instead of direct funding, should create infrastructure to provide full opportunity to every candidate, taking away the privilege, the advantage, the edge or the influence that goes with money. A few steps in this direction are suggested below:

(a) Publicity by the State

Every candidate incurs enormous expenditure on posters, cut outs, banners, bills, boards, and all that. The purpose of all these is to identify the candidate and to link him to a particular party and his election symbol. The objective will be achieved if a common chart for each assembly or parliamentary constituency is published and prominently displayed in its area by the Electoral Officer. This common chart of all the candidates in a constituency should have the photograph of each candidate on one side and his symbol on the other with his name written in between in bold letters, so that the electorate can be informed about all the contestants, their respective parties and the symbols. This will effectively serve the purpose, prevent the wasteful expenditure and ensure equal publicity for all the candidates. No candidate will be disadvantaged on the ground of lack of funds. This will also obviate misappropriation of public funds, a risk to which the state funding is exposed. In the bargain it will also save the nation from huge waste of paper, and the walls from being defiled.

(b) Allotment of Time on Radio and TV

Time should be allotted to candidates on government and private radio and TV channels. It should be made mandatory to divert time over all the TV channels during prime time free of cost during election days for the period to be determined by the Election Commission. The returning officer should hold a meeting and allot time to all the parties and the candidates by draw of lots, if they cannot reach any agreement otherwise. The programme should be broadcast every alternate hour, so that those who may want to watch and listen, may know the schedule well in advance.

(c) ***Manual Propaganda***

The heaviest cost out of the legitimate expenditure is on hiring of vehicles and volunteers for going to places shouting slogans and persuading the people as also organising and conducting meetings. This involves very large expenditure on the part of a candidate and also leads to wastage of petrol and diesel, which involve valuable foreign exchange. The alternative is that the government should prepare permanent platforms in villages and 'Mohallas' in cities and towns. The candidates should address the people from such platforms alone. The system is designed to function as below:

The government should create one or more platforms in each village/*mohalla* in a city depending upon the size of the population. A *pucca* brick stage can be constructed which will be a permanent structure. Candidates should be able to book their time through local administration. Security could be provided by the state and the programme could be displayed prominently. The candidate should be allowed to put up the public address system (PAS) one hour in advance, so that some of his supporters could inform about the meeting and collect the people. The administration should ensure that boards are put up in the village at various prominent places so that the moment the stage is booked by a candidate, his programme could be displayed on this board automatically and immediately. A candidate may bring his own PAS and may decorate the stage, as he likes. No charge need be levied by the state for this stage.

The creation of platforms right up to the village level will require some planning and expenditure; details of numbers required have been worked out in the Table below.

Table: Statement showing the number of Platforms required

State/U.T.	No. of villages	No. of Assembly/ Constituencies	Rural Population	Urban Population	No. of platforms Rural	Urban	Total
1	2	3	4	5	6	7	8
Andhra Pradesh	27221	294	55223944	20503597	40520	4101	44621
Arunachal Pradesh	2973	60	868429	222688	2973	44	3017
Assam	22224	126	23248994	3389413	16605	677	17282
Bihar	67566	324	95122327	14665897	67566	293.3	70499
Goa	-	60	675129	668869	575	134	709
Gujarat	18275	182	31697615	18899377	22553	3780	26333
Haryana	6731	90	14968850	6114139	10341	1222	11563
Himachal Pradesh	16916	68	5482367	594881	16916	119	17035
Jammu & Kashmir	6503	76	7564608	2505309	6503	501	7004
Karnataka	26826	224	34814100	17919858	26826	3584	30410
Kerala	1268	140	23571484	8267135	17850	1653	19503
M.P.	70883	320	60903155	20277919	70883	4055	74938
Maharashtra	35778	288	55732573	41019734	40330	8203	48533
Manipur	1949	60	1818224	570410	1949	114	2063
Meghalya	4583	60	1853457	452612	4583	91	4674

1	2	3	4	5	6	7	8
Mizoram	-	60	450018	441040	310	88	398
Nagaland	960	60	1635815	352821	960	70	1030
Orissa	46992	147	31210602	5496318	46992	1099	48091
Punjab	12188	117	16043730	8245556	12188	1649	13837
Rajasthan	33305	200	43267678	13205444	33305	2641	35946
Sikkim	215	32	480488	60005	308	12	320
Tamil Nadu	15735	234	34869286	27241553	30651	5448	36099
Tripura	4727	60	2648074	543094	4727	109	4836
U.P.	112561	425	137849547	36682874	112561	7336	119897
West Bengal	38074	294	57734690	22486481	41141	4497	45638
A&N	390	60	239858	116407	390	23	413
Chandigarh	26	-	92118	808796	56	162	218
D & N Haveli	72	-	169995	50456	105	10	115
Daman & Diu	-	-	100740	57319	45	11	56
Delhi	243	70	963215	12819761	791	2564	3355
Lakshadweep	10	-	33647	26948	20	25	45
Pondicherry	333	30	325596	648233	333	130	463
All India	575936	-			631856	57085	688941

Note: Data is based on 2001 census and the states of Bihar, M.P. and U.P. include Jharkhand, Chhattisgarh and Uttranchal respectively.

Size of population in a village/*mohalla*, determines the number of platforms required. Requirement of rural and urban platforms has been worked out statewise in columns 6 and 7 and total requirement is reflected in column 8. The figures have been worked out very liberally at the rate of one platform for every 1500 persons, with a minimum of one platform for each village irrespective of the numbers. For urban areas, there is a uniform provision of one platform for a population of 5000 persons.

The number of urban platforms comes to 57085 only, making a total of 6.89 lacs. But actual number of villages is fewer as every state has at least 5% villages, which do not exist, on ground. Thus, the effective number of platforms required may not exceed 6.5 lacs.

These should be created in schools or other such common public places belonging to the government or the local authority or Panchayat and the same could be used for community purposes or by school children, when elections are not being held. The added advantage is that these platforms will provide a focal point for local gatherings. Once created, these platforms will be permanent. The size of a platform could be 12 ft in length, 8 ft in width and 3 ft in height, with a foundation 1 ft deep. The cost of such a platform would be at about Rs. 10,000. The project could cost Rs.650 crores all over the country. Besides some more infrastructural items may cost another sum of Rs. 2000 per platform or a total of Rs. 130 crores raising total expenditure to 780 or say 800 crores of rupees. At the national level, this is a very insignificant amount, which can be funded by the Government of India as one time grant though the maintenance and reconstruction, whenever required, should be left to the State Government or local-self governing authorities.

However, the above would not be possible if the number of candidates is very large but the first two measures will restrict the number of candidates and make the state funding feasible.

The added advantages are that state funding is in kind or in the form of services and hence not capable of misuse or misappropriation like the direct cash funding. This will of course obviate the need for slogan shouting and hiring the people and the huge fleet of transport for the purpose. In the bargain it will save the society from many types of pollution, which is the biggest nuisance during electioneering.

4. Prohibition

Free flowing liquor is the biggest extraneous undesirable influence that mentally subverts the simple voters, particularly in the last phase of any election. If there is no liquor, there will be no rallying point and no such subversion. For this, complete prohibition for a week before elections should be inbuilt in the election laws. During this week the police and excise department should conduct wide surveillance of the entire area going into the elections, to ensure that nobody stockpiles or serves liquor.

5. Security Deposits

To contain the number of candidates, the amount of security deposit and the cut off point for its refund need be raised considerably, so that some of the non-serious candidates are eliminated automatically and the practice of putting up dummy candidates for various purposes is also discouraged. It is well known that the dummies are put up both for political and financial considerations. Political considerations are to divert and cut the votes of opponents. It may be a political necessity, but it is not a sound practice, so the candidate must pay. Financially, it is resorted to as a stratagem. It is widely believed that ever since the Election Commission enforced the stringent measures to check expenditure, dummy candidates are put up in large numbers, expenses are shown to have been incurred by them, but funds are actually diverted to the main candidate. It is not possible for the Election Commission to check at every stage. The system of raising deposits may not check it fully, but it will, certainly raise considerably the costs of fielding a dummy and can make this practice uneconomic. The eternal true economic principle of low demand at high cost and vice versa will probably ensure a lower number of dummies if they do not disappear altogether.

6. Electronically Charged Photo Identity Cards (ECPIC)

No method of preventing booth capturing or impersonation can be foolproof, particularly where the staff on duty also colludes. However, the electronically charged photo identity cards could be the biggest deterrent possible, and not even one bogus voter will be able to cast vote after introduction of photo identity cards. It is widely known that votes are cast in absentia by just stamping the ballot paper or pressing the button in case of Electronics Voting Machine (EVM). Now that the EVM is available at every booth, if like ATM of a bank the machines are so programmed that these will not respond without the charged identity card being inserted into these, there would be no voting without the ECPIC. Organising at any appreciable scale, where cards are snatched and brought without the person, will be very difficult rather near impossible. Even if some photo identity cards were brought, the booth staff would be able to detect the fraud from the photo. Coordination of two-fold events of snatching of card and the involvement of booth staff is a remote possibility. Under such circumstances even booth capturing would also not pay and the role of muscle men would also get curtailed. After issue of such cards, issuing of slips outside the booths by representatives of the candidates would become redundant, cutting down the cost of fighting elections as at present every candidate puts up a number of men outside every booth for the purpose.

7. Fixed Terms for Becoming Member of a House or Member of a Cabinet

No individual should be allowed to continue fighting elections indefinitely for a number of terms. It has many serious implications. First of all a person acquires permanent vested interest. Second, certain people become permanent fixtures and deprive others. Third, one adopts politics as a profession, devoting his whole time to it. He has no time for his profession in case he is a professional. He then tries to hoard money so that when he is out of power or when he retires, he has enough to fall back upon. Fourth, very essence of democracy is that diverse ideas should flow forth and help in nation building. Change is necessary as no single person is the repository of all the wisdom or has ideas to last forever. It is my considered opinion that as on the American model, maximum time limits need be prescribed for Prime Minister, Chief Minister, Ministers, MPs and MLAs. For Prime Minister or a Chief Minister the upper limit should be two terms, which naturally will spread over ten years, but if someone joins in mid stream then he or she be able to assume charge not more than three times, but not exceeding ten years for all the terms combined. If someone completes three terms earlier than ten years, he should not be allowed to run for a fourth term. If he completes the 10-year term in between, he should automatically step down on completion of 10 years. Similar should be the restrictions on Ministers except that if one becomes PM or the CM, the term should be extended. Similarly an MP or an MLA should get fifteen years but not spanning over more than four Assemblies/Parliaments. Once the principle is accepted, the details will have to be worked out meticulously.

8. Police Reforms

It is the ruling party that creates maximum problems in conduct of smooth elections. With law and order machinery at its command, it is normal to use state power to win elections by applying coercion in one form or the other. Besides coercion, even the lawful commands of the Election Commission are not carried out to the full extent. Election violence is a consequence of the blatant misuse of police. With a straightforward and well meaning police force, there cannot be any bungling in elections. It has been observed that whenever the administration and in particular the police see the return of government in power, the bunglings go up.

Basically the police should act as the umpires, but they often act as a party. The reason is simple that this disciplined force is in the hands of the ruling party. Disciplined people normally do not question the commands of their senior masters. Second, people have gone wise and everyone including the policeman tries to cultivate the would be masters. Even in normal governance, this bias is clearly reflected in day-to-day police administration and particularly in handling the matters with political overtones. Law undergoes a change if the rally is of the ruling party or of the opposition. If a rally or a get-together is of the ruling party, the trucks are unofficially requisitioned that too for days. Once in 1977 a deputation of truck operators met me when I was an SP in a district, representing that their trucks had been taken over by the police for 22 days in a month. They were also asked to get diesel to be filled up. What business could they run? I was shocked to realise, but those were my last days in the district as I was under orders of transfer and per chance I never returned to the field after that during next 27 years of my service. That remains a regret as I had resolved not to allow such practice whatever be the consequences. Returning to the problem, if the rally is of opposition, all tricks are applied to stop . The movement of lawfully plying vehicles belonging to the opposition parties or carrying people on their behalf is obstructed. This leads to tension and violence. This most potent and visible arm of law behaves more as a party functionary rather than an arm of law. Framing false cases is also the usual routine affair. I have witnessed this affair right from 1969 onwards.

But it is not possible to alter this equation unless police is freed from the executive/political control. Once police are on their own, they will feel accountable and act as per law and their independent judgment and conscience. It does not mean that they will have no control or accountability. The accountability should be very strict, but not to an individual, or a particular political party whose government may be in power, but to a body consisting of members from various denominations of society, to be constituted into Police Control Board as visualised by the National Police Commission in 1980. In the civilised democratic world police has to be the instrument of law and not a weapon of control in the hands of the executive, but unfortunately in India the colonial system of absolute control over police still continues. Though the commission made its recommandations over a quarter century back, but still its implementation appears to be a distant dream. Every successive government has only appointed a fresh commission or committee on police reforms, including the present Congress led government.

Perhaps when in power it suits the rulers and when in opposition one can flog the same actions committed by others. In the bargain the police and the people down the line suffer.

The recent judgement of Supreme Court may bring the necessary changes, but till such time police reforms take place not much improvement is possible in the polling process. But before this fundamental change is brought about, what can be enforced immediately is to place the state under Governor's rule before elections.

If police are placed under a board, it will have another positive effect. Once police is not privy to the actions of the ruling party, they would be able to act impartially; their investigations would also be fair. It would not be wrong to make a person resign from public office or debar him from fighting election if he is found to be guilty in the preliminary enquiry by the police, which would emerge as a responsible, non-partisan entity upholding law and incapable of being misused and mishandled.

9. Youth and Politics

Should the youth join politics at a very early age making politics a whole time career? The question has been agitating the thinking minds in this country. A person, who joins at a very young age, naturally searches his livelihood in politics. Polìticial activity in India emerged out of fight for freedom. Freedom fighters were the selfless people not seeking any favours or returns and left a tradition of sacrifice. The great tradition of sacrifice and selfless service could not be maintained. The young people who were not settled in any career kept on joining politics and searched their bread out of politics. Acquiring an office of profit became all important for the elected representatives. Besides the money the office gave power that could be used for the welfare of the constituency and it also gave an occasion to misuse it to serve the personal ends both noble and ignoble. Demand was so high that slots had to be found or even created to accommodate the large everswelling ranks. The present office of profit controversy is the culmination of that process and has engulfed the political class including the Speaker of Lok Sabha and other stalwarts from various political parties. However, the facade of service was still kept up. They could not be rewarded officially in any way even if the party they had joined was in power. If they were in opposition, then of course everyone was waiting to come to power. In practice they converted politics into a sort of business that had to yield returns. This was nothing but corruption, which got institutionalized. If young persons join politics, they will seek livelihood in that, and would turn mercenaries bereft of any ideology. Politics without ideology is to be dreaded. No wonder the politics abounds in *Aya Rams* and *Gaya Rams* and unprincipled alliances take place day in and day out, but that should only be expected from the mercenaries. It is high time the youth was barred from entering political parties before attaining certain minimum prescribed age. They should have sufficient time to settle in career, profession and life so that they join politics fired with ideology and not to convert the impending power into money. Minimum age to enter electoral politics in my view should be 35.

On the same ground political parties should be barred from entering the universities and colleges. In the elections to student unions, the big money, violence, liquor and all other aberrations play significant role as in assembly or parliamentary poll. The reason is simple. The political parties dominate the student elections and elections are fought along party lines. The student politics also gets equally contaminated as the real politics. Once the criterion is fixed at an advanced age, it will be easy to refrain political parties from entering campuses and they will realise that in the changed circumstance, their purpose is not served.

10. Mid term Referendum on Government Functioning

As per the Indian Constitution, the Lok Sabha and the State Assemblies are elected for a term of five years. It is often complained that the elected members do not bother about the constituents in between this long period of five years. No doubt, given that long a period for next round of accountability, any candidate can easily go idle for at least initial three years on the premise that public memory is short and he will make good during the last one or at the most two years. Besides, those who are on looting spree by converting the power conferred by the people into wealth, have a field day for long years and do not mind the possibility of being eased out after having utilized their five years gainfully, as the time is money to them. It is bound to happen in all the insensitive or the budding democracies. Sometime there is a talk of recall of members but it is a very tedious process. It requires expression of public opinion, i.e. a sort of election leading to another poll for selection of a new member. Thus, for change of a single elected member, conduct of the poll twice is a must, which is not practical as most of the states will always be in the process of election in some constituency or the other. The other remedy is the shorter term for a house, say, three years. Even in a sensitive democracy like America, the general elections are conducted after every four years. In India we cannot afford the luxury of election after just three years, as that will saddle the already strained exchequer. However, an unwanted government should not be allowed to continue as sufferance of a government that does not command the confidence and faith of the people amounts to negation of democracy itself. The best way out is to hold a referendum after 2½ years in place of elections. In referendum people will express their opinion whether they want to change the government. If the answer is no, the government can continue, but if the people express a desire for change, the regular elections should be held immediately after imposing the President's rule. Detailed rules can be drafted in this context. Referendum will cost very little as there are no candidates. The only publicity should be one or two limited speeches by the CM/PM and the leaders of opposition. The referendum can be held all over the country together in one go with local resources. Only the umpires, i.e. observers could be deputed from the centre. Such referendum could be held on a holiday say Sunday so that the business of the government is not dislocated. The results could be announced by the next day. Referendum could be held also for centre simultaneously.

Many advantages will accrue. It will keep the parties and the governments on their toes. Since accountability will start immediately after the elections, the governments will be under pressure to perform from the day one itself. They would not be able to indulge in wrong practices, as the day of reckoning will always be very near. People will also become demanding and would exert their right. The mercenaries may opt out of the political arena as facing the people time and again may not be feasible or worth for them. Above all, the people will be able to utilise their democratic rights most effectively without losing any time or money. It will have the similar effect as election at the end of 2½ years but save the nation from the expenses and the efforts that go into conducting one.

11. Central Rule During Elections

The elections are conducted by the state governments both for union parliament as also for state assemblies. So there are allegations of favouritism and bungling against the state governments and such allegations are on the rise. Worst aspect is that such allegations are often true irrespective of the party in power in a particular state at any time. To stem such and similar other problems, the states should be brought under the Presidential Rule, say three months before elections. As it is, even now, all initiatives are stopped and no development works are allowed to be pursued in this period. The administration is practically taken over by the Election Commission when the model election code comes into force. Governor will provide a better administration in place of a lame duck and an ineffective CM. This will bring to an end much of the mudslinging that goes on as part of the election campaign and will provide level playing field to all the contestants. Since the level of VIP security would come down, the voting would be much more relaxed and people will be able to vote without fear as the presence of any security force builds up an atmosphere of fear. The lesser the need for security the lower will be the fear in the minds of people.

The government at the centre need not be disturbed, as there is no direct involvement of the centre in the process of the conduct of elections. Moreover, the police is under the control of the state and it is the state which makes arrangements for elections to union parliament also. The provisions contained in the constitution appear to be tailor made for this purpose. It appears that the framers of the Constitution appreciated this finer point and did not provide for President's rule at the centre. That indicates their maturity.

12. Only National Parties to Fight Elections to Parliament

We are witness to the contemporary pulling and pushing by various partners in the coalition governments at the centre. The craft of coalition politics has been reduced to blackmail, bunglings, threats etc., holding national interests at bay. The municipal matters have come to the forefront at the national level pushing the bigger questions to background. The regional or local parties are concerned with the personal matters or the local issue at the most. In parliamentary debates such matters are now dominating and in allotment of resources the regional parties have the upper hand. To keep them together appeasement has to be resorted to, but that is nothing but clear corruption, more often. There is an urgent need that only the national parties are allowed to fight elections to Lok Sabha and all the regional parties and independents be debarred from contesting. That will take care of many other problems as well. The burgeoning number of candidates will be reduced to a manageable number, say around five for a constituency as all the national parties do not fight all the seats in every state. The disciplining or the purging process as detailed in this chapter earlier will become manageable and enforceable. Elections may attain certain degree of fairness and eliminate the freaks straying into the national political arena.

13. No Mid-term Poll

At present the Constitution provides for dissolution of the parliament or the state assembly by the respective cabinets at any time at their will. This provision gives immense discretion of blackmail to the CM/PM at the state cost, whereas the expenditure and the inconvenience has to be borne by the people. Every time there are elections, under the model code, all development works come to a halt and the governance practically ceases three months before elections and next two months are required by the new ministry to pick up the threads again. On an average, states are undergoing through the elections every 1½ to 2 years. It is a strange situation that for 25 to 33 per cent of the time, no development work can be taken up. With frequent elections our democracy is proving an instrument of condemning the people to perpetual backwardness or in other words to perpetual doom.

Elections should be held on fixed time and both the Union and the State elections be held together. If at the state level, the Government cannot be formed by the political parties, let there be central rule till the next elections and at the centre if no party can form the government, let there be a national government under the President.

These are a few suggestions for fulfilling the urgent objectives on the process of voting alone. These will definitely produce very healthy effects and remove some of the fundamental problems that the electoral process faces, and may possibly break the vicious circle of the role of black money, the criminals, the musclemen and the mafia and restore sanctity. It may also help the society to get rid of some of the unhealthy attitudes that have become part of its thought process.

References

1. "*The Pathology of Corruption*" by SS Gill, Harper Collins Publishers India 1998 page 166
2. *Economic Times* dated 29.9.1992 Article titled 'Timeless Existence' by K Subramaniam.

9

Unhealthy Attitudes

Attitudes of the people in a society towards its problems, their seriousness to face and to resolve the same, their will to uphold the value system, their capacity to set higher goals and their determination for achieving the same, shape its destiny. That factors determining the attitudes may lie deep in psychology or history or somewhere else are not within the scope of this work. The attempt here is to enumerate, analyse and examine the most prominent of these attitudes and their effect on fundamental issues, like corruption and the resultant black economy and to analyse *inter alia* why we have become tolerant towards all these vices.

All pervading corruption is like a sensation in our body that its separation from us looks unnatural. In Seventies AG Noorani described this phenomenon as *"AZHIMATI"*, a Malyalam term that denotes a sort of sensation that is even painful, but the body becomes so used to living with it that life without the same does not look possible. In due course, like the demand for drugs, the body politic requires higher dosage of corruption, just to sustain itself. Corruption is seen by certain sections as indispensable to sustain the very economic, political and social superstructure of the country. One wonders whether the system will crumble without corruption. Though, on the other hand, it is also a forgone conclusion that the end of an addict is clear and near. I may sound like a prophet of doom, but these warning signals are written on the wall in very bold letters.

The idea that ruled the sixties through the eighties that like a mild dose of inflation, a mild dose of corruption provided wheels or grease to decision-making in government and hastened faster growth of the economy is absolutely outdated. All well-meaning people now see corruption as the biggest enemy of any society. Instead of working as grease, it has mired the very wheels it was supposed to rotate. We, in this country, have reached a stage where our attitudes have become self-centered, tolerant of and protective towards corruption and the corrupt. By and large, those sections of society who matter have turned corrupt, though at the same time it is also true that voice to fight corruption can be raised by these very classes only, i.e. the lower middle and the middle class in particular. Those who are further lower down have no voice and even if they have, it is too feeble to reach the ears that matter. Deterioration has gone deep to the extent that even organised protection is available to the corrupt. No wonder we are continuously sliding down on the scales of honesty and integrity. We have been feeling so since quite sometime and now the Transparency International (T.I.) has been quantifying the same. Indian score has been between 2.7 and 2.9, whereas China has progressed from a mere 2.16 to 3.4 between 1995 and 2005. The top score every year has been between 9.5 and 10.00. The Transparency International allots ranking to all the countries it surveys and India has been way below near the bottom and on continuous decline whereas China is constantly on the upswing. It is a well-known fact that in the recent past, they have made conscious and serious efforts to fight corruption and have been imposing heavy penalties extending to death on the delinquents. Besides China, some other countries that made serious and conscious efforts have also improved.

Greed, which is limitless, is the prime mover for corruption. Greed propels the capable people who have resources of the state at their command, to divert these towards themselves and misappropriate everything by means, fair and foul. The fifteen per cent upper crust of the population exploits the eighty per cent (in varying degrees), who are perpetually at the receiving end and see no light at the end of the tunnel. The above remarks will be unjust to a limited minority in the society who are either not greedy by their conviction or have developed strong inhibitions and some may suffer from the apprehension i.e. they may be too timid to be corrupt. The number of all the three categories combined is very small and may not be more than five per cent.

The upper crust of society considers it as their right to appropriate to themselves the wealth of India to the maximum, in order to live in the regal style. The middle classes motivated by demonstration effect emulate them, but whenever they find the going difficult, they create a smokescreen of morality around themselves and take to criticism of those beyond them and the criticism can be quite scathing. The corruption continues to grow progressively and defies any action against the corrupt for which part of the responsibility lies on our typical attitudes. It will be interesting to state and analyse in details some such responses of various people.

Perception of Corruption at the Highest level

Corruption was a big problem in 1951 itself as per Gorwala Committee Report. It is well-known how the spate of scams and commissions starting from 1948 continued through the fifties and sixties, during the Nehruvian era even. When confronted with all pervasive corruption, Nehru, the then Prime Minister, exhorted the people to concentrate on creation of more wealth, as the money involved in corruption was within the country only. What exactly he meant by these remarks is not known. It is not clear whether he had in mind some future plans for distributive justice, or legal action against the delinquent but his statement legitimised the corruption and the corrupt activities, which surely he did not intend.

The scandals and corruption continued to grow unchecked. Subsequently, when confronted with a similar question, Indira Gandhi as Prime Minister described corruption as a worldwide phenomenon. By implications how could India alone be free from this malaise and also what was so serious or immediate about this universal phenomenon?

Later in 1996 Prime Minister Deve Gowda took shelter behind the similar argument that corruption was there in every country and so was in India. He was surprised why all of a sudden so much commotion was being made during his tenure when corruption had flourished in India in all the earlier regimes. He went on to deprecate all the institutions (including Ombudsman) and Judiciary fighting corruption, whose efforts were futile and bound to end in smoke.

How wrong our PMs were. Nehru expressed satisfaction that the hush money continued to remain within the country, but how slowly and steadily it kept on being siphoned off to the Swiss and other banks and in other forms abroad up to Rs. 119 lac crores or 2550[2] billion dollars in Swiss banks alone as some estimates claim. Again it has been proved wrong that corruption was a worldwide phenomenon. Transparency International has shown that corruption free countries do exist in this very world. Second, all over the world, the countries that meant business and had a will to cleanse their stables have fought back the monster of corruption and contained it. Several former PMs of Italy and Japan and a President of Korea have been put in jail on charges of corruption. A chief of police of a Korean state was sacked for visiting a golf course, which was prohibited for civil servants[3]." In the eyes of ordinary South Korean, the Golf Course is the place where crooked businessmen and politicians discuss ways to rig economy. President gave up the sport." Singapore, Hong Kong, Malaysia and Australia have also taken strong measures against corruption. If it is a worldwide phenomenon, fight against it is also worldwide.

The Transparency International now measures corruption every year. The Scandinavian countries along with New Zealand are the cleanest and have been sharing the top honours, scoring full 10 marks or near that on the scales of Transparency International. Many other countries maintain high scores, which indicates that these are comparatively free from the menace and also that their number is on the rise. We, unfortunately, are sliding down. It falsifies the contentions of our successive Prime Ministers that it was a worldwide phenomenon or that nothing could be done to fight it or that all the institutions fighting corruption will end in failure. Every country that had the will and resolve to fight has succeeded and there is no reason why India should not succeed.

'Leave Me Out' the Middle Class Syndrome

The typical middle class attitude is 'nab others, leave me out'. The middle class cries against corruption and the corrupt, but when it comes to corruption by themselves, they insist that their corruption is need based, only for survival at a particular level, an existential compulsion. In their justification they put forth, *prima facie,* convincing arguments, that only they pay tax on incomes as salary earners, that corruption in high places is not checked, whereas they are dealt with severely.

The middle class may advocate rationale of or justification for their conduct or their corruption, but still they perpetually suffer from a sense of guilt. They have, as such, always criticized and have led fight against corruption, whatever little worth it might have been. Is it a pointer to some hope? Can some positive contribution be expected from them if ever the cleansing process begins? Pawan Verma illustrates the point well,[4] "As the victim of this escalation, the average middle class person was a vehement critic of corruption. But in the general erosion of ethics, many of the newly corrupt were people from his own class. Ironically, even a person thus enriching himself would never miss a chance in private conversation to condemn the increasing corruption of those at the very helm of the nation. The denunciation of corruption of a greater magnitude and at a higher level, fulfilled the psychological need to minimise his own divorce from ethics. Hypocrisy grew, but guilt was allayed."

In the recent past this class appears to be abandoning its inhibitions rather fast. With rise of consumerism, greed of this class has gone up. Volume of corruption indulged in by this class has grown over the years as this class soon realised that,[5] "...it is better to swim with the tide than to remain for ever marooned on an island of principle." This class could have given a tough fight and surely prevented the slide, but it took cover under the shield of super corruption by the higher classes and cried 'Why Me. Leave Me Out', but sort out the problem. With the exposure of corruption at high places, the aggressive attitude of the middle classes towards the higher classes sharpened further. It is for this reason that any action against corruption finds praise for the agencies leading the fight. Till such time the lower section of society acquire both the comprehension and the voice, the middle classes would continue on their corruption spree, but once the lower sections raise their voice or start opposing the higher sections effectively, the middle classes will revert to their traditional shield of principles, values, ethics and all that. They are as such the fence sitters and would jump on to crusading brigade as soon as the crusade begins. This could constitute the bedrock and will also lead the struggle at lower and middle levels. This very class all over the world fought the evils in the society, brought about the revolutions and change, but unfortunately in India these classes are at the moment themselves stuck deep in the mire and are unable to lead fight against corruption.

Disobedience of Laws and Soft Enforcement

Generally in India, people do not like to respect law or the established systems; rather they feel a sense of adventure, romance and achievement in breaking the same. This could be the legacy of the Civil Disobedience Movement of pre-independence days, but we have not overcome the hangover, though now we are an independent nation with democratic system for which rule of law is the essential ingredient. The more one can violate the law, or say the socio, legal and economic norms, the more one rises in one's own estimation as also in the estimation of the people around him. The one, who grows rich by violating with impunity all the laws of the land and in particular those pertaining to economic offences, is seen as a hero and an achiever. This is what happened in case of Harshad Mehta, who could corner the big fortune. He was invited for a TV show. The intention of the organisers might have been to grill him, but strange enough, as he appeared in the studios, the audience spontaneously applauded him, extending to him a hero's welcome, as if it was a tribute to his capability to circumvent/manipulate the laws, the rules etc., and make big money by befooling everyone. Did they perceive their own reflection in him and imagined for a similar opportunity for themselves? If only they had believed that he would be punished severely they might not have extended him that ovation.

Our attitude towards enforcement of the laws is the weakest link in the chain of our unhealthy attitudes towards the society, the nation, the system and the rule of law. However, the arm of law is used for perpetuating the wrong acts and converting the power, conferred by the law, into money or other privileges.

This frame of mind and the infrastructure have led us to the following weaknesses in our thought process:

a. *Non-cooperation with Enforcement*

Whenever a scandal breaks out, the media demands immediate action, that too instantaneously. There will be all round bashing up of the investigating agency and meanings will be read into why the case is not being worked out. No doubt the investigating agencies in India are slow, but some minimum time has to be granted even to the most efficient ones. On the contrary, the moment the case is worked out and action under the law is proposed against the offender, there comes an immediate shift in perception and the media starts reporting against the investigations. It takes no time to mould public opinion against the so-called harsh action. Perhaps the media reflects the public opinion itself. The core point is that the enforcement agencies have to be opposed under all circumstances. Roots of non-cooperation may lie deep in colonial days when the arm of law had to be opposed as it belonged to the foreign ruler. Is that the reason that when the action is taken, the society stands up to defend the culprit? Is it that perhaps the culprit is seen as a native, but the enforcement machinery is still perceived as belonging to the masters (i.e. the aliens)? It is unfortunate that six decades after independence, the same legacy and the mindset continue. May be the functionaries of these agencies have failed to identify themselves with the people and could not win their confidence, or may be still they function under the ruled-ruler syndrome.

b. *No Strong Action*

Every vibrant country enforces firmly whatever law it enacts, but in India, the law is enforced softly and the enforcement is highly selective. If the enforcement or the investigation is thorough and complete, that shakes us instead of reassuring. Since people from upper and middle classes are generally not clean, it is possible that they visualise similar treatment in store for themselves tomorrow, which they want to avoid. This is very obvious and marked when we come to fighting corruption or economic offences. Efforts are made to devoid every economic law of the sting or the punch. The people, whose voice has requisite decibles to be heard, do not like any strong law or strong action against the corrupt in particular.

Lihaz (Regard)

A.D. Gorwala speaks of *'lihaz',* which literally means regard or consideration to be shown for one's position, wealth, status or such like other attributes, as against the principle of equality. It may be feasible to some extent in other fields, but turns ridiculous and creates complete mess when *lihaz* has to be shown in the enforcement of laws. Such an attitude is nothing but a part of the feudal ethos that still survives. Even in investigation of crime or in the case of fight against corruption in high places, one is supposed to show extra regard or *lihaz* for the position of the person, which is clear negation of equality before the laws and cuts at the very root of the principle of rule of law. The quantum of regard depends upon the influence he can exercise and also on his monetary standing, as if the position confers some sort of basic right to indulge in bungling, misappropriation or corruption.

The concept of regards is extended to the ridiculous limits. In this poor country every state runs its emporium. The ostensible reason is to help market the produce of the small producers, who are not capable of marketing on their own, and to popularise products of the state. The emporia get subsidies as they run perpetually in losses, but still they allow freely VIP discounts ranging from ten to thirty per cent straight and could be as high as seventy to eighty per cent through underhand methods by showing the stock as damaged and condemned. Such rates of discount are managed even on fresh arrivals. I discovered in one emporium that if a VIP liked a particular article, the supplier was asked to give a fresh bill on lower side even upto fifty per cent with the promise that the loss would be adjusted in some other purchase from him. Even the communist ruled states are not free from this virus. The concept of regard applies to the process of acquisition of articles as well. If the articles are supplied through some dignitary, they are paid necessarily higher rate, which raises the price level in these subsidised shops even, but the *lihaz* has to be shown to the dignitary both ways.

When the same concept of *lihaz* or regard is extended to the field of Criminal Law, the consequences are not only grave, but fatal.

d. *Patronage*

A. D. Gorwala pointed out as early 1951 that in the Indian society, a person in position of influence or power has to take care of his family, *biradari* (clan), village etc., and has to consider many other factors that are irrelevant in any civilised society governed by rule of law. The basic tenet of patronage lies in extending favours to those who do not deserve these, if fair practices were followed. This could be in the field of employment, admissions to educational or professional institutes, or even in the field of criminal laws by protecting accused persons of one's own village, caste, etc. The essence is that the people connected with this functionary should get everything irrespective of the fact whether they are eligible or not. Once one goes on wrong track in extending patronage, one is tempted to encash it for his own benefit as well.

An important aspect of all this is that the politician, the administrator or the investigator who wants to put up a strong fight against corruption, is naturally not accepted by the system. Equitable and strong enforcement of laws without *lihaz* or patronage is dubbed as stupidity, immaturity and tactlessness, as if the maturity or the tact lies in the capacity to compromise, capability to conceal the dirt, to suffer by softening one's conscience all those vices against which one should stand up and fight. Ironically, a person becomes a participant in things one is supposed to fight.

Colonial Legacy of Secrecy

In government there is absolute secrecy even in absolutely open matters pertaining to the most ordinary issues. When the country is looted, some government servants will invariably know, as some of them will always be involved. If moved by the zeal to cleanse the system, someone of them wants to give out the information he is prohibited by the conduct rules. Even pointing out such issues in a meeting constitutes misconduct. A public servant is expected to suppress and protect all the bunglings that go on around him. The tradition continues from the colonial era where all public servants functioned in the interest of the RAJ, so every action of the servants of the government was an internal matter. Since government was different from the people, the latter had no right to know what was going on inside. Continuing the old tradition, even now any information going out is viewed as a leakage and viewed very seriously as an attack on the government, enough to attract disciplinary action, or at least an inconvenient transfer, or prejudicing him in matters like allotment of house, grant of reward, being ignored from promotion, etc. Fear is so severe, that an honest civil servant refrains from even dealing with matters pertaining to corruption, what to speak of exposition. Faced with such ugly situation and finding no better alternative, he may proceed on leave.

In a free country, in national interest, the law should encourage a public servant to bring out truth i.e. uncoloured facts. Corruption can be exposed only by those who have inside knowledge and access to the official records. If officials cannot expose the patent bunglings, the truth will never come out. The honest government servant, under present dispensation, finds the going very difficult and the system can turn him crazy. He cannot digest the bunglings, but if he exposes, he runs the risk of disciplinary action. The system is such that it may digest the worst of the corruption, but any deviation leading to exposure is treated most seriously. It takes no mercy in finishing the deviant. He starts wondering if he is still living in the colonial era as the regulations and the mindset, given by the colonial masters, still continue to rule the roost. It is his grit, his conviction, or sense of commitment to truth or nation that sustain him.

Blind Obedience to the Top Boss

This is another retrograde remnant of the same colonial legacy that as a good subject, he should not question the top boss, including the illegalities, improprieties etc., committed by him, and just acquiesce to what he desires. I myself witnessed a number of police officers swear that they would even kill someone if asked by the Chief Minister. Similarly I heard the members of the administrative service saying that they would do anything if the Chief Minister so bids—from dismissing a public servant to allotting some valuables in utter disregard of laws or rules, changing the land records, even if such a manipulation led to murders. As a young officer I had observed, how orders of a Chief Minister would change the very concept or the perception about the facts, which in any particular case are fixed and unchangeable except by manipulation and injustice. Quite often I would ask should the Chief not be briefed about the right and the wrong. Most of the officers did not believe in unnecessarily inviting avoidable trouble. The same thing I found in Government of India, years later in the context of cabinet ministers and the Prime Minister.

Once a Union minister, who was visiting the CBI, narrated how under the executive instructions the extra legal single directive, under which the CBI was to seek permission from the Secretary of the concerned Ministry before registering a case or an enquiry against an officer of the level of Joint Secretary and above, was added to the Rule Book. It was informally decided at the highest level to award contracts of big projects on limited tenders as against calling global tenders, ostensibly to save time and also to identify and get the correct and capable firms, but in reality in order to award projects to certain predetermined firms at the rates of choice.

Some officers felt that it would eliminate competition, expose them to the CBI enquiries and land them in trouble. They were assured by the powers that be that the enquiries would start only if the government permitted. Requisite provision was made that against the decision-taking level officers, i.e. Joint Secretary and above, no enquiry would commence without permission of the government. The same was incorporated in the infamous single directive that was hit by the Supreme Court in its judgment of 18th December 1997, in the Jain Hawala case. The minister was deprecating the bureaucrats that they did not even point out that it was wrong, or that it will lead to the loss of competition and hence result in higher costs of projects. Gently the minister questioned the sense of integrity of public servants, their commitment to principles or the national interest. The minister continued that the sole concern of public servants was for saving their own skin and arrogating privileged position to themselves. After issue of this Directive, project costs rose. It is interesting to note that the number of scams at national level and their size both grew larger when the single directive ruled. This shows that straightforwardness or integrity was not the first concern of senior officers. Once their own skin was safe, their inhibition to do wrong also disappeared. May be that in the process some of them might have cornered some fortune for themselves as well.

The primary duty of the public servant is thought to be not to the nation, but to himself and his master, and whether it is right or wrong, legal or illegal, moral or immoral, is all immaterial.

Hypocrisy

A large number of the civil servants having indulged in all the misdeeds during their service period, suddenly start speaking of values and value system after their retirement. They had flouted all those norms or virtues with impunity, when they were expected to uphold the same, but suddenly rediscover their worth to ensure a place of respectability in the society or may be by repeatedly projecting themselves as such, their sense of guilt is mitigated. The common man is taken in by anybody who cites scriptures irrespective of his real past. This has a demoralising effect on all those who had known him and some of them may be tempted to follow the tainted route to prosperity during service and make-up by preaching the values of ethics and morality after their retirement.

In fact in all the academies training the administrators, the police officers and officers of any other service, the first lesson is that the civil servant should carry out only the lawful orders and not the unlawful ones. But in the field, invariably most of the officers buckle down once they face any opposition. Peers around him also advise to fall in line. The new entrant gives in and feels secure flowing with the tide and learns to maintain a facade of hypocrisy like his seniors. During my stay in CBI a number of times this topic cropped up in informal discussions that whether one should act as per law, whatever be the consequences, or toe the dictated line, a course that may not be according to the letter and spirit of law. The dominant view was that the CBI was also a part of the government and as such, law for its officers was what the persons in authority over the CBI laid down. Some would only quietly listen refraining from expressing any views. I normally found myself alone on the other side opposing vocally such views. The argument invariably got long drawn and ended with advice to me to leave the government job, go out and then make as much noise as I could, as if there was no need for change from within. I have often reflected, whether it meant that as a civil servant, one is only a hypocrite slave whose only job is to protect people in power without any regard to legality or illegality, propriety or impropriety, morality or immorality, relegating all that for the post-retirement period. Incidentally, everyone generally agreed with me that ideally mine was the correct position, but only in theory, whereas one had to be practical.

In a free country, 'where the mind should be without fear' and 'clear stream of reason should flow', this mental slavery is not understood, particularly when they swear by law, truth, integrity and straight action.

Did time prove them right? If I did not leave the CBI on my own, the system shunted me out like a foreign body. In less than three years I was thrown out of CBI whereas CBI does not believe in quick change, mine is perhaps the only exception.

Departmental Gang Mentality

People believe that all departments of the government are corrupt. There may be difference of degrees from one department to another, but the basic conditions are believed to be the same. There are a few honourable, straightforward and honest individuals in every department, but as a group or a service no department is clean including the services like administrative, revenue, judiciary, law enforcement including police, defence, engineering, transport, health or even the education; all have been suffering from the deep malice of corruption, nepotism, casteism, feudal bias, exploitation and the whole train of vices. A survey conducted by Transparency International, India, in 2005 confirms the above. They studied just the 11 services and found all of them corrupt, to whom the citizen confesses to have directly paid a whooping amount of over Rs. 21,000 crores in corruption. This does not include the money siphoned off by the public servants from the exchequer and also paid by the people in collusive corruption like contractors sharing with engineers or administrative bosses or an evader sharing with the tax collector, which basically constitute the volume.

However, every denomination tries to justify itself and its own ways among its members and before the public. Departments have acquired the attributes of any gang of dacoits i.e. each of them protects all other members of one's own gang. Small exploits are individually their own, though major ones are collective and the common booty is shared honestly. The internal wars in a criminal gang normally arise over distribution of the booty, so is true of these departmental gangs also. Complaints come to light only when there are disputes over sharing the booty. Justice Mulla had once called police as organised band of dacoits, which basically applies to all the departments of the Government and other denominations who are deep in the process of looting the people and the exchequer. Remarks of Justice Mulla, if read in the light of Gorwala Committee Report, would rightly extend to whole gamut of administration as also the politicians. As a group, they also harbour the same gang mentality and have tremendous capacity to justify their corruption and other aberrations

The politicians have been arguing over the last five decades that their salaries were very low, not sufficient even to meet the expenses for tea at their residence for people visiting them from their constituency. What prevented them from raising their lawful salaries, instead of perpetuating the hypocrisy that they were honorary servants of the people? Did they create the myth of selfless service of the people as a rationale for their corrupt actions?

Every denomination has its own vested interests in perpetuating the corrupt system, but publically every group swears by honesty. In other countries, unlike ours', such aberrations have been crushed with an iron hand.

The Compulsions

Characteristically in our society, our existence and actions are not our own, but under compulsion. If someone is a criminal, it is out of compulsion. If any public servant is corrupt, it is again his compulsion. Tax evasion is a compulsion for most of us and for business and industry in particular.

The politician apparently is the master of the show, but all his actions including corruption are under compulsion, so much so, that he has to continue in politics also out of compulsion. The business offers baits and candies to both politicians and civil servants and thereby makes tonnes of illegal and illegitimate money, not only out of economic offences, but also out of what is commonly understood as substantive criminal acts; all under compulsion.

The civil servant or the official is the person without whose complicity no corrupt practice can take place either by the politician or the businessman or the industrialist. It is he who examines all the proposals, interprets and enforces all the laws, rules, regulations etc., investigates the crimes, assesses and collects the taxes and finally adjudicates all the matters, as an arbitrator or a judge. His responsibility as such is the highest, but even he has his own unending list of compulsions.

Each of the three sections has its own rationale and each is equally convincing when heard separately. In the process they have wrought havoc and conditioned an average mind and confused him as if all such aberrations are unavoidable and there is no way out except excusing these high and mighty as helpless. It is precisely they who should be the repositories of all the trust and faith of the people, but unfortunately these sections have embarked on ruthless mercenary exploitative activity, and whenever asked for accountability, each section weaves a web of compulsions around itself.

The fourth colluder, i.e. the criminal or the mafia is called upon again under compulsion whenever the trio is faced with any problem, either amongst themselves or from the commoners. The recourse of these sections to criminals has legitimised the criminal activity, not only in politics but also in business and even in administration. A stage has come, when criminals have made their direct inroads into politics as also administration and have started calling the shots, which was the cause of worry for the Vohra Committee. But the governments have their own compulsion not to act against them; as such there has been no substantive followup action on the report.

The sad part is that the judiciary is also under compulsion. Even the mighty judges trying Jain Hawala case were under compulsion not to give out the names of those who had tried to pressurise them. Vineet Narain, the petitioner of Hawala Case, states[6] that Mr. Justice Verma, the Chief Justice of India, had himself spoken on 14th July 1997, from the Supreme Court bench, "tremendous extraneous pressure was exerted on him and his brother Judge", but the Hon'ble Judge refrained from mentioning their names or taking any action against them. One wonders if they were under some compulsion, neither to divulge the names nor to take any action against these worst criminals against justice who had the audacity to try to pressurise the Hon' ble judges of the highest court of the land.

Everybody acts from behind his own shield of compulsions. Are we a *Majboor Rashtra* (helpless nation) where right from peon to Prime Minister, serf to kulak, labourer to capitalist, advocate to judge, clerk to secretary, constable to director general of police, are all helpless, only the excuse (reason and explanation) may differ.

Religion and Corruption

Every religion has two main aspects, first the form of worship and second the code of ethics and values. Worship is the apparent form and varies from religion to religion, but the core of every religion is the moral and ethical set of values that it imparts to all its followers. Admirably, this code of values is common to all of them, but unfortunately the religions, as being practiced, do not lay the requisite emphasis on such values.

In Sanskrit literature the twofold aspects are delineated very clearly as follows :

"Ijya adhyan danani tapa satyam dhriti kshama,
Alobheh iti margo-ayam Dharmasay ashatvidhi samrita.
Tatra purvash chaturvargo dambharthamapi sevayte,
Uttrastoo chaturvargo Mahatmanyev tishthati"

When translated it means *Yagya* (worship), *Adhyayan* (reading of scriptures), *Tap* (penance), *Dan* (charity), *Satya* (Truth), *Dhriti* (right endeavour), *Kshama* (forgiveness), *Alobh* (lack of greed), are the eight-fold paths of religion. Of these the first four are followed by the bad, the crooked, the criminals also, but the last four are followed only by the *mahatmas,* i.e. really good people.

A careful consideration will reveal that the first four are nothing but forms of worship, whereas the last four constitute the set of values. Without following this code, consisting of truth, endeavour, forgiveness and lack of greed there can be nothing religious, but the religious gurus do not lay any emphasis on adoption of these virtues, though they go a long way eulogizing and discussing the other part of the religion concerned with the form of worship.

If religion is godly and purifies the soul, then adherence to religion should dissuade people from corruption and corrupt ways, but unfortunately it does not. The corrupt and the criminal both seek shelter by invoking God and offering money as if it is His share of their booty. Religion and religious preachers have not deprecated greed, corruption, tax evasion, money laundering, adulteration or other such crimes, which are against the humanity, whom religion is supposed to sustain. The religious leaders have quite often used their influence for bailing out their erring followers by putting in a word in favour of their disciples to their other followers who might be influential.

The main objective for undertaking the arduous religious journeys normally is to seek forgiveness of Almighty for the sins already committed, but even the so-called devout religious people have no intention of abandoning such wrong path for future. To my mind seeking such forgiveness amounts to an attempt to enter into corrupt bargain with God almighty.

Though religion is not a substitute for law, but still religious preachers can play a very positive role. When pressed by law, people invariably seek solace in religion. If religion also decries such activities, the concerned person will have no alternative but to refrain from the same. Religion can make direct impact if the respective godmen prick the conscience of their followers. Unfortunately, the great religious people speak only of the first four tenets of religion, practically ignoring the last four. Corruption emanates from greed, which all the religions denounce in theory, but no religion on ground decries it in the context of a corrupt follower.

Ethics, Morals and Corruption

Time and again corruption is described as a consequence of loss of moral and ethical values, and the resurgence of moral and ethical values is prescribed as the panacea to cure all the ills of the society including its worst malady, i.e. corruption. This point of view betrays correct understanding of the problem and makes matters worse.

There is no reason why corruption should not be treated at par with other crimes like theft, robbery, the economic offences, adulteration, swindling, smuggling, and such other offences, and the corrupt as any other criminal. Further, wherever corruption involves coercion, it assumes still greater seriousness. All these crimes are committed with the identical sole object of greed, so all such criminals need to be dealt with at par. Since the problems of corruption, tax evasion and the like are associated more with the elite themselves, the two situations cease to be comparable. However, if the elite adopt these moral and ethical standards themselves, everyone down the line will follow automatically. Who has prevented the higher echelons of society from adopting ethics and morality, but no one can tell them so. The upper sections of society play this ruse and prescribe cultivation of such values by those down the line, in order to avoid any legal action against themselves. Since moral or ethical principles in the ultimate analysis require voluntary submission, sure enough there would never be such a moral regeneration. The history all over the world is a witness. The moot point is, how will the laws be enforced on this top segment of the society, as corruption anywhere has been contained only by the strong enforcement.

The enforcement of laws can be ordered as the Supreme Court did in the Jain Hawala case and other cases in 1995 and 1996. Though it all did not reach the logical end, but still the effort was worth as the theory of inviolability of the highest was exposed. The name of the highest person in the executive hierarchy, the ruling PM, entered as accused in the CBI records for the first time. The change stands ushered in. The subsequent conviction of a former Prime Minister and a former Chief Minister of a state proves the point that law can be enforced on ex-VVIPs at least, but teaching morals and ethics to the most honourable of all the mortals in the country is impossible. Even if these VIPs were discharged or acquitted ultimately, for whatever reasons, still a milestone has been reached and new grounds broken.

I happened to be in The Netherlands in August 2001, for a workshop where I had the opportunity to interact with people and learnt about the economic and social conditions prevailing in that country. The Netherlands is a small country with 1.08% of area and 1.6% of population of India, but it had a GDP of $384 billion, or 87% of Indian GDP at $442 billion. The country is smaller than the state of Haryana, but it claimed to be the third largest exporter of agricultural produce in the world, next only to the USA and France. What impressed me most was, its very high tax collections by central government, which was as high as 42.7% of GDP as against only 8.6% of GDP in case of India. At the highest slab, people of The Netherlands paid income tax @ 60% as against 30% in India. I enquired about tax evasion, which was more or less non-existent. Most of the people, I enquired from, were of the view that it was the result of strong enforcement as penalties were very severe if they were caught evading taxes. It is the fear of law, which has kept them clean. The score of The Netherlands on the scale of Transparency International was 8.8 and she enjoyed as high a ranking as eighth in the world out of 91 countries surveyed in 2001, but the prime mover remains the fear of law. Incidentally, the theft was rampant and we were advised to be very careful about pilferage at all public places. The very first day, purse of a young woman member of our team was stolen from her table in the lobby of a five-star hotel. The theft is there, but no Tax evasion as law enforcement against evasion is strong.

People Get What they Deserve

It is often said that "People get the government they deserve", "people get the police they deserve", "people get the development they deserve" "people get the justice they deserve" and "people get the administration they deserve". I am not aware in what context the original observations were made, but now it is a fashion to extend the same ridiculous logic to all the fields. Various government departments cite it in defence of their own failures and lethargy. This philosophy of status quo is an insult to the helpless people implying that they deserve this corrupt system only. It is a justification created by the vested interests, the tyrants, and the perpetrators of injustice. During British era, its implications were that the Indians deserved to be slaves, so any fight for freedom was misplaced. How wrong, mischievous and misconceived the notion had been. Indians remained the same, but with increased awareness they continued their agitation and won the independence in 1947. Had they rested their oars and not waged the struggle for independence as per this dictum, we would have continued to be in the same state of slavery.

There is need to expose this hollow philosophy and inculcate an inherent desire for sweet dreams. If today people start dreaming, tomorrow they may rise to realise the same. Mahatma Gandhi and others dreamt of freedom at a time when the country was firmly held in the clutches of the colonial power, but they fought for their goal and realised their dream.

God Will Descend To Solve Our Problems

This is a typical attitude with the Hindus that God will handle all their serious problems. They do not even think of mustering courage, combining and fighting out the same. The philosophy is that let the tyranny grow, when it crosses all the limits, it becomes unbearable, decent life appears impossible, the concept of 'Dharma' itself is threatened and people groan under the tyranny of forces opposed to '*Dharma*', then God himself will descend on earth, take charge of their problems, solve them all and establish Dharma (order) back as He did in 'Satya Yug' as Narsimha, in 'Treta' as Ram and in Dwapar as Krishan. We, therefore, watch and wait. We need to realise that 'He' has shown the path an ample number of times and exhorted through 'Gita' to stand up against injustice. If people remain inert, He may be compelled to descend once again rather soon and may have to preach Gita a second time. I see no reason why can't people do away with their helplessness, organise and fight against this demon of corruption and avoid invoking God again and again for these earthy matters.

Corruption for Party or Society

It is a general belief that no blame attaches to a corrupt person if he does not retain the hush money himself, but passes it on for collective purposes like party funds if he is a politician and otherwise for social purposes or charity. It is conveniently forgotten that loot remains loot whatever be the purpose. Ends do not justify the means and much less where such means involve violation of law and commission of substantive crime. The Robin Hood image has no place in a democratic welfare state, governed by the rule of law. A politician, who collects money for the party through questionable means, is no better than any other criminal accused of corruption. The corruption has the same effect irrespective of the fact who commits it or with what intentions.

Unhealthy Attitudes

India had a great tradition of upholding truth, value system and high morality. Aberrations are, of course, natural to human nature, but these were analysed and taken care of. Kautilya's strategies for weeding out corruption are some of the pioneering remedial measures in this direction. Through the Middle Ages, when justice used to be sold in the West, our Panchayats represented a very strong system of justice. What went wrong and where did we fail, are the questions that we need to address. The answers lie in our long spells of slavery. Once foreign rulers take over, they try to subjugate and suppress all the local customs and institutions as that is the best way to divide and subjugate the society. Efforts are made to corrupt local life and to destroy all sense of morality and ethics, as these are essential ingredients of patriotism. It is patriotism of the locals, which any colonial power dreads. With weakening of moral and ethical fibre, the foreign rulers gain an upper hand, hold the people under fear, create a coterie of collaborators, cause a wedge between the collaborators and the patriots and thus divide the local population.

In 1947, we inherited such a society in which certain constituents lacked sense of belonging and commitment. The erstwhile ruling classes felt diffident in mixing with the commoners and continuously looked outwards to the west, whereas their job now was to serve and build the nation and not to rule or exploit. The contradictions continued. In the process even some of the erstwhile freedom fighters and their successors lost patience as they found the same old systems ruling the roost. The dismal pattern that evolved kept on enveloping section after section till we lost all our determination to stick to our moorings. Society and the nation as a whole kept sinking.

However, basic goodness, fellow feeling and nationalism still persist among a large number of individuals who have been able to stay afloat the high tides of corruption, but the country has to be rescued before it is too late. Cultivation of healthy attitudes through education, propaganda, religion, penal laws and many more similar measures constitute the answer. In view of weak attitudes towards enforcement, the agencies have not been adequately strengthened. CBI, the highest investigating organisation in the land, itself requires to be strengthened so that it can work freely, frankly, fearlessly and without favour or prejudice towards anyone. Whereas CBI needs to be fully accountable to law, but at the same time, it needs to be liberated from all other controls so that it could enforce laws effectively. In general our attitudes towards life, crime, justice, fairness and corruption, in particular, have to turn healthy. The next chapter examines CBI in this context.

References

1. *Ministers' Miscoduct* by AG Noorani, Vikas Publishing House, Delhi 1973, Page 230.
2. "Empathy for Guilty" by Olga Tellies in *Observer of Business and Politics* dated 23.11.99.
3. Fair ways and Foul, *The Economist* 9th to 15th September 1995.
4. *The Great Indian Middle Class* by Pavan K Varma, Penguin Books 1998, page 88.
5. Ibid
6. *Hawala Ke Desh Drohi* (in Hindi) by Vineet Narain, Arunodaya Prakashan, page 41.

10
The CBI

The deterrence ultimately comes from the laws and their strict enforcement, which specifically brings the role of enforcement agencies to focus. In our context the law enforcing agencies should include the CBI, the Enforcement Directorate, the vigilance and the anti-corruption organisations of the states as also of PSUs of both the centre and the states, capped by the CVC (Central Vigilance Commissioner), the leader of all the above agencies. Somehow all the above agencies including the CVC are equally ineffective. The CVC is still groping in the dark for its role and relevance.

Finally, it is the judiciary, which adjudicates the actions of all the above agencies. Leaving out the judiciary, all the above agencies that constitute criminal justice system in context of the Prevention of Corruption Act, work with and are basically an extension of the executive performing the quasi-judicial functions. That brings contradiction to their role and renders them all ineffective as has been seen in previous chapters in context of the CBI. What is true for CBI is truer for all other agencies.

The CBI in its embryonic form was created in 1941. The British created an organisation in India, named Delhi Special Police Establishment (DSPE), to look into the charges of corruption arising out of the transactions of war and supply department. With its headquarter at Delhi, it was set up under an executive order of the government. In 1946, DSPE was given a statutory status by

DSPE Act and its jurisdiction was extended to all the departments of the Central Government all over the country. Slowly the economic and some of the other offences were included within its ambit.

In 1963, the Government of India renamed it as Central Bureau of Investigation under a resolution. It remained dependent upon DSPE Act, as all its legal powers emanated from that Act only. At the same time, it was restructured to make it more broadbased and the scope of cases that the CBI could take up, was widened. Meanwhile its workload kept on increasing with increased governmental spending (particularly in defence, development and services sectors), the rise of an ever expanding Public Sector and the nationalisation of banks. The Bureau divided itself into various functional wings and also added more branches at various important centres all over the country, besides a number of central branches located at Delhi, with jurisdiction all over the country.

At present the CBI has three main operational arms or wings viz

(a) Anti-Corruption Wing (AC)

(b) Economic Offences Wing (EOW)

(c) Special Crime Wing (Spl. Crime)

Each wing functions under an officer of the rank of Special director or the Additional director and is further divided into zones. An officer of the rank of Inspector General designated as Joint director (JD) heads each zone and is assisted by two or more DIsG. A DIG has two to three branches under him. His charge is known as a region. Each branch is commanded by an SP, assisted by IOs of the rank of DSPs and Inspectors, besides the supporting staff. The branch is the basic and the executive unit. All officers above the rank of SP have supervisory role, though they may personally take up some important cases themselves as IO.

Anti-corruption wing is the largest with six zones under six JDs, of whom five are territorial and one heads the Central zone, also called the Headquarter (HQ) zone. The central zone gets the most important cases having ramifications all over the country or involving the bigwigs including the VIPs and the VVIPs. The AC wing has zones, regions and branches all over the country.

The EOW and the Spl. Crime wings have three and four JDs respectively. Their branches are normally all located in Delhi at the Headquarters only, though as per requirement their officers fan out.

Besides the three operational wings, there are supporting divisions, which render technical/legal advice, provide training, administrative cover, and scientific services to the CBI. In addition, the Interpol division helps in coordination and liaison work with other police forces and agencies the world over.

The CBI has been functioning under the Union Government, Ministry of Personnel, but following the Supreme Court judgement of 18th December 1997, in the Jain Hawala Case, some organisational and operational role and superintendence has been transferred from the government to the CVC, as the court found that because of executive control over it, the CBI was not investigating the big and the influential people in that case and was succumbing to the pressure of powers that be. It is in this context that the Supreme Court focussed on the question of accountability and tried to liberate the CBI from the control of the executive. The question that arises is to whom should it be accountable. The Supreme Court tried to address this question, but still it does not seem to have been settled finally. The question is vital and needs a thorough examination.

To Whom Should the CBI be Accountable

The CBI has enjoyed a very high esteem ever since its inception and has been treated as the last word on investigation in this country, though from time to time, it was dragged into controversies whenever a case with political overtones was assigned to it. Irrespective of the party in power, the Opposition has always accused it of obliging the rulers. However, the CBI continued to steer clear its way and the controversies died down with passage of time. The moot question still remains whether the CBI really functions according to the dictates of party/government in power and are its investigations really steeped in their colour or is it unnecessarily dragged into such controversies, or is it the infrastructural arrangement that renders it vulnerable to the charge?

In 1994, the Supreme Court when engaged in hearing the public interest petitions in Jain Hawala Case came to the conclusion that the CBI was not taking up the investigations, as bigwigs were involved. The court inferred that the CBI was not able to work impartially because it was under the influence of the government. They tried to identify some alternate agency, which could be impartial, beyond the influence of the government in power, but ultimately settled in favour of the CBI. However, for purposes of the Hawala Case, the court directed the CBI to report directly to it without reporting to the government. Besides corruption aspect, which was the responsibility of the CBI, the case involved FERA angle, and also the unaccounted money, the subjects of Enforcement Directorate and the Investigation Wing of Income Tax respectively. The court also asked these agencies to report directly to it. The court felt that the three departments would be able to conduct themselves impartially under these guarantees and the protection the court had afforded. Further, the judges made it mandatory for closure reports, if any, to be laid before them.

The court tried to ensure an impartial conduct from all angles, by protecting the agencies and exhorting them again and again to follow the dictum "Be you ever so high, the law is above you" and also by reserving the discretion for closing the case to their own scrutiny, but still charges of corruption against all the accused persons ended in miserable failure. With my first hand knowledge, I have tried to analyse in depth the reasons for failure and reached the unfortunate conclusion that the CBI could not investigate those who were its own masters i.e. the government. This narrative has earlier amply demonstrated how investigators were not allowed by the top CBI brass to look into and collect the evidence. The agency managed to throwaway and scuttle the scam despite all the safeguards prescribed by the Supreme Court. In order to avoid the sharp scrutiny by the apex court, chargesheets were filed against all, practically without any evidence. The main evidence in the chargesheets was of entries in the diaries. The trial court discharged everybody between the years 1997 and 2000, on the simple ground that evidence of entries in Jain Diaries was no evidence under the Evidence Act or under any other law of the land. It was not a new finding and was already very well-known in the CBI. The CBI files were replete with the same opinion since 1995 at least and this position of law was well-known to the then director CBI K Vijay Rama Rao and the subsequent director Joginder Singh. The issue was formally repeatedly examined in great detail during the time of Rao and it was unanimous opinion in the CBI that by themselves, the diaries would not stand, as they did not constitute any evidence. Corroborative evidence of payments, motive or favour was essential and in absence of the same, no chargesheet could be laid. Direct evidence of payment is impossible to find in such cases, but the evidence of motives and favours was possible and *prima facie* visible, and could be collected by examination of projects.

Under such circumstance, any investigating agency worth its name, will turn to their Disproportionate Assets (DA), which presupposes immediate searches, maintaining complete surprise, but both the Directors, Vijay Rama Rao and Joginder Singh, dared not venture on such a risky step which would put a questidn mark on their personal loyalty to their respective mentors. Basically the CBI has always behaved like any other department of the government taking care that the interests of those in power in high places were fully protected and that nothing was brought against them on CBI files.

Reverting to the basic question of credibility of the CBI, there is no escape from the fact that CBI investigations into the matters pertaining to high and mighty were generally coloured and since corruption is conversion of power into money, the bulk of corruption is at the highest levels where there is more concentration of power and the CBI remains diffident or crippled in taking any action against these very people who consider it as the boy from their backyard at their service. In its present form and organisation the CBI is incapable of investigating those who control its own destiny. The Supreme Court took note of this aspect, though very gently in the following words.

[1]"This experience revealed to us the need for the insulation of these agencies from any extraneous influence to ensure the

continuance of the good work they have commenced. It is this need which has impelled us to examine the structure of these agencies and to consider the necessary steps which would provide permanent insulation to the agencies against extraneous influences to enable them to discharge their duties in the manner required for proper implementation of the rule of law."

The court, on advice of a specially constituted committee under Shri Deshmukh, a retired civil servant, worked out a system placing the CBI under the Central Vigilance Commissioner (CVC). The CVC has been made a statutory body and assigned the responsibility for efficient functioning of the CBI, but at the same time, the Government will remain answerable for functioning of the CBI. The director CBI is to be appointed under the normal procedure of Appointments Committee of the Cabinet (ACC) but is to be recommended by a committee consisting of the CVC as chairman, the Home Secretary and the Secretary Personnel as members.

Whereas the court had initially started with the idea of freeing the CBI from any extraneous control, but in the end, it landed wherefrom it began as is obvious from the above procedure set for selection of the director, and from the court's observations that "government shall remain answerable for the CBI's functioning."[2]

Further, a nodal agency has been created under the Home Secretary with director CBI and heads of other enforcement agencies as members "for coordinated action in' cases having politico-bureaucrat-criminal-nexus". All big and important cases will have such nexus. Have not the CBI and all the other enforcement agencies been placed back under the Executive from whom these were to be liberated? The Executive is there to guide and obviously direct all the important cases as the government or in other words the minister in charge is answerable for the CBI's functioning. Also, a committee of three members had been recommeded by the Court but CVC Act has raised it to five for selection of the director of the CBI. Two of its members are the officers of the Executive and the other three are the bureaucrats of yester years. Any officer of and above the rank of JD is to be selected by this same committee. How is it going to change the public perception or perception of the officers of CBI that they will not be subjected to any pressure or influence?

The Supreme Court has further diluted its own findings and earlier observations when it observed,[3] "the constitution and working of the investigating agencies revealed the lacuna of its inability to perform whenever powerful persons were involved. For this reason, a close examination of the constitution of these agencies and their control assumes significance. No doubt, the overall control of the agencies and responsibility of their functioning has to be in the executive, but then a scheme giving the needed insulation from extraneous influence even of the controlling executive, is imperative."

Thus, there appears to be some contradiction that CBI has to function under the executive and that insulation from the control of the executive is also to be provided. The court does not lay down any mechanism for the same. Further, in CVC Act, the CBI has been placed under the CVC only for the cases under Prevention of Corruption Act and not other work. Corruption cases are covered by one of its three operational wings. Executive will thus have full control over CBI personnel and hence the CBI.

The CBI is already accountable to law. But if, as per Supreme Court judgment "overall control of the agencies and responsibility of their functioning has to be in the executive", then how does this judgment make any difference? Incidentally so far as investigations are concerned, courts have clearly ruled against any interference. The Supreme Court upholding the principle quoted the Kerala High Court order in director CBI Vs Nayamaved 1995 CRLJ 2917, "no court has power to direct the investigating officer to include a person as an accused in the case while investigation is in progress". The court regretted "the tendency to interfere in the investigation which was on the increase and courts should be wary of possible consequences."

But, in spite of clear provisions reiterated again and again and specific protection extended by the apex court itself in the Hawala case, the agencies including the CBI could not cast aside their predetermined course and the mindset. They could not ward off the pressures on them. With full knowledge, deliberately the bogus chargesheets were filed in spite of clear-cut advice to the contrary, available on the files of the CBI. Justice Verma, after his retirement, regretted, "though the chargesheets were filed against many persons at the initiative of the court, the court came to the conclusion on the basis of the same that no *prima facie* evidence existed to try them." He continued his lament, "Even after full insulation, if they could not perform, it was a human failure and exposed their infirmity."

It has been amply demonstrated that it was not a lapse on part of the CBI, but these were the deliberate and calculated acts, a continuation of its routine and the mental conditioning. The directives of the apex court could make no difference. In the existing infrastructure and mindset of these agencies, nothing revolutionary can be expected from them even after the verdict. No wonder, though both the directors—K Vijay Rama Rao and Joginder Singh—were fully aware of the importance of looking into the assets of the highly placed accused persons, but they took the agency tangentially off whenever such questions arose. Even at the risk of repetition, it is worth mentioning that even when Vijaya Rama Rao had information and documents about a Minister having assets worth many crores, still he did not allow investigations, though it was purely within his discretion only.

Despite stating that[4] "It is settled that statutory jurisdiction cannot be subject to executive control", the Supreme Court judgment has failed to address to the question of ensuring an infrastructure in which the CBI has freedom to function strictly under the law. How is the new arrangement, as laid down by the Supreme Court and further diluted by the legislature/executive, likely to make any difference to the mindset of the CBI when it is still subject to the similar executive control and directions? What difference does posting of a CVC in between make? The committee consists of an independent person in CVC and two officers of the executive itself, representatives of the Union Government. These two are the members of the same bureaucracy and take their instructions from the same executive whom the court was trying to muzzle. In any case they were in the system earlier before the judgment as well. They are equally good slaves in our system just like the director CBI is. Can two slaves guarantee freedom to a third slave? No wonder the appointment of the CVC has made no difference at all to the CBI working as no influential person has been chargesheeted ever since the institution came into existence since 1998. Further, treatment of Tehelka, Judeo, Ajit Jogi cases and the Quattrochi case proves the point beyond any doubt that the CBI has been in the same mould and the same mindset.

At the end, the judgment does not lay down any structural changes, which could give a distinct identity to the CBI free from executive control. Instead of one, the CBI now has four bosses namely the CVC, the committee as constituted by the Supreme Court, the minister as mentioned by the Supreme Court and the Home Secretary as coordinator between different agencies. The arrangement is not going to guarantee either (a) the functional autonomy or (b) eliminate interference or (c) enforce better accountability. To my mind, the only revolutionary steps the Supreme Court has taken are, first to remove the operation of extra legal single directive and secondly to ensure a two-year tenure for the director. Even the two-year term is no guarantee as the committee that basically consists of the executive, can meet any time and recommend removal of the director, if so desired by the chief of the executive. Even if the CVC musters courage to oppose, the majority can overrule him. So long as it remains under executive control, it will naturally and rightly remain vulnerable to the charges of partiality even if it functions in a completely straightforward manner, though that by itself cannot be visualised.

Interestingly, the single directive has already been smuggled in via the statute route by including it in section 6 A of 'The Central Vigilance Commission Act 2003.' This section is discriminatory and is as such against the principle of equality as enshrined in our constitution, but strange enough the detailed reasoning on grounds of discrimination as relied upon by the apex court could so conveniently be ignored by the Parliament. Situation is worse than it was earlier. As part of the executive instructions, the violations were possible, but now these are on the statute book. Even under executive instructions it was very difficult to obtain permission of the competent authority under single directive. I recall that in case of telcom department the permission was consistently not received despite half a dozen recurring scams that were referred to the

Secretary. Each complaint covered wrongful loss to the tune of Rs. 100 crores to the government but still a series of reminders to the Secretary drew no response. However, one such case was registered through oversight and was also investigated. When referred to the same Secretary of the department for prosecution sanction, the response was immediate, though in earlier cases about two dozen communications had fallen on deaf ears. Sh. Vittal, the then Secretary promptly raised the question of violation of single directive by the CBI. I as joint director replied at my level bringing out in details how the denial of such permission by the Secretary was blocking the course of justice. The last sentence of my D.O. letter to the Secretary was "if the permission under the single directive is still not granted, it will be presumed that the Ministry is aiding and abetting corruption." I was expecting a flare up by the Secretary, but strange enough nothing was heard till I held the charge of that zone. Neither permission nor any order on prosecution sanction or any further reactions were received.

Now that we have lived for quite sometime under the CVC regime, but unfortunately it has made no difference to the corruption prevalent in the society. My first-hand experience also stands witness to it. I made a complaint against Joginder Singh to the CVC Sh. Vittal that he as director CBI had bungled the investigations in many cases. Under my signature I furnished him five instances on 1st January 1999, and that too demi-officially. I met him half a dozen times and sent an equal number of reminders, but the only response that I received under the signature of a Joint Secretary of the Commission was that the comments had been asked for from the CBI. Despite pursuing the matter for full two and a half years, I could draw no positive response. During my last and perhaps 5th interview on 20th December 2000, when I complained of inaction on part of the CVC, Sh. Vittal shot back saying "What can I do........Government does not listen......CBI does not care......"I was dumbfounded for a moment. Here was the roaring lion, who makes bold claims in public, how he was so helpless. Collecting myself I made certain observations and suggested at the end that he should have left the *Gaddi* (seat of power) and resigned if he felt so helpless. I followed it up by summarising the gist of our conversation and advised him what he could have done. That was the last communication and meeting. I did not feel worth writing or requesting him any more, but till this day nobody has approached me to enquire. Enquiry normally starts with the statement of the complainant. It is obvious that nothing has so far been done in this case. One paragraph from my letter of 27.7.2001, may interest the reader "....It is true that there could be many obstacles in the way and also you are lacking in infrastructure as you require an investigation wing in your office, but such lament on 26th December 2000, that the government were not supporting your organisation and the CBI was not caring for your directions and that none was happy with you, are of no avail or of satisfaction to me and many others like me, who might have lodged complaints with you. If you felt so handicapped, you could have considered in time, whether to continue or not. You would have jolted everybody and done a great service to this nation."

The control of the CVC over the CBI is partial and shared. Recording of the ACRs is with the government, the supervision and superintendence of CBI in all cases other than those of PC Act is with the government and CVC has nothing to do with that. The CBI has problems of multiple bosses, whereas CVC cited his own problems. The CBI needs to be freed from the executive no doubt, but the organisation need not be placed in the hands of any individual or a small group of individuals and nor with any toothless, ineffective organisation as that will only boomerang.

This clearly brings out that the body controlling the CBI should be high powered, effective and a larger one so that all oddities and biases of various individuals cancel themselves out. The body controlling the CBI should have about a dozen independent members. Under any circumstances it should be absolutely free from any kind of the executive control.

In no country that appears high on the scale of Transparency International, the agency entrusted with the task of investigation of graft, functions under the executive. It is recognised the world over that the agency has precisely to investigate the same very executive, both the bureaucrat and the politician. In parliamentary form of government the Prime Minister is the Chief Executive, so the chief investigating agency functions either under the head of the state or under the parliament directly or through a parliamentary committee, but definitely not under a minister or the prime minister. In countries like South Korea, Hong Kong and Malaysia such agencies function under the head of the State whereas in the UK and Australia, they function under the control of a parliamentary committee. The essence is that the system should ensure full functional autonomy, do away with any external interference and should be able to take strong action against its own erring members so that none, not even its own chief, should dare to take any undue liberty with its systems.

The system in the USA is altogether different as no representative elected to either house under the US Constitution can hold an office of profit. The President proposes the name of the Attorney General (AG), who supervises the FBI. His appointment is further subject to the approval of the Senate. The Attorney General is a constitutional entity and is independent. Under their system, he is not subject to any political or administrative pressures from the executive, so there is no need for him to interfere into the affairs of the FBI, though he can guide and check it in certain matters. Independence of the office of Attorney General has been proved time and again. The latest in the series was the appointment of an independent Attorney by him to investigate President Clinton in Monica Lewinsky's case, something un-thinkable in India.

It compels us to think of an independent system for the premier investigating agency so that it could really be free from all sorts of pressures and still more important the agency should not appear to be labouring under any pressure, and nor should it appear to be vulnerable by way of any infrastructural disabilities. The following few alternatives can be suggested:

1. **Under Direct Presidential Control**

   In some of the countries that have successfully fought against corruption, the supervision and superintendence of such agencies has been entrusted to the head of the state in place of the head of the government. Since head of the state is beyond all politics, the agency is unlikely to be vulnerable to any pressure and also will be seen by the people as independent of the executive as the agency not only needs to be fair, but also needs to appear to be fair. All the functions in context of this agency vested in the government could henceforth vest in the President. Only the annual report of the Agency could be placed before the parliament.

As the President is the constitutional head, a question may arise whether such an arrangement would be legal, practicable and desirable. In countries like Malaysia that have constitutional monarchy, this system is functioning well. In India only an amendment to the constitution is required, and should present no problem, once there is seriousness. Details of how the President will exercise his powers and rules of business for the agency can be framed and approved by the parliament.

2. Under a High Powered Constitutional Head

The director of the CBI, like CAG, could be given an independent constitutional status. The director could function independently and be accountable in the same manner and to the authority as the CAG is at present. Its report could be laid before the Parliament so that the sovereign body is kept informed of the activities of the chief investigating authority of the country.

3. Under a High Powered Board

The CBI could function under a High Powered Board constituted either under the constitution itself or under a statute. The CVC, as envisaged by the Supreme Court in its judgment dated 18th December 1997, in the Jain Hawala Case, is somewhat on similar lines. This Board should be a pluralistic body whereas CVC is only a three-member body, though in reality it is a single member Commission as all the discretion is vested in one man i.e. the CVC himself. A single person commission or body to supervise the CBI is not a good alternative and will not, serve the purpose. Second, a committee selects the CVC, whereas members of the Board as visualised here should be thrown up by the system automatically and there should be no element of selection so that the members are not obliged to anyone. Third, in CVC system, the selection of the director CBI and the other senior officers is again left predominantly to the members of the executive only. This discretion and all other powers, now being exercised by the government should be vested in the Board itself. The Board could have about a dozen members as follows:

i. Last retired Chief Justice of India.
ii. Last retired Comptroller and Auditor General of India.
iii. Last retired director of CBI.
iv. Last retired Chief of Army or Navy or Air Force (one of them).
v. Last retired Chairman Bhaba Atomic Energy Commission.
vi. Last retired Chairman University Grants Commission.
vii. Last retired Governor Reserve Bank of India.
viii. Last retired Cabinet Secretary.
ix. Last retired Speaker of the Lok Sabha or Deputy Chairman Rajya Sabha, who must have finally retired from active politics (One of the two).
x. Last retired Chief of Central Board of Excise & Customs or the Central Board of Direct Taxes (One of the two).
xi. Serving director CBI as the member-Secretary.

The Board would thus have 11 members with a quorum of seven but the presence of the Chairman and the Secretary should be mandatory. The Board must meet once a month or more often.

Chances of pressurizing such a broad-based body are reduced to the minimum. All the members are high dignitaries retired from diverse fields and such positions of responsibility that collectively they will neither commit any indiscretion themselves nor allow any being committed. Since they would represent a number of disciplines, the CBI would be able to get specialised guidance in various spheres, which may enable it to conduct investigations better.

All the operational and the administrative powers would be vested in this Board, including grant of prosecution sanction, selection of director and other officers. The Board could delegate such powers as it thought fit to the director.

After the approval of the Board, the Secretary (director) would send the annual report of the bureau to the parliament and could also appear in person before the parliament whenever desired by the speaker and place before or explain to the sovereign body any particular documents or issues.

4. Under Parliamentary Control

The Parliament could oversee functioning of the CBI either directly or through a committee. Direct supervision may pose problems, as the parliament is not a body that makes day to day decisions. It could exercise its supervision through an all party Parliamentary Committee, say Joint Parliamentary Committee (JPC), constituted specially for the purpose. The CBI, on the pattern of the Australian model, could be made accountable and answerable to this committee, as adapted to Indian conditions. It is this committee, and not the minister or any other member of the executive, who should guide the affairs of this chief investigating agency. Rigorous qualifications and restraints could be prescribed in order to ensure that the committee has persons of integrity who mean business. The committee should exercise all the powers that are vested in the government at present. The committee should have no powers to interfere in the investigations, which should remain the responsibility and the prerogative of the investigating agencies and the law courts alone.

Parliamentary control will give certain advantages. As the committee would represent all or at least all the major parties in the Parliament, both from treasury as also the opposition benches, no one individually would be able to give any order to the CBI, but at the same time, the CBI would also have to stick to the law and that by itself would act as its shield. It may be said that even on the committee, the ruling party will be represented in majority so the decisions could swing in its favour. However, with the presence of members of other parties, the questioning and discussions would be threadbare. With access of all the members to CBI records, even the absolute majority will find it impossible to bulldoze the truth and law. Moreover since all the major parties are to be on the committee, none will be able to blame it of any political bias or vendetta. At present, it is a standard practice to make allegations of political victimization even in case of the most professional action taken by CBI. However some safeguards against brute majority could be built in the system like prescribing maximum number or percentage beyond which no single party can have representation on the committee irrespective of its strength in the parliament. Second, the director CBI could have a right to demand hearing by the full house if he does not agree with the decision or the directions of the committee. Such proceedings of the house should be fully telecast over all the TV news channels, so that the people in general could judge the issues for themselves. This will act as a big deterrent by itself.

The Parliamentary Committee could consist of say fifteen members, ten from Lok Sabha and five from Rajya Sabha, apart from a Chairman and a Vice-Chairman. Presence of either the Chairman or the Vice-Chairman should be essential for chairing the committee along with a quorum of eleven members. The Vice-Chairman would exercise the same powers as the Chairman while presiding over the committee meetings.

Following categories could be debarred from the membership of the committee in order to keep it clean :

a) Any member who has any criminal case or that of evasion of taxes pending in any court or tribunal in India.

b) Any member who has any criminal case pending with police of any State or any other specialised Central or State Agency.

c) Any member who has been convicted/fined for any criminal offence or on ground of evasion of any tax of Central or State Government.

d) If he is holding any office of profit such as a minister, a parliamentary secretary or any other.

e) The membership of JPC will automatically cease if a member accepts an office of profit or resigns from Parliament or when Parliament is dissolved.

The JPC could perform the following functions:

(i) Recommend appointment of the director CBI.

(ii) Exercise superintendence over the functioning of CBI.

(iii) It will have right to examine the evidence in an open house only.

(iv) The committee may approve any reports to be printed.

(v) The committee could call any papers, persons, or records from CBI to monitor and to review the exercise of its functions.

(vi) Report to both the Houses of Parliament, with such comments as it thinks fit, on any matter pertaining to the CBI or connected with the exercise of its functions to which, in the opinion of the Joint committee, the attention of Parliament should be drawn.

(vii) To examine each annual and other report of the CBI and report to both the Houses of Parliament on any matter appearing in, or arising out of, any such report.

(viii) To examine trends and changes in corrupt conduct, practices and methods relating to corrupt conduct, and report to both Houses of Parliament any change that the committee thinks desirable to the functions, structures and procedures of the bureau.

(ix) To inquire into any question in connection with its functions referred to it by either House of Parliament, and report to it.

(x) To consider the cases for Prosecution sanction.

(xi) Refer such complaints as it may think fit for enquiry/ investigations by the CBI.

Provided nothing authorizes the Committee:

a) To reconsider a decision to investigate, not to investigate or to discontinue investigation of a particular complaint or a case, and

b) To reconsider the findings, recommendations, determinations or other decisions of the bureau in relation to a particular investigation or complaint.

Either House of the parliament by resolution may refer to the bureau any matter that it may like to be investigated or to obtain any information. The CBI will be duty bound to investigate fully and present a report to the House in respect of the offences included in the schedule.

In case of disagreement between the director CBI and the committee, if the former feels, for reasons to be recorded in writing, the Speaker of the Lok Sabha may permit a discussion in the House where director could present his case. Decision of the House shall be final. Whichever of the above systems may be adopted, the government will have certain rights. First of all the Central Government will have co-terminus rights to refer any complaint to CBI for investigation/enquiry. It will not require permission from JPC or Board or any other authority for causing such investigations/ enquiries and nor will CBI wait for any clearance from the JPC or the Board, but shall only inform such Board or JPC at the first available opportunity. The Supreme Court and High Courts, of course, have their original jurisdiction under the Constitution. As such any case referred by them will have to be entertained. Once registered, the cases referred by the Supreme Court, the High Courts, the Union Government, the Parliament, the JPC or those registered by the CBI on its own, would all be treated at par. Second, a copy of the annual report of the CBI would be sent to the government as soon as it is ready. Third, a monthly diary will be sent to the government in order to keep them posted about the activities of the CBI. A copy of the proceedings of the meetings of the Board/JPC will also be sent to the government for information.

When the CBI takes up an investigation or an enquiry, neither the police of any state, nor any other law enforcement agency shall investigate any such offence or complaint. Any such case/ complaint, which has already been registered by any police force or by any enforcement agency and is pending investigation/enquiry, shall stand automatically transferred to the bureau.

Only the countries, where the anti-corruption agencies have freedom of action within the ambit of given laws, have been able to fight corruption. It is absolutely essential that the agency should be liberated in order to liberate the country from corruption. Any of the above four models will make the CBI accountable to law through the courts of law and to the people in general instead of the ruling classes and will also help in shedding the mindset of protecting the people in power. Conditions in states are rather worse. In almost all the states the anti-corruption organisation functions as the hand-maid of the party in power. It will not be an exaggeration to say that the anti-corruption agencies of the states, by and large, function as an extension of the party apparatus or another wing of the ruling party. Once the CBI gets organised, states could follow. Once CBI becomes effective, states will have to tone up their agencies under pressure of public opinion. Accountability of the CBI to a body that does not pressurise it, is the first and the foremost requirement.

The Size of CBI

The CBI is a very small organisation as compared to the quantum of crimes committed in the country. This has a bearing on its effectiveness. In 1996, the FBI had 11,400 investigating officers, while CBI had only 1,031. Even a small entity like Hong Kong the size of which geographically, demographically or crime-wise is infinitesimally small, had as many as 684 investigators on rolls of Independent Commission Against Corruption (ICAC), which is the counterpart of CBI. At present the CBI keeps on refusing to take over cases, some of which it has to accept later on either under court orders or under the pressure of the public opinion, but still significant demand remains unfulfilled. By the time it takes over the cases, lots of evidence evaporates. It so happened in Assam LoC scandal, in Bihar AHD scam and in many other cases.

The CBI should expand by at least twenty per cent every year for the next ten years so that its cadre of investigators grows to 6000 strong by the end of the decade. Keeping in mind the magnitude of the problem, if possible the strength needs to be added by a thousand personnel every year for three to four years raising the number to about 4000 investigators. The supporting staff also requires to be reduced from 3.75 per IO at present to 2 or at the most 2.5. However, if in our system we cannot reduce supporting staff that should not hamper the work of increasing the number of IOs. Under all circumstances, the CBI has to improve its disposal performance in investigations. Only certain innovations have to be introduced and its officers have to exert. Similar is the position in the field of trial of cases. I worked out a model for trial disposal and carried it out in Jabalpur branch and the results were spectacular. With cooperation and efforts of all who were relevant, the disposal of the branch, could rise as high as twenty to thirty times from exactly the same infrastructure. It is a pity that no more Jabalpurs have been repeated. In CBI disposal of cases under trial even within the given infrastructure can at least be doubled in just one year with sincere, systematic and innovative measures coupled with close monitoring and timely guidance.

With massive tax evasion and corruption in all the departments and in every nook and corner of the country, strong and effective presence of CBI is needed. There should be three-pronged attack on corruption. First, the spotlight should focus on those occupying high places in government and are primarily involved in the big deals. Such deals, as also their assets need be kept under watch. Secondly, cleansing should begin at points where public suffers the most and the public outcry is the loudest. A good beginning could be made with departments such as Railways, Telecom, Oil and Gas sectors. Third is the sector of tax evasion. Centre levies four most important taxes—the Income Tax, the Corporation Tax, the Excise Duty and the Customs Duty—and all the four suffer from big bunglings and merit special attention. The CBI very badly but urgently, requires to be strengthened both in physical as also mental capabilities so as to measure up with the grave situation.

To reduce pressure on the CBI and to make it more focused an organisation the Special Crime wing should be taken away from the CBI and constituted into another organisation under the Home ministry as that is the proper place for such cases. Specialised squads could be developed there to deal with different types of serious crimes. The CBI in the very nature of its basic functions would never be able to develop such specialisation. Ultimately this will leave the CBI to concentrate on its twofold functions of Anti-corruption and the Economic offences.

Corruption Prevention and Education Wings

All sorts of impediments are faced in fighting or preventing corruption. People lack education about the anti-corruption laws and procedures. They also have little knowledge about their rights and duties. There is an urgent need to educate the people about laws and procedures related to prevention of corruption, and how they can cooperate with the concerned authorities in the fight against corruption, rather than being mute spectators or be a party to pulling and pushing the investigating agency. Since ordinary people are not aware of the provisions of laws and procedures, it is easy to drag every case into controversy. At present a case follows the following pattern:

i. First of all registration of a case is resisted by some and advocated by others. A public debate ensues whether the case is made out, and if so, should it be registered or not. Despite clear provisions of section 154 CrPC and the Judicial Rulings, the case is not registered immediately and the interested parties are even able to create much confusion so that the case is never registered.

ii. After registration, allegations and counter-allegations of politicisation and political vendetta are freely traded and the debate then turns to the demand for handing it over to CBI.

iii. If the case was registered in a state or with any other investigative agency, it is transferred to the CBI at a late stage and steeped in controversies.

iv. The investigation does not take off if persons involved can manipulate the levers of power.

v. Whenever investigator collects evidence, the debate ensues whether it should be chargesheeted or not. Subsequently there is debate on grant of prosecution sanction.

vi. Court battles ensue; the stays on all judicial processes are sought at various stages. Whether the stay is granted or not, delay can always be managed, which could run into years and serve the intended purpose.

In the meantime, the accused gets enough time to set his house in order, destroy the evidence and win over the witnesses. Evidence in any case is a highly evaporative commodity. With loss of time, in this rigmarole, the valuable evidence is also lost. With loss of evidence, the accused is able to show that the case against him was based on flimsy grounds or that all the action against him was motivated or malafide.

Education will make the people aware not only of their rights, but also of the legal position and their responsibility towards the law and the society. The community can pressurise various power centres to keep away, enabling the CBI to take its decisions in the light of relevant laws on registration, investigation, chargesheeting, trial etc., and also relieve it from the accusations of siding with one or the other party. More importantly, the CBI would appear to be taking its own decisions independently, which will go a long way in reposing the trust of the people in the agency and its impartiality.

Prevention is better than cure. Foolproofing of procedures, advising various institutions and the people and disseminating information relevant for checking corrupt activities, constitute some of the preventive steps. A thorough honest and deep investigation by itself acts as a deterrent by making punishment more probable.

It has been recognised the world over that the agencies engaged in fight against corruption should have full-fledged wings for prevention and education. The ICAC (Independent Commission Against Corruption) Australia and the ICAC Hong Kong, have three wings each i.e. investigation, prevention and education. It is also recognised universally that plugging the loopholes is a continuous process so as to make the very act of commission of corruption very difficult for which specialised research into the methods and procedures of various departments becomes obligatory. Studies to evolve and enforce such measures are being conducted the world over. Pavrala in his book[5] *Interpreting Corruption* quotes Carino and Guzman, who in the context to Philippines, have suggested the following measures:

i. Procedural changes to plug loopholes conducive to corruption,

ii. Reducing the area of discretion of the officers,

iii. Increasing visibility of transactions,

iv. More effective monitoring systems,

v. Attacking the Administrative culture of a particular agency:
   - Political and administrative culture
   - Ethico-cultural and economic systems

vi. Salary reforms of public servants.

Besides the above, several other measures typical to Indian conditions require to be examined and enforced strictly. Delays, for instance, are endemic to Indian system and are one of the most important factors that sustain corruption. There is an urgent need for continuous research and its application so that corruption becomes more and more difficult to take place. Creation of the specialised wings in the CBI is unavoidable.

In Hong Kong, the emphasis on prevention can be gauged from the fact that a sixty-man strong force of specialists from various fields i.e. Engineering, Accounts, Science, Investigation, Taxation etc., are hired by the ICAC to provide consultancy in matters relating to reducing corruption opportunities, not only to government departments or public sector undertakings, but also to private companies whose requests continuously pour into ICAC offices from the fields of industry, commerce, education as also welfare organisations. Majority of references are from manufacturing and trading who are advised in as diverse fields as[6] "purchasing, inventory control, cash collection, sales and accounting controls, and the legality of offering or accepting rebates and commissions by employees.......They go to top security prisons (to stop the entry of contraband), to kitchens and restaurants (for health inspections), to custom control points (for smuggling controls), to temporary housing areas (to monitor clearance operations), and to morgues, funeral parlours and graveyards (to study undertaking and grave allocation practices)". So much "so that one officer once spent a day as a film star because she was assisting a client in producing a video tape on private sector building management". The ICAC takes up System studies to cut delays as also to tighten the procedures, to curtail and eliminate corruption.

Besides Corruption Prevention, role of Education or Community Relations Department, as it is referred to, in Hong Kong by ICAC, is most important. It not only educates the people about corruption and how to prevent it, but also enlists their support. This wing carries the anti-graft message to the people through all available media. It has a highly trained staff of 200, out of a total strength of 1200 for the whole of the ICAC. This gives an idea of the extent of importance that a small territory like Hong Kong attaches to education in fight against corruption. The staff of 200 is distributed into eight regional offices in the small area that Hong Kong covers with a population of just sixty lacs.

The wing imparts moral and ethical education to the public, the trade, the industry, the government etc., and formulates codes of conduct, organises training courses i.e. tries to instill positive values like honesty, through appropriate techniques for various levels right from the kindergarten (with cartoon booklets and activity sets), to the university level. At secondary level, specially designed moral education packages (with videos and games) are employed to cultivate correct attitudes. Talks are delivered on anti-bribery laws and work ethics to graduating students in secondary and vocational schools as well as in technical institutes and universities. Effort is concentrated on young people as they imbibe these values easily, whereas resistance is tremendous in greedy grown up people. There are similar systems in Australia and other places where the fight against corruption is taken with the seriousness it deserves.

In India, the CBI does not have either the Corruption Prevention or the Education wing. CVC at one stage made a beginning by putting certain placards in various offices. The step may be very well intentioned, but it does not serve the intended purpose. Most of the grown up people, by and large, will only ridicule the lessons in morality. The efforts at primary school level with right earnest will bear fruit fifteen to twenty years later and at high school level will yield comparatively quicker results, but their response will not be so profound and effective. Education produces slow results initially, but is an extremely potent weapon in the long run.

The CBI should immediately create a Prevention Department with some 50 and an Education Department with 100 experts in respective fields. The departments should be expanded in future in proportion to the expansion of CBI cadres. Both these departments should have more and more of experts and as little supporting staff as possible.

The department of prevention may be created under a JD, expert in investigation, with specialists drawn from various relevant fields. Besides these, experts could also be hired as consultants for a particular job from a particular department or the organisation, whenever the need arises. The Department of Education could be headed by a media person at the level of Joint director of CBI, with a team of experts from various fields including investigation. Like prevention directorate, the education directorate could also hire consultants from other fields.

It is an integrated approach of these three wings that will create internal resistance in the society against this nefarious crime, and will build a bulwark against criminals who indulge in corruption with impunity. Besides, the sense of being free to act as per law only, can create determined cadres within the CBI to fight this evil in the most effective manner.

References

1. Supreme Court judgment dated 18.12.1997 in Criminal writ petition 340-343 of 1993 in case of Vineet Narain and others vs Union of India.
2. Ibid
3. Ibid
4. Ibid
5. *Interpreting Corruption* by Vinod Pavrala, Sage Publication 1996 page 170
6. *Introduction to ICAC*, Hong Kong, September 1996. An introductory booklet published by ICAC, Hong Kong.

11

Strategies to Combat Corruption

We have continued to skirt the biggest problem that the country has been facing during the past six decades since Independence. The excuses advanced from time to time for not sorting out the problem are of no consequence. Mahatma Gandhi pointedly focussed on it time and again till his death and exhorted the people to refrain from corruption and warned against its destructive potential. His last warning came in his prayer meeting on 29th January 1948, just a day before his assassination.

A D Gorwala alerted the nation against corruption in 1951, and Pheroz Gandhi led the crusade in mid-fifties. The Government of India set up Santhanam Committee, which made shocking revelations in its report submitted in 1964. In the meantime the Government of India established the CBI that has since developed into a fine, highly professional specialised body, but unfortunately its fight has remained effective only upto the middle levels of bureaucrats and politicians. It has not been able to storm the citadel of the influential. Jayaprakash Narayan (JP) took over the role of crusader during the decade of 1970s but his health did not allow him to have a firm grip on the movement and he died before long. The 1980s and 1990s witnessed corruption at the peak and were plagued by havoc of scams and scandals culminating in rising outflow of capital through underinvoicing and over-invoicing in external trade, outflow of black money through Hawala channels, and a dramatic increase in the outflow of high spending tourist traffic and in many other ways, whereas the will to fight this evil fell to the lowest evels.

Moral regeneration of the society has been overwhelming and recurringly prescribed as the panacea for containing corruption, thereby discouraging and discounting the apparatus and the action as visualised under the laws. As discussed in details earlier, the problem of corruption is a legal one and can be fought and contained through legal measures alone. Imagine, what a revolution would have been ushered in, if even half a dozen big people in Hawala scam had landed in jail. That would have demolished the protective walls built around the big and sent the message straight home that everyone including the highest was subject to law. We would have been transformed into a vibrant nation. After all, "punishment is divine". Even gods had to suffer punishment in divine order for their delinquent behaviour. Every single country, which meant business, has fought corruption through legal means and contained it. The morality and the ethics took over and re-enforced the fight later. Laws are not against morality and ethics; the three are intricately woven into each other.

Certain infrastructure needs to be created and enforced formally with the following objectives in view for any meaningful fight against corruption:

i. It should become difficult to take or to give hush money.

ii. It should become difficult to store the hush money or illegal assets by the taker, both at home or abroad.

iii. It should become difficult to spend the hush money i.e. enjoying the fruit of corruption should be made difficult if not impossible.

iv. The system should be sensitive and should come heavy immediately whenever somebody tries to flaunt his illegal wealth, either by word of mouth or by conspicuous consumption or by display in any manner.

v. The system and the infrastructure should make it easy to detect corruption, catch the corrupt and bring him before the laws speedily. Further the system should ensure swift trial.

vi. Court procedures and practices need be reoriented and freed from technical and other roadblocks derailing substantive justice.

vii. The infrastructure should include a system of educating the people about the laws, the rules and about their rights and duties. Transparency should become the rule and people should have a right to know practically everything, except if the information affects investigations adversely and helps the accused.

viii. The system should have a corruption prevention mechanism so that it is able to prevent corruption before it takes place rather than only investigate and prosecute.

ix. Finally the system should create awareness and resistance in people so that they resist corruption in place of becoming a helpless party to it.

A great debate has been raging in the country from where to begin the crusade and in the process each interest group passes the responsibility on to the other. Vinod Pavarala[1] depicts this phenomenon in an interesting manner through his empirical studies. He draws his sample from five distinct groups — bureaucrats, businessmen (including industrialists), judges, journalists and politicians. Responses of bureaucrats, businessmen and politicians, who are the active participants in the sordid drama of corruption, differ or converge depending upon their self-interest and perhaps requirement of their own business/job. Judges and journalists being in the chair of passing judgment have different perception altogether.

The bureaucracy blames the nexus between the politicians and the businessmen as primarily responsible for corruption that has[2] "negative consequences for the economy, creating distortions in development objectives of the state and contributing to the generation of black money."

The businessmen[3] "blamed the politicians and bureaucrats .... and tended to minimise the contribution of corruption to black money problem." He is right to a large extent as the politician and the bureaucrat both wield the administrative power and run the show. The former is also the master of the show and can take action against all others who err. However no rationale has been brought out to say that corruption does not lead to and perpetuate black money.

The politician places the basic responsibility with the bureaucrat and the businessmen. He cites the finances for costly elections as a rationale or compulsion and wants to be understood that he is not the worst specimen, but is under compulsion. He denies political factors in corruption and explains it as rival propaganda at character assassination. He denies that[4] "bureaucrats are victims of politicisation, opposition politicians frequently accuse politicians in power of trying to politicise the bureaucracy".

All the three combined pass the buck on to the system and the mafia. System is abstract and mafia is secondary, so out of the three, everybody goes on shifting the major responsibility, putting forth own compulsions, describing own role as marginal and thereby saving own skin.

Judges and journalists do not spare any group and see very fatal effects of corruption as[5] "...corruption has severe economic consequences, including distortions in development, generation of black money, scarcity of resources and slow industrial growth. Corruption, in their opinion, also has an adverse effect on the functioning of the administration, alienating people from their government."

Every section has its own perception, but except the business, all advocate waging a fight against corruption. The industrialist feels that the costs of waging such a war would be too high. He is also opposed to any coercive action against the corrupt, the politicians are silent about strengthening of enforcement or taking any coercive action. Bureaucrats advocate social boycott of the corrupt. Judges and journalists support him.

The perceptions are bound to differ as these are largely the matters of own self-interest, but a redeeming feature is that at the end everyone, by and large, realises the adverse consequences that corruption has on the economy, but it is intriguing that none of the five groups advocates strict legal action against the corrupt. It is understandable, as all the constituents have been drawn from the elitist class who generally think themselves above the law. The elite cannot imagine any action against themselves, their relations or friends. Sample of Pavrala is not representative to cover the entire society. Still all are agreed on fatal consequences of corruption, only the groups are shifting responsibility to each other. This crack in the elitist thinking could be utilised by a responsive and well-meaning administration, in its fight against corruption to further deepen and widen it and use it as an effective and potent instrument in fight against corruption.

Liberalisation and Corruption

Liberalisation in the field of economy or privatisation is seen as the *gurumantra* (panacea) for all the economic ills of the country. It has immediate bearing on corruption and other related matters like black marketing, smuggling and money laundering. Liberalisation in India has come to be interpreted as complete abandonment of all the functions by the state in relation to the economy, a complete turnaround from the past when even the micro level decisions in detail fell under the control of the government. It is conveniently forgotten that private enterprise is based on self-interest, with greed (in general term) as the propellant charge. In pursuit of greed, some people are likely to break all the rules and norms. There have to be strict laws and more important these have to be enforced vigorously so that the pursuit of self-interest does not degenerate into immoral and illegal actions.

Hong Kong has no public sector and has a very small bureaucracy, but it has created a vast anti-corruption organisation that also oversees the activities of the private sector and ensures adherence to laws by them. The organisation is independent of the executive and as such brooks no pressures, entertains no favours and no prejudices. It is this ICAC that has brought about prosperity and respectability to Hong Kong. Why does our business want complete liberty? There are laws and rules to which all business has to conform in any country all over the world. There has to be some authority to enforce the rules of the game. The more the liberty and freedom, the regulations have to be tighter and also have to be enforced strictly, so that everyone gets level playing field, no more and no less, and that any violation attracts immediate notice and is proceeded against. Every vibrant economy leaves business decisions to private enterprise, but regulates the environment and enforces the laws strictly and firmly. Indians visiting abroad pay tributes to strong enforcement in the USA, in Singapore and in other countries, but resent such enforcement in India, as it impinges on them and curtails their privileges.

It is in this context that responses of the elite have to be understood. It requires penetrating examination before policy decisions are taken at government level. But it has to sink in our mindset that strong enforcement must accompany liberalisation if we are not to be exploited and drained as a nation.

The Combat Strategies

The responsibility for corruption cannot be compartmentalised. Corruption is a joint venture, by at least two or more major groups (of Pavrala) at any given time. Aberrations by all the three groups viz. the politician, the bureaucrat including the judge and the businessman including the industrialist have to be tackled simultaneously.

The mafia is adjunct to all the groups and plays the secondary role whenever assigned by one or more of the three basic players. If any one of the basic groups desists from corruption and decides to fight it, the other two cannot indulge in corruption though the business may find itself on a little weaker wicket as compared to politician and bureaucrat as they can individually stand up on their own and cleanse the system of corruption, which business by itself cannot.

Obviously there is need to wage war on all fronts with particular focus on the collection of due taxes and plugging of financial loopholes to prevent drain of resources abroad. During the freedom struggle, the patriotic economists led by Dadabhai Naoroji had raised voice against this problem and propounded the drain theories. Now the quantum of drain has surpassed all records of the pre-independence era. The system should concentrate on this aspect before the country is turned completely empty.

It is often suggested that the people should rise against corruption, but no mechanism for the ordinary people to raise their voice has ever been suggested. As an abstract phenomenon it may all sound very good, but when its implications are analysed, it amounts to uprising of the people, lawlessness in the society and breakdown of law and order leading to anarchy. When confronted with such implications of an uprising of the people, no one has any answer. Such a thought should have no place in a society boasting to be governed by the rule of law. What for, then, have the laws been enacted and institutions for enforcement, investigation, prosecution and trial created? Even when people rise against corruption, still the law will ultimately have to come in force and take action against the corrupt. Uprising of the people by itself is no solution.

Comprehensive steps have to be taken in order to strengthen the laws, to enforce them, to educate the people in fight against corruption and to prevent its very occurrence. Steps, which can ensure the nine-fold objectives enumerated earlier, can be grouped under the four broad headings, (a) Enforcement, (b) Regulation, (c) Education and (d) Prevention. Action that can be taken under each is discussed below in form of recommendations.

ENFORCEMENT

Our laws may have some weaknesses, but the most serious problem that we face is in the field of enforcement. The enforcement is tardy, discriminatory, perfunctory, believes only in window dressing and is loaded with patronage and feudal bias. Basically the impartial enforcement is alien to our mindset and the system. The suggestions below try to visualise a few practical tips that in conjunction with some updating of the regulations side by side may be able to contain corruption.

Declaration of Assets

All gazetted officers of the Government, both at the Centre and States, should declare their assets every year. This should cover judiciary as well. Even the non-gazetted officers of the government from the enforcement departments like Police, Excise, Taxation, Revenue, Industry, Judiciary, Urban Development and Customs who make deep dent at the cutting edge level, should also file the returns regularly. The same regulations should apply to Boards and Public Sector undertakings of the government. Besides the government employees, the elected representatives also need to file their annual property returns with the speakers of their respective Houses. This will cover all the MLAs, MPs, Ministers, etc. As per chapter on elections, all elected representatives would have already filed such returns before elections at the time of filing their papers with Electoral Officers. A fresh return should be filed before swearing in and renewed every year. Any lapse should disqualify him from entering the House and should be a sufficient cause for termination of his membership of the House. The system of filing of property returns does exist in the government services, but it is really in shambles. These are not filed regularly. Further either these are not scrutinised at all or scrutiny is not thorough and nor any follow up action is taken. The return is just received and consigned to records.

Examining the property returns is a laborious task and also the person dealing with the same risks creating enemies if he points out any irregularity or takes any action. Introduction of computers can make a qualitative difference, if only the information can be fed into it. Special software designed for the purpose could throw up all the irregularities automatically; nobody can then ignore or stop action on the same.

Again the examination in office will only throw up the inconsistencies in the returns. For the real picture, it will have to be verified on ground, but it is just not possible to check back each return on ground. Even if some surveyor is sent, he may not find any undeclared information. This problem can be tackled in two ways. First, that the information regarding assets of every person who files property return be put on the website either of the concerned department or of the respective vigilance or both. The public, in general, should be invited to inform the concerned department if they have any further information of more assets or any other relevant information about the person concerned as someone or the other always knows about both the undeclared as also the Benami assets of every single person. Second, since the reach of Internet is still very limited and the problem of corruption is too widespread, the returns should also be published in the newspapers. The returns of junior persons could be limited to local papers, middle levels to state level papers whereas, the returns of seniors could be published in the national papers or alternately the departments could issue directories of the assets of its employees. The system will bring out the hidden assets to the fore to a large extent. Similarly for Ministers, MPs and MLAs, the Speaker should issue a directory, publish in the Press and also place on the website.

The privacy angle may be advocated against making assets of an individual public. Only the speculators can legitimately fear such declaration, which no officer of the government is expected to be. If a government officer is already declaring these assets to the government, the matter is no longer confidential in the sense of privacy as so many in line are already in the know of the same. The objection would come only from those who have something to hide whereas the government as a whole, including ministers and civil servants, need to be transparent, in line with the present doctrine of transparency.

The proforma for the return should be simple and computer savvy, so that it could be fed into the computer directly. It should elicit comprehensive information regarding assets of all types and incomes earned from all possible sources within the country as also abroad during the year. Alongwith bank balances, the account numbers of bank accounts also need be declared which however need not be made public.

If the spouse of an employee is earning some money from agriculture, business, industry, gifts or from any other source and is not filing a separate property/tax return, the return of the employee should mention her/his earnings. If no such mention is made and if she/he is not filing an independent return, it will be presumed that all that income belongs to the employee and will constitute his disproportionate assets in case the employee is investigated. It is necessary in order to curb the black money or money arising out of corruption, being transferred in the name of the spouse. It applies equally well to the ministers and the MLAs.

Besides the government employees and the employees of the PSUs, the same procedure and provisions need be extended to the organised private sector. All their CEOs, the directors and the employees should file similar returns with their respective organisations e.g. CII, FICCI, ASSOCHAM, etc. These organisations should maintain their record, place these on their respective websites as also circulate/publish on the model of the government. This should be made mandatory, and any violation should attract severe punishment. Further any violations of Income Tax or any other law by any employee should also be notified to the concerned departments/authorities.

Forfeiture of Undeclared Assets

No one should be able to misappropriate or keep with himself or with his family, the illegal gains. Even after the death of a person if some illegal/undeclared assets are unearthed, the family should not be allowed to enjoy the same. All undeclared assets unearthed by the government department should after due verifications lapse to the government automatically and stand forfeited. Laws should be updated to that effect and applied most firmly. If nobody is allowed to enjoy the fruit of crime, the crime should cease to be a profitable business, and then people will not indulge in it. Forfeiture only takes away the fruit and does not punish for the act of bungling. So it is necessary to impose steep and severe penalties in addition to the forfeiture of the ill-gotten assets.

National Property Register

Cash, gold and the real estate are the most popular repositories of black money kept within the country. Transactions in black economy are conducted in cash, but it may not be possible to have any check on cash holdings except through periodic raids. However, real estate transactions are all recorded, though there are lots of frauds committed and cheating of the exchequer in the process. The registration authority plays no lesser a role in this loot. The bunglings at registration office are manifold; the rates of property are depressed for purposes of registration, the identities of sellers and purchasers are not ascertained, so the transactions turn 'Benami'. Further, it is well known that whenever government sells/ allots any house for economically weaker sections, the land sharks purchase them in the name of poor people by paying them some pittance and after the mandatory minimum period, get it transferred in their own names. A few years later palatial buildings come up on the site. This is what happened to Madangir, a colony in South Delhi, that now boasts of the palatial marketing centre. Further, lots of money can be concealed by way of luxurious specifications in the buildings, which again is difficult to verify and assess. The shark decentralises his properties and that too in different names, ensuring that detection and accounting are almost impossible. The crucial point that emerges is to bring all these properties at one accounting place.

Till a few years back, it was unthinkable to compile and compute such property transactions, but now with advancements in computers it has easily become possible. Computers of almost unlimited storage and processing capacity are available. Data regarding all registrations all over the country can be stored, processed and retrieved as per requirements. With suitable software it is possible to process the entire range of data in the desired manner. The system can function as detailed below.

All property transactions and other transactions relating to assets should be entered at tehsil and district level computers. These district level computers should be linked to the state level computers, which could retrieve information from district computer directly. The network could similarly extend to the national level computer chain, managed by NICNET. These days all state governments are connecting the state headquarters with districts, sub divisions and tehsils, so retrieval of information over this network is possible at every level. This computer network is visualised as the National Property Register.

The registering authority should obtain legible and decipherable fingerprints alongwith photographs of the purchaser as also of the seller. The prints should be classified generating a separate file for each such individual and then only the registration deed should be executed. All properties in the name of this particular person will get collected in the computer at one place in this file generated on the basis of his fingerprint classification. In his file, a reference can be made to all such files of his family members, so that all the family properties can be located. Besides property, the details of all the bank accounts holders could also be stored in this register. For the purpose, the bank should obtain and forward the finger prints to the NPR where these will be classified and fed into the computer just like the property transactions. At the time of investigation of a disproportionate assets case, search can be mounted on the national hook-up all over the country. The accused cannot then hide the property transactions in his name or in the name of any other member of his family. For purposes of conducting search, the law should provide that in investigations of a registered criminal case under Prevention of Corruption Act, the family members of an accused should be obliged to give their finger prints. This will enable the IO to trace all the family assets. Further, only the person whose fingerprints are on record should be allowed to make a sale. That may reduce dependence on Benami as this person has to account for and receive all the payments through cheque or bank draft. Transfer back to the real owner, in case of 'Benami' transactions may pose-problems and discourage the people from indulging in such activities. The computer will be able to link an individual to the property and vice versa. If a property cannot be linked to the person in whose name it is ostensibly registered, it should lapse to the state. Introduction of national property register may curb speculative purchases of real estate and release lots of properties from the clutches of the sharks. It may also arrest the soaring property prices, particularly in urban areas.

Joint Raids by CBI and Income Tax Department

The income tax department conducts raids for locating tax evasion. The people, however, do not keep their booty in cash only, but in various forms of assets. So the taxman prepares a full inventory of all the assets of the subject and investigates them from all possible angles. This is precisely what an investigator from CBI also undertakes. If the subject is a public servant, a case under anti-corruption laws is automatically made. They can conduct joint raids, but the information and the evidence so obtained can be processed separately from their respective viewpoints. Since possession of unaccounted money constitutes separate offences under Income Tax Act and the Prevention of Corruption Act, both the taxman and the CBI Investigator can take action simultaneously and the accused/defaulter can face axe from both sides under the law. Similarly when the CBI officers organise a raid, they should take officers of income tax department with them so that they can process the case from tax angle. Statement that the subject makes before the CBI officers is inadmissible under the criminal law, but the statement made before a taxman is admissible. The investigations may draw some benefit on this account.

Joint raids would be very effective as the expertise of both the departments will be pooled together which would help unearthing the assets hidden in any possible way. This will also reduce the possibility of the oft-levelled allegation that the riding party misappropriates to themselves part of the unaccounted cash, which the subjects gladly offer. With different organisations involved, it becomes difficult to keep secrets as every department tries to keep up its own image in the eyes of others and more so the CBI.

Till such time joint raids are conducted, sharing of complete information between the two departments should be made a rule with immediate effect.

Attachment of Assets to be Made Simple

After uncovering the assets, which *prima facie* are disproportionate, no purpose is served unless these are rendered beyond operations and manipulations by the subject under investigation. Provisions for attachment of property do exist but these are very cumbersome during investigations and not simple even when the case has been chargesheeted. Moreover the process allows enough time to the subject to dispose of the same while investigations are on. Normally an investigator likes to avoid attachment as it adds to his problems. Cases of disproportionate assets are very unwieldy even otherwise, as the information has to be culled out of a plethora of record from a number of sources and angles and yet there is a possibility of some issues being left unattended. The investigator, therefore, likes to avoid taking unmanageable risks and all the problems that do not expose him immediately. He knows the trial takes long. Even if the accused is convicted by the trial court, probably he might have retired by then. Judicial processes for whatever reasons can be relied upon for delays. Further, at the end, the processes and procedures are also so difficult that the IO who goes to court for attachment of assets, only stands in the dock. The attachment proceedings require to be made simpler and then the IO needs to be held accountable if properties are not attached despite requirement.

An added advantage of attaching the property is that the accused may like to expedite the case as at the end of the trial, he may expect some part, if not whole, to return to him. He may not put usual obstacles in the process of trial.

Assets Management Commission

It is often said that any article taken into possession by a government department is as good as lost. It may be damaged; its parts may be removed or may be replaced by something inferior or may just wear out lying unattended. If it is a factory, it may have to close down and create problems, not only for the owners, but also for the employees. Courts as such are normally reluctant to attach assets. There is a need to create an Assets Management Commission. All the attached properties should be handed over to this commission, which should maintain the properties or run the same, if it happens to be a business concern. The commission may run it on its own or could give it to some expert professionals. The decision should be left at the discretion of the commission according to its best judgment. So far as land is concerned, it will be the responsibility of the commission that the title, the possession, and the use of land are not altered in any way. The commission will be entitled for maintenance or running charges, which it could recover side by side if the asset is an income yielding one, or could recover the same from its sales proceeds or from the owner in whom it is vested, at the end of the trial, by the court. In the last case, the court will have to pass a suitable order. This provision will remove the most powerful argument against such action. The courts then may not hesitate in ordering attachment if otherwise they think it is justified. It may relieve the investigating agency of the task of maintaining it, which is neither its work, nor part of training of its personnel.

Accountability of the Executive

Firm and strong enforcement requires the members of the executive to be held accountable for their respective actions. The executive has to ensure that the work is disposed of in accordance with the rules, procedures and the laws of the land, expeditiously and honestly. Taking example of Police Department, the officers have to ensure that all the cases are registered properly. The law specifically provides in Section[6] 154 of Code of Criminal Procedure that any information to the Police regarding commission of a cognizable offence will be reduced into writing, in the form of FIR and investigations will commence immediately. The judicial pronouncements on the subject have left no doubt. Still, it is well known that a layman feels that it is not an easy task to get a criminal case registered at a police station without either 'Sifarish' (recommendation) or bribe. After registration, the case has to be investigated properly and thoroughly, but the reputation of police for quick and impartial investigations is also no good. It should be possible to hold the guilty officer accountable for non-registration or for non-investigation or for incorrect or improper investigations. Third stage for the executive is the prosecution. Similar responsibility lies on the prosecution as well.

The accountability should be for the following factors, which are essential:

a) Integrity] Personal as also of subordinates working under a
b) Efficiency] particular officer.
c) Capacity to take work from subordinates.
d) Capacity to deliver in lawful ways.

Since the politicians also take decisions in all executive actions, they should also be held accountable as above. Further whenever an important case against an influential person ends in closure, acquittal or discharge, it should automatically stand referred to a committee of three retired distinguished senior Police officers, known for their investigative abilities and for their integrity. They should go into the details and see if there was some lapse or a wilful effort to hush up the evidence. The deliberate omissions or commissions should attract severe punishment under scrutiny of the court to whose notice it should be brought invariably. If some bonafide omissions occur, no action need be taken, but the case could be looked into afresh once again.

The examples given above are from the domain of criminal justice, but can *mutatis mutandis* be extended to all the other departments in accordance with rules, procedures and legal provisions governing their functioning. On the ground, conditions are no better in any other department as well. The basic principles of accountability as enunciated above, apply to all without any exception.

Accountability of the Judiciary

The criminal justice system can be effective only if judiciary is firm, effective, impartial and quick to deliver. The sentence awarded should be exemplary so that it produces deterrent effect. The judicial system for such delivery has to be honest, efficient, impartial, fearless and firm. But unfortunately the system has not responded to the requirements and is lacking in many respects.

The most important issue that transcends all others is that the trials are full of delays. No purpose would be served by citing delays of various cases or the cumbersome statistics as everyone in India knows that the trial is a highly languishing process from the lowest to the High Courts, and that no one here is accountable for delays. As per, Leila Seth, retired Chief Justice of Himachal Pradesh High Court, the house of judiciary is in such a mess that the justice has become a rare occurrence through these temples. Honest advice of this judge to her husband, who had been denied his lawful claims of salaries by his employers, is revealing:

[7]"Take half, take one-third, even take one-fifth, but settle. You have a good case, but if you take them to court, you certainly won't get anything now, if you have grandchildren, they might. Apart from that, you will lose sleep and get high blood pressure when you hear lies being treated as truth and frivolous adjournments being taken by the other side to delay the matter. I know that I will have to bear the brunt of it, as you will keep telling me what a frustrating and useless exercise the whole process is". Reflecting further on the consequences, she observes, "I often think

about how litigation or the threat of litigation affects people. It takes over one's whole life. The fear of the lawyers and the courts, the delay, the tension when you have to appear and all too often- the complete lack of reasonableness of the prosecutor or opponent are horrible realities. It is time consuming, expensive and nerve racking".

The courts must function under complete freedom so far as trial is concerned, but they cannot escape accountability. The higher courts should hold the lower one's responsible and accountable for delays. The judges who fail to deliver, need be proceeded against and punished departmentally or be weeded out. After all, there has to be some decent limit to pendency, which should never be allowed to be crossed. As the police have to complete investigations within certain time period, so also should be the case with judiciary, but unfortunately the sense of urgency is missing with the judiciary. A judge grants stay at the drop of a hat and it continues indefinitely. Either no hearing is fixed or dates are perpetually postponed. Either party and most often the prosecution could keep applying for early hearing and the court may continue to reject, wasting time, but the real issue will seldom be addressed.

Further, once police custody remand is granted after due consideration, the defence keeps on moving applications on one pretext or the other and the court goes on fixing dates and adjourning the substantive trial, resulting in loss of time. Once remand is granted, there should be no review except on the appointed date. The stays, the bails and such like other processes contribute to lots of avoidable delays.

In context of the huge pendency in our courts, the number of judges in India is often compared with their counterparts in the USA. Following the 120th report of the Law Commission, the stock argument is that the number of judges in India is abysmally low at @10.5 as against 107 in the US per million of population. It is conveniently ignored that their number has no correlation, whatsoever, with the population. Hypothetically, if the cases instituted in courts were to fall to nil, whatever be the size of the population, the requirement of judges will fall to zero i.e. not even one judge will be needed. Some 107 judges per million of population will constitute an army of 1,17,700 courts. Taking the staff strength of a court on an average at 20 as it obtains in Haryana, the total strength of judiciary will soar to 23.54 lacs, almost double the strength of entire gamut of the defence forces or equivalent to half of the total employees of the central government including the mighty Railways—a fantastic situation.

Despite lower population levels, the number of filings in the USA in 1999 was 938 lacs and the number of judges 29,000 as against 130 lacs filings and 13,000 judges in India. A substantial portion is of part time judges in the USA and 557 lac filings are minor in nature. Even if all these are excluded and all the US judges are taken as full time, still out of 387 lac major filings, the annual load per judge works out to 1335 as against 1000 in India including minor cases as well. The annual institution of cases is much lower in India, but disposal here is abysmally low in comparison to the USA and cases pile up year after year.

The number of miscellaneous applications, which are either for delaying the justice or for expediting it or for similar other matters, occupies not less than twenty-five per cent of the court time in the morning when efficiency is at the peak and substantive disposal can be the maximum. Delays over delays require more and more time every subsequent year as miscellaneous applications regarding expediting the trial also pile up besides the usual one's for stays, bails, etc. At the top of it all, someone or the other will be absent and the process of granting fruitless adjournments continues endlessly.

The moment a case is registered delaying tactics start for:

a) Quashing the F.I.R.

b) Staying the F. I .R.

c) Staying investigation

d) Repeated putting in bail applications

e) Challenging jurisdiction of the court

After completion of investigation the delaying tactics may be by way of:

1. Challenging the chargesheet.
2. Stay at any and every stage right from the beginning to the end of the case.
3. Frequent adjournments as delaying tactics.

Such like many more tactics.

Obviously it is more so in corruption cases or wherever big names are involved.

Even if the accused may fail at all the steps, he would have achieved his goal of delaying the proceedings, enjoying liberty and the fruit of crime. With the passage of time the evidence evaporates, witnesses can be won over, and some of them may die or may be eliminated. Many such things can happen and then in all fairness, the case would be closed by the court with clear conscience, but undermining the confidence of the people, impairing their will to assist the system as the impression goes that the justice is only a mirage.

A judge is the nodal person and the umpire in everything so far as enforcement and interpretation of procedures in a court are concerned. The law lays down the broad parameters and it is upto the judge to run his court within those parameters. Because of the discretion placed in him, he is in a position to guide everything happening in his court. So, all the delays are also his responsibility. If he disposes of the applications for various processes meant for delaying the case expeditiously and does not allow blanket stays, the advocates will stop approaching him for the same. Though the stay for a short period could make sense, but there can be no justification for a prolonged stay for years or decades. When a judge allows stay, it should be for a limited period and a limited purpose only and the court should review it on its own instead of getting bogged down by further presentation of petitions. The blind stay by itself amounts to denial of justice. Relevant issues should be sorted out in the given time and the trial should proceed further within the time schedule.

The power of stay needs be exercised with restraint and for a limited period. In criminal cases, there should be no stay beyond two, four and eight weeks in case of district courts, High Court and the Supreme Court respectively. Total stay on all accounts and including all the stages, in any particular case should not exceed fourteen weeks. The judge should be duty bound to decide the matter whichever way, within this period. In criminal cases, the law intended the stay to prevent immediate miscarriage of justice, but it need not convert itself into a vehicle of injustice as they say, "the justice delayed is justice denied".

It may be advantageous to cite a couple of cases to bring home the effect of such avoidable delays. A criminal revision petition No. 184 was filed in Gauhati High Court in 1981 challenging the jurisdiction of Prevention of Corruption Act in a case registered in 1973 and chargesheeted by CBI in 1976. The High Court in 1990, after keeping it pending for full nine years, ruled that "The case has been pending for more than 14 years for no fault of the accused person. There has been enormous delay and the sword has been hanging over the heads of the accused persons for more than 14 years. It is true that offences of that kind should not be allowed to go unpunished... quick justice is sine qua non of article 21 of the constitution of India. ...Considering the overall circumstances of the case.... the trial or prosecution of....accused persons are hereby quashed."

Another case W.D.C. No. 223 of 1995 of Patna High Court in Kamleshwar Thakur Vs SPF registered in 1969 was referred for prosecution sanction after investigations. The same was received from the concerned authorities in government in 1982 and chargesheet was filed in 1983. The judgment lists the causes as non-appearance of one accused or the other leading to 'several adjournments', so that the charges could not be framed. After sometime, following the Supreme Court ruling in Antulay Case laying down emphasis on quick justice, the accused filed petition for quashing the trial. On 2nd Feb. 1994, the High Court asked for disposal of the case within six months, but no progress was achieved. The court cites the reasons in the judgment as advocated by the prosecution counsel, "delay was because the accused persons, who in conspiracy with each other, avoided appearance before the court on various dates fixed for framing of charge. Part of the delay was caused according to his submission, because the lower court record called for by this court had not been sent back for considerable time, but much delay was caused as several adjournments had to be given, because all the accused persons in the case including the petitioner did not appear before the court on the various dates for framing charges. Now the criminal case seems to have been instituted about 26 years ago in 1969 and I find that despite direction given by this court for concluding the trial within 6 months period and extension of that period for 18 months, no substantial progress has been made in this case and in a way earlier directions of this court itself seem to have been violated." The High Court quashed the case. SLPs were filed in the Supreme Court, but the same were summarily dismissed in both the cases.

This judgement also takes help and cue from Article 21 of the Constitution, like the earlier one of Gauhati High Court and quashes the trial on ground of delays. Questions that arise are:

Under the constitution or otherwise, who is responsible and accountable for delays during court trials. Should it not have been incumbent upon the High Court to fix responsibility for the delays and hold the guilty accountable whosoever he may be? The first case remained with the same High Court for nine years. If the accused is not at fault, who is at fault? Is the victim at fault? If the accused is set free without even trial, what for has the victim taken all the trouble, waited, spent money and also suffered Initial losses? Is the responsibility of the court limited only to the accused and is the court accountable to the accused and not to the society or the law? Can a victim not look for or seek justice under the same article 21 of the Constitution? In a civilised society, is it the prerogative only of the accused to get justice? Should the victim fall both at the hands of the accused and subsequently at the altar of criminal justice system? Does victim also have some human rights or those pastures are the preserve for accused persons only?

In the second case, the CBI and the Prosecution Sanctioning Authority took fourteen long years, for which the court should have hauled them up. Ultimately in 1983 the case shifted to the courts. The lower court could not manage to summon the accused persons for the next eleven years. The court has powers under the law to compel their presence. Why did the court not utilise such powers for eleven long years when in the meantime it became a delayed case. The High Court did allow eighteen months, but the clerk of the High Court did not return the record and therefore the lower court could not proceed with trial. Why action should not be taken against the lower court and the clerk of the High Court? The lesson is that the accused should manage the delay and the case will get scuttled. The judiciary has to honour its responsibility in these cases on at least following four counts:

First, it should have asked the government to explain why the Prosecution Sanction took so much time. Strictures were due against the sanctioning authority.

Second, why the lower court did not manage to organise its affairs well, so that the trial proceeded in time?

Third, why did the High Court clerk not send the records immediately? Does it require months and years at end to just dispatch a few papers? If a clerk does so, should the court not take any action against him and throw away the case instead?

In the end, the victim has been denied the basic right of justice under the Constitution, holding the society, the law-abiding citizens and the victim to ransom despite the concept of swift justice as enshrined in various judicial pronouncements. Court needs some self-introspection instead. Such cases and such decisions encourage the criminals to commit offences of corruption, make money, use this money in delaying the proceedings and enjoy this ill-gotten money that will keep on growing with passage of time. Ultimately, the accused can interpret the sacrosanct Constitution in his favour and project himself as the sufferer, a victim, on whom the society and the prosecution, all have perpetuated tyranny. Long judicial delays have turned the scales of justice upside down.

No wonder today we witness a naked dance of corruption. Initially the executive commits delays. The courts can check that, but what if the judiciary itself is the delinquent? Whether it is the executive or the judicial indiscretion, its effect on the system is the same. Soft enforcement by any agency aids and abets corruption. No doubt all organs of Indian state behave as very soft. Though it may appear strange, but a soft judiciary at the end becomes the biggest liability for two reasons. First if any other organ goes soft, the judiciary can pull it up and secondly all deterrent actions of the state, under the law, have to culminate at the altar of judiciary only. If the deterrence that the punishment is able to generate disappears, the criminal can commit crime with impunity, and get away. Both delays and corruption have great capacity to subvert the justice and hence the system.

Reverting to the other case, whereas all the constitutional rights of the accused should be respected, but if he does not present himself before the court, the due processes of law including issuing warrant for getting him arrested and keeping him in jail should not be spared. When the accused persons did not appear in the court for years, why did it not feel responsible to issue warrants on its own? This should squarely be the duty of the judge, who runs the entire show in the court and is responsible for giving justice. In Gauhati High court, it was a small matter disposable in a few minutes instead of nine long years. The judge, in all fairness, should have introspected his own role and not thrown away the case with contempt. It amounts to ridicule of the system, of the statute and of the constitution itself.

A para can be made mandatory in all the judgments where the judge should discuss the causes of delay and fix up responsibility. In a transparent system it is essential and perfectly in order. Apart from warrying parties, it will bring the role of lower as also the higher judiciary into the focus.

We have seen how quick the system is in the USA. In Hong Kong too, the bulk of the cases are decided within six months of filing. So is also the case in Australia. As per Australian Institute of Criminology, sixty per cent of the cases brought under trial before various courts are disposed of within six months and disposal within eighteen months of institution of cases is as high as ninety- five per cent, which by Indian standards is unthinkable.

It is possible to cut the delays in India also as was experimented in the CBI court at Jabalpur in 1995 and 1996. The experiment was a grand success and the Jabalpur branch of the CBI has been continuing with its high disposal rate. I specially picked up this branch out of the six branches under my charge as Jabalpur had an exclusive CBI court and it had an energetic senior PP (public prosecutor) and the SP, who responded to the call immediately. The disposal of cases under trial used to be one or two in a year but rose to 15 in 1995, 35 in 1996, 42 in 1997, 45 in 1998 and 46 in 1999, after certain critical areas were identified and acted upon. The judge encouraged the prosecution when plan was unfolded and felt happy that CBI had initiated a good move. He undertook to perform his part of the act well. Some major causes of delays along with the actions taken are discussed below:

i) The CBI took one to three years in supplying copies of documents meant for the accused. It was made compulsory that the copies should accompany the chargesheet. SP was made responsible personally to check that legible copies accompany the chargesheet and he should send a certificate to this effect to the JD through the DIG.

ii) The service of summons was not being ensured, with the result that the witnesses would not turn up. Again the service of summons was also made the personal responsibility of the SP and every failure to serve was to be reported to the JD through the DIG.

iii) The accused would absent and obtain a number of adjournments, which the court accorded as a matter of routine. He would then appear after six months or so and absent himself again. If there were more than one accused persons, they would take turns in appearing, so that the case could make no progress, as all the accused persons are required together for the trial to proceed. The PPs remained silent spectators and the court permitted endless adjournments in routine. The PPs were exhorted to take up the question and apply for non-bailable warrants against absenting accused persons and also to brief the court on ill-effects the routine was having, so that the court also acted tough.

iv) The most important issue was that only one or two witnesses were being summoned and examined on the date allotted to a case after an interval of a few months. The court was requested to fix a case continuously for three to four days and finish with Prosecution evidence. If it were a long case, there could be hearings over two to three continuous sittings, but prosecution evidence that normally spread over half a dozen years, could close down in a period of two to three months only.

v) The advantage of quick and continuous recording of evidence was that the judge would remember the evidence as also the demeanor of the witnesses and the accused. The prosecution also took advantage and would drop the repetitive witnesses immediately, which was not possible in case of long adjournments as he would not be able to remember readily what each witness exactly deposed.

It had the salutary effect. Not only did the number of cases disposed of accelerate to thirty-five in 1996, but also continued to grow further in the subsequent years. The process gathered momentum. Jabalpur has shown the way that the coordination between the judiciary and court officers has been of great value and service. This model could be studied further and followed in other exclusive courts for the CBI as also in all other courts in general.

Apart from the sharp rise in quantitative disposal, there has been great qualitative improvement as well. The conviction percentage in Jabalpur hit the highest levels ever in the CBI in the country and stabilized at eighty-five per cent. The judge had started appreciating the dimensions of corruption better and the quantum of sentence shot up so much so that in one case the court ordered recovery of full amount bungled and awarded rigorous imprisonment for 11 years, alongwith fine, to each of the two accused persons.

The time has come for the courts as the organiser of trials and the umpires of overall show, to take initiative to expedite disposal of cases pending with them. There is no reason why their output cannot increase substantially very soon within the existing framework and the infrastructure.

Last, but not the least, the issue is that punishment needs to be commensurate with the extent of bungling in corruption cases. For a bungling of rupees two lacs, the fruits of which the accused might have enjoyed for twenty long years, the punishment of one to two years in jail and a fine of Rs. 10, 000/- only, hardly matters. Over the twenty years, the accused might have reaped twelve times the advantage amounting to rupees twenty-four lacs. What does a fine of ten thousand or even a lac mean to him? Where is the bar to recover the entire twenty-four lacs apart from inflciting a prison term on him.

Acceptance of Gifts

Rules regarding acceptance of gifts do exist. A gift of value beyond certain limits has to be declared by the public servant. But during festive season and particularly on the occasion of Diwali, all the limits and restraints on the numbers or the value of gifts go haywire. Delhi the seat of power of the Union Government goes mad. In Delhi for two years I was living in a first floor flat, the person downstairs was the Chief of Central Board of Excise and Custom (CBSE). On the last two days of Diwali alone, I counted upto 1000 persons carrying gifts of various sizes. I noticed that some of the persons, would take out from their pocket or the dash board of the car, the typical jewellery boxes covered with velvet cloth and would slide the same inside the big pack in which they had kept a slot. Value of such packs cannot be assessed. They were not aware that someone was watching them from the window overlooking the entrance of the ground floor house.

In fact there are three issues; one, the gifts are costly; secondly, the movement is one way and third, these are recklessly accepted from all, which shows the extent of favours that might have been done or would have to be done in future. A bar needs to be placed on all such gifts, which are not from personal close friends, or close relations where it is exchange of gifts. One way gift, except from some senior close relations, is in the nature of corruption. Unfortunately Diwali has been converted from the festival of lights to an occasion of internal or mental darkness.

Besides, it also applies to gifts given in the garb of dowry. In view of mounting dowry deaths, a time has come, when dowry as gift should be registered and recipient should be subject to tax on this additional income. It is also necessary from the angle of regulating the black money. Once registered, it will check the dowry itself, as the large dowry is normally in black money. Secondly in case of a problem, the bride will always have a legal right to recover that amount. She will be saved the trouble of proving what she brought in dowry. This may also prompt some to record the dowry amount correctly so that in case of any dispute the bride is able to recover in full the declared amount. The fear of full recovery itself would act as a deterrent against the forcible dowry seekers. It may perhaps check dowry deaths as well.

All dowry items with their value should be declared in the property return of both the giver and the taker. If not declared, no concession need be extended in future on any pretext and the amount be treated as unaccounted money and assets constituting disproportionate assets.

Enforcement of Ethics

A number of countries have framed their codes of ethics and re-enforced the same with the power of statute. All the business, both in government and in private, is conducted as per these codified ethics. In the USA, George Washington, the first President, prescribed ethics as early as the 18th century. The same were amended by the 'Ethics in Government Act, 1978', further strengthened by the Principles of Ethical Conduct for Government Officers and Employees 1989. Under the auspices of OECD, twenty-two advanced countries adopted a code of conduct since 1997. Australia and the European Union have also codified the ethics and efforts have been made by some countries of African continent, as also OAS (Organisation of American States).

In India it is fashionable to preach voluntary morality or ethics to be practised by an individual, but no one puts the same into practice. We should shed the hypocrisy and codify the ethics, just like the rules of the game, enforceable by law, violation of which should attract penal consequences. It is no use waiting till eternity for moral regeneration and then to discover the axiomatic truth that in money matters, the ethics do not evolve unless enforced by strength of law.

Regulations

Regulation and enforcement go side by side and can only be effective in tandem. Certain suggestions and recommendations primarily for amendment in the statutes are proposed to be enumerated in this section. These may overlap with previous section on enforcement, but it is unavoidable as making the laws and enforcing them are two consecutive links of the same chain.

Publication of Assets of the Accused

During investigations, when the assets of an accused are *prima facie* found to be disproportionate, the investigator should be allowed to advertise the same in the media and public be exhorted to extend help by giving information if they are aware of any more assets of the accused or any member of his family. At present, the investigators mainly depend upon the informers and the records seized during search or on analysis of bank accounts of the subject, which may preclude properties or bank accounts held in other cities that may not be known locally. Further, the subject may keep his records including details of his bank accounts elsewhere or in another city. The investigations will draw a blank in such cases. People in the city of location of property/account will know and may choose to respond if an advertisement is published in the press or shown over the TV. It may also bring 'Benami' properties to the fore. A provision to this effect needs to be inserted in the Statute Book, as at present, if properties of accused are advertised, he may invoke his right of secrecy and may claim damages.

Severe Imprisonment for Tax Evasion

The punishment of imprisonment for tax evasion exists at present also, but it is not so severe as to act as an effective deterrent and is imposed only in exceptional cases. Exemplary rigorous imprisonment commensurate with the amount of evasion requires to be incorporated in the statue along with laying down the minimum scale. In absence of any such provision, no wonder, the collection of tax revenue of central government as percentage of GDP at 8.6 per cent is one of the lowest in the world as per World Development Report[8] 2000-2001 of the World Bank and as of now is around 9.5%. This reflects the degree of evasion. To curb this tendency, rigorous and heavy prison sentence needs to be provided. Effects would be immediate as tax evaders are all soft targets and cannot tolerate any physical discomfort. It may not be necessary to use it widely as people will respond immediately when effective intentions are known. Incidentally, some countries of the third world have tightened on the above lines and achieved spectacular results. In a span of 6 to 10 years countries like Ghana, Philippines, Peru, and Bolivia have augmented their tax collections from a meagre 4 upto 16 per cent. If only we had the will to follow!

Exemplary Punishment for Disproportionate Assets

One may indulge into any amount of financial tyranny, tax evasion, exploitation, smuggling, corruption and may accumulate any amount of assets, but when charged for disproportionate assets, even of Rs. 100 crores, there is no provision for any special sentence at some augmented scale. It is the same varying between one to seven years. For just a crore of rupees, many people will not mind going to jail even for seven years, the highest possible sentence, if they can retain the money and what to say if the booty runs into tens or hundreds of crores. Since the minimum sentence is just one year, the judge normally gravitates towards a single year only and does not go beyond three years. There is need for providing a graded scale of minimum punishment for possessing disproportionate assets beyond certain limits.

China has even imposed the death penalty, which of course, may be foreign to Indian ethos and sensibilities, but the minimum that could be done in India is to introduce life imprisonment if D.A. with someone is beyond rupees ten crores, fourteen years if D.A. is over rupees five crores, seven years for over rupees two crores and five years for over rupees one crore, besides forfeiture of D.A. in full along with its fruit that the accused might have earned and enjoyed during the period of possession. Some sizable penalty over and above also needs to be imposed. At present section[9] 16, Prevention of Corruption Act 1988, lays down for the fine to be commensurate with the amount of bungling, but the provisions are softly interpreted and softly enforced. The court should have no discretion, but to forfeit the entire ill-gotten asset and its fruits, besides the penalty. Basically it is nothing revolutionary as many countries are following such norms. However to be fair to the ascused persons, the financial limits may be revised after every 5 years.

Banking Secrecy Laws abroad

There is no doubt that slush money moves abroad in bulk from the third world into the banks of advanced nations. It is not possible to know its extent, nor can it be recovered by any indigenous government agency. The kickbacks are often credited into the accounts abroad in order to avoid detection. Money, duly laundered, may sometime be brought back to India through normal banking channels, by showing it as gift from some relative or friend, or simply the payment earned through exports. There are innumerable ways prevalent in murky export-import market. Several other advantages may be drawn by way of incentives and even the money can be remitted back if that serves their financial interests. Even if the money comes back, it is sure to get lost into the blind alleys of black economy. The countries of the third world suffer heavily on this account as it causes a great drain on their economies and they have no option but to borrow strong doses from abroad. If outflow of their resources could be checked, some of the countries of the third world, like India, may have enough of foreign exchange as also the resources and may not borrow at all. This drain will continue unabated unless there are certain structural changes.

Indian resources get transferred abroad where these are invested to generate employment and incomes. Other countries develop and prosper at our cost. No wonder Switzerland has the second highest per capita income, with banking industry in the lead.

The holdings abroad, whether in cash or in real estate, or in any other form, cannot be checked as banks cover themselves with the veil of secrecy. This aspect has been discussed earlier also, but is worth recapitulating in brief even at the cost of repetition. However the slush money arising out of drug trade is being treated as different. If it is suspected that the money in a bank has some relation with the drug trade, the secrecy laws stand automatically relaxed, as these have been amended to that extent. It was done on insistence of the big western powers, as drugs are their problem. After attack on World Trade Centre in New York on 11th September 2001, money held by terrorists has also been frozen. For countries like India, all economic offenders including the corrupt are the

'Financial Terrorists'. The major problem of the third world is corruption, and the secrecy laws aiding and abetting it. It would not be an exaggeration to say that the people of countries like Switzerland are acting like receivers of stolen property and are leading parasitic existence. This hypocrisy does not go well with their famed high stance on morality. They should abandon such laws and throw their banking business open and transparent. India should take up this question with Swiss banks, the western world and with all possible international organisations, including the U.N. The countries of the third world, and India in particular, should agitate for relaxation of banking secrecy laws in cases of corruption.

Apart from bank accounts, another dimension is that property or some other assets could be purchased abroad. Since the agency of one country cannot conduct investigations in another country, some rules need to be framed so that the particulars of deposits or properties held abroad could be known to the mother country, in the name of whose citizens these may stand.

Following measures are suggested in the Indian context, but the same hold good for all other countries similarly placed:

a) Whenever a bank account is opened by an Indian citizen abroad, the particulars of such account should be communicated to the Indian authorities, through its embassy/high commission in that country. The account number and other details should be fed into the National Property Register (NPR) immediately and could also be compiled in the CBI.

b) If the person is found involved in some crime or a criminal case, particularly of corruption or any other white-collar crime registered against him in India, then the particulars of balances in account and the copy of the account, if asked for authentically by an investigating agency, should be supplied. In this context the authorised agency should only be CBI. If any state agency or any other agency of the government of India needs some information, it could approach the CBI. The foreign bank/government should have no discretion but to supply duly certified copies of accounts/ information whenever demanded by the nodal agency, CBI in this case.

c) Whenever an Indian purchases a property abroad, its details like those of bank accounts be informed by the registering authority there, to the Indian Embassy/High Commission, who will transmit the same to India. This information could also be fed into the National Property Register and also compiled in CBI and used when required.

d) Details of all the properties and the bank deposits held abroad by the Indian citizens at present should be supplied to Indian Embassy/High Commission in the respective countries.

e) Further, on instructions from CBI, the accounts should be frozen, the lockers, the properties and other assets sealed and ultimately these assets be disposed of as per directions of the Indian courts.

f) For obtaining/supplying such information, the dual criminality may not be insisted upon, as corruption is a crime everywhere, only some technical details may differ. Similarly, the blanket sovereign guarantee of reciprocity may be executed once at the level of the governments and should not be insisted upon for every case as that causes tremendous delays.

Once this happens, hiding black incomes abroad will become very difficult and practically impossible. India will start looking up immediately. But to get such amendments to their rules, India has to take other countries of the third world along, prepare a lobby and initiate very persuasive and aggressive propaganda underscoring the point that we are readily helping them in their fight against drug and terrorism.

It will not be easy to take any step in this direction, as the first obstacle will come from Indian elites, who are holding such accounts/ assets abroad. They will oppose any such move tooth and nail. But no meaningful fight against corruption, black money and plethora of economic offences can be really successful without such radical measures.

Exemption on Agricultural Income

Agriculture is subsidised the world over and concessions are extended in various forms. Such concessions are being provided in India also and should be continued as otherwise agriculture will cease to be profitable and the country will suffer heavily. But the income tax on agriculturists falls in a different category altogether, as only those whose income is beyond the normal exemption limits, would be required to pay the tax. After all, once income has accrued, it belongs to the individual and the source is basically of no importance. Even if exemption is granted on the grounds that agricultural income is uncertain, the exemption should then be extended only where there is no other source of income. This has become the most misused provision under the statute. Heavy returns are declared from agriculture, no tax is paid and thereby huge amounts of black income are converted into white without payment of tax and even if the source of income may lie in crime, one can cover it under the broad shield of agriculture. So the industrialist, the businessman, the politician and the civil servant, all run for acquiring agricultural lands that ensures continuous laundering of ill-acquired income.

A time has come when such blanket concessions require to be withdrawn. The exemptions may be continued as it is, but only if agriculture is the sole source of income. The moment there are some other sources also from which an individual draws his income, the mixed income should be subject to tax in entirety. All those for whom agriculture is the only source of income, or whose combined income falls below the taxable slab, it will make no difference. It will cut across a big chunk of those who keep on laundering their black income/through agriculture.

Prosecution Sanction Should be Abolished

There is no justification for provision of prosecution sanction to remain on the Statute Book as the concept has lost its meaning, import and relevance altogether ever since the fall of colonial rule in this country. This retrograde provision was inserted for the protection of their loyal subjects/slaves who might have indulged into corruption, but otherwise helped the British in perpetuation of their Raj. Strangely it continues as a great protector for the corrupt in free India. It is well known that corruption exists at all the levels, then how can any level in the same department of the ministry exercise objective judgment whether a case should be tried or not. Sanction by the same department or ministry these days when corruption is a collective/joint venture and where all levels are involved is a farce and denial of justice to victims. Even in more serious crimes, in which punishment is much higher than corruption, it is not required. This provision needs to be removed from the statute. However, if still it is thought that we cannot perform any major surgery, still there is need to vest this discretion in objective hands like CVC who should look into the cases of prosecution sanction and not the concerned department or the concerned ministry, secretary or the minister. Though basically there is no need for such a provision.

The Structure of CBI

The law needs to restructure the CBI as per special chapter on it. In Indian Constitution separation between the executive and legislature has not been effected. Under the US constitution no elected member of either of the two houses can hold any office of profit under the government. Executive and legislature function independently and separately. In India this overlap of executive and legislative functions, causes various complications making it imperative, more than anywhere else, that the CBI should be completely independent of the executive/ministerial control.

Constitution of Higher Judiciary

All agencies dealing with laws and legal matters finally have to report all their actions and submit all their reports to law through judiciary, which is the final destination where all the actions are weighed and adjudicated. Unless the judiciary is honest, just, impartial, efficient, fearless and firm, no law-enforcing agency will be able to make any dent or stand for any length of time. The agency, will collapse, turn inactive and inert or may turn hyper and take the role of judiciary into its hands. Since there is right of appeal against the judgment of lower judiciary and higher judiciary has power to comment upon, alter, stay or even negate the decision of lower court, it is the higher judiciary that in this country, or for that matter in any other civilised society, is supreme, nodal and the ultimate in the field of criminal justice.

Judges are also human and their judgments will be conditioned by their mindset, which in turn will depend upon their background, their mode of recruitment and the perception of their charter of duties and the role. Their recruitment and past conduct should be in consonance with their important strategic role. Those who join from legal/judicial services are fully judged for their suitability and integrity for being promoted to higher judiciary, but those coming from the bar are not judged thoroughly for their integrity and efficiency.

Unfortunately, the honesty has ceased to be the high point with judges for which the judiciary should be known. The retired judges have been going astray occasionally in arbitration matters and they went berserk in the Oil Selection Boards, which used to allot gas agencies and the petrol pumps. But recent tales of high court judges of Delhi, Punjab, Rajasthan, and Karnataka have been highly disturbing. The Chandigarh CBI court and the Ahmedabad experiences of lower courts are equally shocking. Leila Seth regrets about the dishonesty of high court judges and co-relates it to faulty recruitment system and illustrates it with appointment of one judge.[10] "These cases appear to me to be the result of the faulty system of appointments. If there were transparency in the process, Mr. Madan certainly would not have been appointed. The bar as a whole was aware of Mr. Madan's misdoings and misconduct as a lawyer, and brought it to the notice of the judiciary, but powerful connections prevailed and he was duly appointed.......I hope that the National Judicial Commission, if and when it comes into existence, will be more transparent in its process of selection. I think it will be a better method of appointing a judge, rather than leaving it entirely to the senior most judges and the politicians."

Integrity has become a serious problem with the judiciary. The proposed judicial commission should not only look into the appointments and such like matters alone, but also to go deep into the entire gamut of judicial functioning as visualised by Leila Seth, the distinguished judge. Affairs of judiciary are too serious and of far reaching importance and consequences, to be left to politicians or the legal profession itself. The commission should consist of a majority of non-jurists and it be headed, not by a judge as is the common practice, neither by anyone connected with the legal profession, nor a politician or a bureaucrat, but by someone who is learned, a man of proven integrity and holding respect amongst the people. The commission should have full time dedicated academicians, intellectuals, administrators, judges and jurists who are capable of full analysis of the entire issue and can really grapple with it. Since Police is the biggest client of the judiciary and whenever we talk of criminal justice system, human rights, fundamental rights, police becomes relevant. Police should also find place on the commission as otherwise the point of view of those who implement the most serious of the laws will be lost.

It is a very urgent and the most important problem. Justice is the corner stone of any democracy. In the words of George Washington, "the administration of justice is the firmest pillar of Government", so let us prevent it from shaking and save our democracy.

It is a well-known fact that a number of lawyers do not issue receipt for full amount that they charge from their clients. Quite a substantial part is unaccounted for and constitutes their black money. If such a person becomes a judge, his mindset will not allow him to take any action against any person accused of tax evasion or other economic offences. He will identify himself with every such person and will fear that if some such person is punished today, it may be his own turn tomorrow. For judging others one puts forward self as the standard and that constitutes his conviction. For instance the land ceiling Act has not been enforced to any appreciable extent anywhere in the country. One of the main reasons is that amongst other organs, the judges also did not have conviction to enforce such laws.

A tax evader, a man who has handled black money at any stage, a man hiding incomes, a man flouting laws, particularly welfare oriented laws, should never be made a judge. The minimum that can be done is that a declaration on oath i.e. an affidavit can be taken from him, that he always issued receipt for full amount that he charged during his practice, that he never evaded any tax, that he did not hide any assets in his name or in the name of his family from the law and that he never handled black money for himself or any one else. Unless judges are themselves clean, they can never do justice in cases of corruption, disproportionate assets and the other economic crimes.

Prevention

The general duties of corruption prevention wing have been enumerated in the narrative on CBI. Those actions are dependent upon creation of such a wing, but the steps recommended below can be taken immediately to have salutary effect in fight against corruption.

Fixing Realistic Tax Rates

The rates of two taxes i.e. Stamp Duty on registration of property and VAT are very high and naturally so are the returns on evasion of such duties. The rate of Stamp Duty in various states that averaged around fifteen per cent are being cut down in some states. Parties employ all sorts of methods to declare the value of property as low as ten per cent of the actual transaction or the market price. The sale is transacted on market price but registration is for just ten per cent of the consideration, pushing down the effective rate of registration duty to the tune of 1.5 per cent or so. In practice, the Stamp Duty is paid by the purchaser, though as per law, it is payable by the seller. The purchaser does not want to incur this heavy additional liability. Till the rate was around five to seven per cent, the extent of evasion was low, but when duty rate was hiked to double figures, the amount declared progressively saw a steep decline and the corresponding escalation of black money in the economy. The seller too received money in black on which he also saved income and other taxes. Even if there were no savings for him, he became a willing conspirator against the perceived tyranny of the state that charged unduly high rates.

Similarly, the rate of VAT on certain items is very high. On most of the building materials, the rate of VAT is twelve per cent but the tragedy is that in private sector for most of the items, not more than ten per cent of the building material purchased, is actually billed. Even the patent items like cement and steel are sold and purchased without any bill. Billing in electrical items is as good as non-existant. When transfer of material is interstate, bills are issued to meet checks at the border, but if the consumer can manage crossing the border without a bill, there is no question of any bill. Even when a bill is issued, it may be for fifteen to twenty per cent of the value of the goods. Even in case of government constructions, the contractors pay practically no tax on the articles or items that they purchase. Their payment of tax mostly remains restricted to the statutory deductions from their bills by the government departments. The market for furniture constitutes another grey area where payment of taxes is just unknown. Government collects tax from its own purchases or the company purchases only. A dining table set or a double bed in Delhi market priced at Rs. 40,000, would be billed for Rs. 2000 to a private purchaser. Whereas the tax on full bill amount would have been Rs.5000, the tax actually paid is just Rs.250/- that too if a bill is issued. At Rs.250/- it is just 5 per cent of the due amount of Rs. 5000/- or 0.625 per cent of the value of the goods as against the rate of 12 per cent.

When a purchase is made with black money, no one will like a bill. So is also true of the land transactions, but in the market, because of high rates of taxes, certain otherwise honest individuals also go in for taxless sales/purchases, turning their white money into black which some of them may not like to, if only tax rates were reasonable. In case either of the parties does not agree, bills will have to be issued. Incentive could be provided by lower rates, coupled with education of the people.

Checks to Cut Delays

It is said that, in general, delays are the root cause of corruption, but no studies have been conducted to root them out. Further, nobody is held responsible for delays, and when in some stray case, it comes to taking action against someone, some functionary down the line is made a scapegoat. Senior officers do not look to the disposal aspect on a continuous day-to-day basis. Similar is the treatment of complaints that are marked down by the officers. Then in due course extending to weeks, months or years, some routine reply may be communicated to the applicant. Officers are, by and large, markers i.e. they mark the papers down and forget. Down the line, it is not taken seriously except at the pain of disciplinary action.

An interesting incident occurred when I was district SP at Jind in Haryana in 1976. I had just taken over, when one Lachchman Singh (LS) appeared before me stating that he with his family was working in the fields of one Anant Ram (AR) for the entire Rabi season, but when it came to harvesting, the latter kicked him away. Out of the total produce of 280 quintals he was entitled to 1/5 or 56 quintals. I marked his application to concerned SHO for immediate enquiries and necessary action. After 15 days, he again appeared as nothing had happened, nobody had visited the village till then and his family was going hard even on food, as he already had borrowed to the hilt and none was prepared to extend him any more credit.

His application had been disposed of and returned to District HQ. The Head Constable appointed as the enquiry officer by the SHO is supposed to have visited the village and found no substance in the application after spot enquiries. On the other hand the applicant was reported to be a perpetual complaining type, not interested in work and a blackmailer. The DSP on behalf of the SP filed the same in routine and that was end to it.

I endorsed another application to the SHO and asked for thorough enquiries. After three weeks L S came instead. To my surprise he was coming out of jail where he was sent on charges of breach of peace. He stated that he was summoned to the Police Station one morning, was made to wait the whole day, was arrested in the evening and was produced in the court the next day. Since there was no one who could stand surety for him, he continued to languish in jail for next two weeks. When his wife located him in jail, she sold their young buffalo at throwaway price, hired an advocate with this money and earned his freedom. I summoned the SHO and the Head Constable, immediately. On questioning, the HC admitted that he had never gone to the spot and had not verified the facts, as it was the usual way to keep the lower sections of society away from harassing the respectables. Accordingly the challan was forwarded to the court by the SHO.

This was the usual routine he had witnessed during his twenty-five years of Police serving, he added.

The facts were then *prima facie* verified, and the version of L S was found to be correct. A case under section[11] 406 IPC was registered against A R as he held the share of LS in trust. Now it was the turn of AR to go to jail. The court appreciated and did not allow immediate bail. AR then instructed his family to give LS his due. Once the grain was transferred to LS, AR naturally got bail. It all could happen because of the dogged efforts of LS for which he had to suffer as well. Despite my commitment, I remained a marker, till I was sensitised by Lachchman Singh.

The moral of the story is that the senior officers and ministers just mark the papers, do not keep a track of their disposal and much less about the quality of disposal. Ultimately everything boils down to individual initiative, but still the system can be such as should compel the individual officer to look into the details. The system should have an in built mechanism to hold him responsible and accountable for delays not only by himself, but also by his subordinates. The system of entry of a communication, its marking and disposal is such that the senior officer does not get the total picture as to what is happening and how things are moving. Studies into these and other related systems could prevent delays. Finally the officers need be punished if there are delays under their charge. Punishing one Joint/Deputy Secretary or an equivalent officer in any department, irrespective of regard for his rank or cadre, will do the trick in Central or State Secretariat and will set an example for all the departments as well. Cutting down the delays is the foremost step in curtailing corruption, particularly at the grassroots level.

Corruption Prevention Wing

All anti-corruption agencies in the country should have a corruption prevention wing to advise and work on the pattern of similar wing in the CBI. Like the CBI, they should also take the innovative men and women of proven integrity and efficiency on their staff on deputation from various disciplines. The Assam LoC scandal, as also AHD scam of Bihar, would not have escalated if such a wing existed in Assam and Bihar vigilance bodies. They would have taken up the matter suo-motto as the news initially spread. The preventive systems would not have allowed escalation at all and would have nipped the evil in the bud itself.

Ombudsman

There can be no escape from setting up the institutions of Ombudsman both in states and at the centre known as Lokayukta and Lokpal respectively for catering to corruption particularly at the highest political levels in government. An objective and vigilant eye is required to oversee the exercise of executive powers at all levels. All corruption, as described above, is only the conversion, translation or encashment of power. Whosoever exercises power, needs to be watched. In the west where there is a crusade against corruption, they have either ICACs, or Independent Commissioners as also Ombudsman in one form or the other, who exercise jurisdiction over the big political bosses, and other institutions take care of services down the line. In any fight against corruption, two ingredients are very essential namely the agencies be independent so that these are not vulnerable to allegations of administrative or political biases. At present the agencies in India are subject to executive control and as such are open to charges of partiality, favouritism and all that. Politicisation of even the obvious patent misconduct is the best defence available and is being exploited to the utmost limits. Secondly the agency should have power to take suo-motto cognizance of the allegations and cause investigation into the same on its own. The institution of Lokpal with the twofold discretion can prove very effective.

Transparency

Transparency by itself is the most potent internal and external check in and on any organisation. In India, following the legacy of colonial days, all processes of the government are kept under wraps. Even the innocent matters pertaining to official establishment are classified as top secret and so are also other matters of routine. The underlying idea is that if the employees do not know how, why and what for a decision has been taken, they would not be able to pose any challenge to any action howsoever bad it may be. The person dealing with the matter can indulge in any manipulations. The victims would be compelled to grease the ever-dry palms of the concerned officials. It then leads to the court cases. If the results of selections, departmental committees, the panels prepared etc., were made public at the first opportunity, perhaps half of the cases in service matters that dominate the High Courts will never come about.

To my mind, in establishment matters, there is nothing that should be concealed from concerned employees. Only the original records should be out of bounds simply for the reason that someone may not alter or tamper the same. Now in computer age, all such records can be fed into the computer and every employee can have access to the same and get justice.

The court procedures in such cases are amazing. First the employee has to prove the existence and then contents of the record and has also to produce the same. When it all is secret material, why and how, can the petitioner be expected to produce it? Why should the state not produce all the documents on its own? The state need not behave like a party to the suit, but be more like a mother for all its employees, so that its warring children could feel satisfied and get internal justice that in turn will prompt and inspire them to give further justice to others. To quote famous Urdu poet Sahir Ludhianvi, *'Denge Wohi Jo Panyenge Is Zindgi Se Hum'* (we will return to society what we ourselves get from it). The employees constantly talk of the injustices at the hands of the state, and the common people groan endlessly against these very employees.

The Central Administrative Tribunals were established to give quick justice, but they also unwittingly followed the dictum that create long procedures and then blame the system'. If in CAT 'cases the department is asked to produce, in the first instance, all the records and documents connected with the case on its own irrespective of the fact whether these are secret or not, the disposal would take one or at the most two hearings. Cases will be decided in five weeks in place of 10 years. Real justice would be meted out, without compelling the employees to resort to underhand methods to procure evidence or secret documents by hook or by crook.

Similarly, in matters involving financial transactions and awarding of contracts, the rates come down wherever transparency is introduced. Tendering parties put a charge for everything that is not clear or is uncertain, whereas transparency gives a clear picture and imparts certainty. Any favour to anyone will be contested and fought. This fear and the fear of being exposed will by itself ensure honesty and correct action.

The instances given above are by way of examples. Transparency has its crucial role in all walks and aspects of clean governance. The process can be extended to all the departments of the government.

As an extension of the principle of transparency, the works could be physically examined by the specially constituted public committees, which could visit the sites of the works in their own area and could ensure quality as also the costs. They could also verify the materials being used, labour being deployed, etc. Boards could be prescribed, for display at site, which should have statistics about the work and number of workers, stock position, costs, etc. The boards and the records should be open to inspection by any person from the public. That may also bring to the notice of the enforcement agencies any bunglings and in any case it will be a good confidence building measure.

Education

The duties of the education wing or the 'Community Relations Department' as is known in ICAC Hong Kong, are rather broad based. It is not only the publicity department of the agency fighting corruption, but is also the best friend of the people advising them on their problems relating to government departments, and making them wiser about merits of a clean society. In short, it is meant to bring them out of the dark recesses of ignorance, so that they could grow more responsible and become conscious of their rights and duties. Some of them may join the fight and also assist others.

In India a beginning has yet to be made. To start with, a few points are outlined below:

Education regarding Anti-Corruption Laws and Procedures

First of all, the wing should educate the people regarding the ill-effects the corruption inflicts on the society and the economy. The wing should educate the people about the provisions of anti-corruption laws and the anti-corruption work. Public knowledge about the laws is very scant. Ignorance gives rise to fear. For reasons deep rooted in history, they are afraid of approaching any government functionary exercising legal powers. The role of anti-corruption laws and agencies has to be projected and appreciated as crusaders. Once people feel assured, cooperation will start flowing automatically.

Apart from the laws, the intricacies of investigations and the procedures need to be explained. So long as these remain shrouded in mystery, the citizens will continue to get intimidated. Once people know, they would be forthcoming and it will automatically ensure transparency. The recalcitrant members of state agencies will also have to fall in line as otherwise they would stand exposed.

Doctrinate the Young Minds

It has been brought out that the mindset of the Indian society is conditioned by its colonial past. Over half a century of independence has not made much difference. Efforts to change this mindset have to begin from the early childhood. The education wing should target the children right from the primary school and should travel with them right upto the university or the higher educational institutions, with suitable changes in the programmes at every successive stage. From school days they should be made aware about ill-effects of corruption. Young children take the teaching in the school as gospel's truth. They will not only imbibe the value system themselves, but would also act as teachers and policemen for the parents erring on scales of integrity, morality and the law. As they progress in their studies i.e. graduate to higher classes, constant dinning of morality, ethics, legal provisions, nationalism, expectations from them will be required into their ears. All such efforts produce results in the long term.

Apart from young people in schools and colleges, youth in universities and business schools need be targeted. Education on business ethics should be imparted to them. This part is relevant for other sections of public as well when we have embarked on the system of privatisation or liberlisation.

Education of Women on Futility of Gold and Diamond

It is no secret that the consumption of gold is the highest in India. The country spends a staggering amount on gold imports. Indians may go anywhere in the world, they bring back gold from there as if destination of whole gold production of the entire world is India alone. Demand is ever rising and even the recent unprecedented steep rise in prices has made no substantial difference. We are supposed to have over 3.5 lac outlets for jewellery, processing and selling 800 tons or 8 lac kgs. of gold that is supposed to be lawfully imported, which gives an average of 2.3 kg. per outlet per year, the sales proceeds of which would be worth Rs. 23 lacs at present price level. Ostensible margin of a jeweller or a goldsmith is not more than 20% on sales proceeds which also includes all his fixed as well as variable costs, including labour. The earnings per outlet work out to Rs. 4.6 lacs a year. Diamonds, pearls and silver, may add another equal amount to his income from gold raising it to Rs. 9.2 lacs per annum or Rs. 75,000 per month. Even a small goldsmith cannot defray all the charges, the staff salaries and earn a livelihood on this turnover, whereas every single city has a large number of them rolling in wealth. Obviously more gold and other valuables creep in through unaccounted sources than the World Gold Council can vouch safe. It does not appear to be an exaggeration that the entire 3000 tons annual gold production of the world gravitates to India by imports and smuggling in bulk as also in bits. Exact arrivals into India would only be the guesswork, but even if it is 2000 tons, it would be worth a staggering Rs. 2,00,000 crores as against Rs. 80,000 crores as per the published figure of 800 tons of World Gold Council. Besides gold, there is craze for the high value items like diamonds and platinum among the higher classes. When added to gold, the national bill for jewellery may soar to something like Rs. 4 to 6 lac crores every year.

Our womenfolk require education about futility of wearing and possessing jewellery not produced in the country and import of which, through whatever means, retards the nation's growth. If gold and diamond etc., in that magnitude, were not imported or smuggled, and the money so saved had been invested to import machinery or utilised for other gainful economic activities, the country would have progressed faster. The education wing needs to motivate the patriotic side of women and exhort them to come out of their blind passion for gold and diamond. Women's organisations need to be enlightened and involved actively in the task.

Make People Demand Quick Decisions/Justice

If people demand expeditious disposal, no administration in a democracy can deny this. Even the courts will have to fall in line. The education wing can educate the people to demand their right for quick decisions and quick justice. This will be the best guarantee against corruption as delay is the mother of corruption. In the final analysis, people can take help of judicial activism and form organisations, which will compel the powers, including judiciary, to be sensitive to law and the expectations of the people.

The task of preparing the people is a continuous process. The wing has to target various groups in various ways like imparting information and preventive education, organising training programmes in various organisations and holding seminars where the floor should be thrown open to all for even the inconvenient questions. The Education Wing should target the women, the students, the politicians, the civil servants and the common people, utilise all available means, lectures, seminars, audio and video screening, newspapers, newsletters, for disseminating relevant information. The electronic media should be bound by the law to allot time for this wing, free of charge, in national interest.

These are some suggestions. This is not an exhaustive list. Various learned people have suggested lots of ways, perhaps after prolonged research, whereas I have made a humble attempt on the basis of my deep involvement in CBI at a very crucial juncture, solid experience in state vigilance for four years, besides having watched the contemporary scene for nearly half a century as a keen observer. I hope the above suggestions alongwith those discussed earlier, would contribute towards fighting corruption successfully.

References

1. *Interpreting Corruption* by Vinod Pavarala, Sage Publications 1996.
2. ibid page 226.
3. ibid page 226
4. ibid page 228.
5. ibid page 228

6. Section 154 is reproduced for ready reference of the reader, "Every information relating to the commission of a cognizable offence, if given orally to an officer in charge of a police station, shall be reduced to writing by him or under his direction, and be read over to the informant; and every such information, whether given in writing or reduced to writing as aforesaid, shall be signed by the person giving it".
7. *On Balance* by Leila Seth, Penguin, page 349.
8. World Development Report 2000-2001, table 14, page 300.
9. Section 16 PC Act 1988 is reproduced for the benefit of the reader, "Where a sentence of fine is imposed under sub-section (2) of Sec. 13 or Sec. 14, the Court in fixing the amount of the fine shall take into consideration the amount or the value of the property, if any, which the accused person has obtained by committing the offence or where the conviction is for an offence referred to in C1.(e) of sub-section (1) of Sec.13, the pecuniary resources or property referred to in that clause for which the accused person is unable to account satisfactorily."
10. *On Balance* by Leila Seth, Penguin page 410
11. Section 405 and 406 IPC dealing with misappropriation of property in trust read as under:

    405. Criminal breach of trust

    Whoever, being in any manner entrusted with property, or with any dominion over property, dishonestly misappropriates or converts to his own use that property, or dishonestly uses or disposes of that property in violation of any direction of law prescribing the mode in which such trust is to be discharged, or of any legal contract, express or implied, which he has made during the discharge of such trust, or willfully suffers any other person so to do, commits "Criminal breach of trust".

    406. Punishment for criminal breach of trust

    Whoever commits criminal breach of trust shall be punished with imprisonment of either description for a term, which may extend to three years, or with fine, or with both.

12
Conclusion

The corruption and the collosal drain from our country have to be stopped as our wealth cannot be allowed to disappear into other countries leaving us way behind in development, progress and growth in all the sectors despite our vast resources. World is making great strides on all fronts, economic growth is exploding in the developed countries and per capita income of some of them is nearly 100 times as compared to ours, though our resources are equally comparable if not better. Problems are likely to multiply further with India opting for liberalisation. That adds to the urgency to fight corruption and lay down and implement strong regulations and enforcement as otherwise foreigners will fish richly without any restrictions in our muddy waters. In India we are very soft on enforcement whereas in the developed world any violation of law is very firmly dealt with.

The present mess, if allowed to continue, threatens the very integrity of our nation. The disadvantage groups are becoming more and more conscious of their rights. They are resorting to militancy expecting to break the economic shackles, but these uprisings have the seeds of political break up of the nation. During the last few decades, the rationale of militancy has been identified to the lack of development in the area and the unemployed youth is identified in the forefront of militancy everywhere. Ultimately it is the special economic package for the area that settles the issues. It is imperative that we develop, and the precondition for this measure is to contain corruption.

It is possible to retrieve the situation, to prevent corruption and to stop the drain of resources of the nation. However, it can be neither through slogan shouting, nor by displaying boards and hoardings, but by strict and equitable laws and their firm enforcement without fear or regard for any one's status or position. It is strong unwavering action against corruption and the corrupt, which really will make the difference and change the mindset. India will not be the first country to recover. Hong Kong was mired deep in corruption till 1974, when strict and meaninful fight against corruption commenced with the establishment of ICAC. By 1996, 98.8% citizens felt that Hong Kong was free of corruption. It happened through the meaningful and unsparing action against corruption and the corrupt. Hong Kong boasts of 15th position out of 159 countries in 2005, with a score of 8.3 on the scale of integrity in the ratings of Transparency International.

The seriousness in India can be gauged from the two instances practically enacted by the establishment. The Lokpal bill was first introduced in the Parliament in 1968 and the process has been repeated in each Parliament ever since but the bill is never taken up after its introduction in the house and lapses with the term of the house. The shade of the government or the party has made no difference. Similar is the fate of single directive. The Supreme Court held it ulra vires and discriminatory but the same is already back as part of CVC Act. This has been brought back by the NDA government; the BJP had criticised the directive when they were in opposition, but enacted it when in power.

Any country, which made sincere efforts, has been rewarded. It has been amply demonstrated that corruption is basically not a moral or an ethical problem, it is a crime, a legal problem, and has to be firmly dealt with, as such. The legal and procedural infrastructure will have to be changed wherever such changes are required in the interest of justice. The impression that corruption cannot be contained has been disseminated deliberately in order to foment the spirit of helplessness. If Hong Kong could recover, if the US could come out of gangsters' decade, any country can recover. It is a question of the will of the people to enforce the laws strictly. It is improper to say that one has to wait till moral or ethical regeneration of the society, or to view it as a problem that the revolution will take care. Some may consider revolution as the ultimate solution, but its route is too circuitous, meandering through lawlessness, destruction, anarchy, bloodhsed and many more destructive channels, which any sensible person should dread. Further the revolution only breaks the existing system and the new one has to be evolved. It can be achieved by the legal and the mental revolution that needs to be ushered in. The only option, which is tried, tested and recommended through the ages, is the strong and firm enfocement without favour, fear or bias.

The Judiciary has to play a greater role, as punishment is the only ultimate deterrent. If other progressive countries can go to the extent of imposing death penalty or imprisonment for life and recovery of all the bungled amounts along with penalty, we should also get firm. Judiciary has to redefine its procedures to cut delays and review its norms of passing sentence within the legal framework. In corruption cases till now, the system in practice has been to award the minimum punishment prescribed for the crime and to impose token fine allowing the fruit of crime to remain with the criminal.

The democratic system in India is often held responsible for nurturing corruption and protecting the corrupt. Basically, I feel no system is allowed to work honestly in India. China was doing better in communist mould and is doing far better after liberalisation and opening up. We also opened up at the same time, but are left far behind. Any system will perform well if it is adopted honestly; no-doubt a better system will give better results. But take away the honesty, even the best of the systems will fall, crumble and fail.

Even in India the facade of strong enforcement is enacted with every change of government. All new governments promise a clean administration and a complete crusade, but in reality it is limited to vendetta against their predecessors and the opponents. The anti-corruption agencies are made to act beyond the laws and the available evidence that leads to controversies and mudslinging on political plane, but in the bargain brings bad name to investigating agencies, which demoralises their personnel and kills their will and inititative to uphold truth. They tend to lose their soul and tend to be dead instruments that are musused by their handler. These agencies themselves need to be liberated and so restructured that they become independent of the executive and are able to work purely on merits, precluding any interference from outside.

A strong and determined Prime Minister can make all the difference, liberate these agencies and give their soul to them. Very few persons are required for the task of cleansing the rot and there is no dearth of such people in this country. Only they have to be placed in right positions. They will create suitable infrastructure as recommended at various places in this book. No doubt, the vested interests, both from administrative and the political class will oppose any such moves, but there can be no cause for fear from any angle, as the P. M. can take the nation into confidence. People are impatiently longing for such a leader and once the action commences, the fence sitters will get converted. It will shake the corrupt political and administrative establishment who will initially oppose such measures, but will soon be on the run for cover. A corrupt person is very weak from inside. I am sure once cases against disproportionate assets are taken up in right earnest, the message will go home that the state means business; the corrupt, the tax evader and such whole lot will run for safe places to dump their papers concerning black transactions, wads of notes of hush money and their weighty possession of jewellery and other such items. All we require is a straightforward, effective, honest, firm, bold and a well-meaning Prime Minister for a few years at least.

Annexure A

Central Bureau of Investigation

D.O. No. 79/AJD(N)/CBI/95

GOVERNMENT OF INDIA
C.G.O. COMPLEX, BLOCK NO.3
LODHI ROAD
NEW DELHI-110003

Dated August 1, 1995

B. R. LALL
JOINT DIRECTOR (NORTH)

Dear Shri Rao,

I am grateful to you for sounding me in advance on 19th regarding my transfer. Nobody has a title to any post and one has to serve wherever posted. Some people get attached to certain posts but as I told you that day, I have never clung to any post, but only upheld the principles wherever I have served with the result that during the 24 ½ years, since I was promoted as SP, this is my 26th transfer, that too despite the fact that I spent 12 years in 3 so called insignificant postings (where one's straightforwardness does not hurt others), i.e. 3 years in ITBP, 4 years as SP (Vigilance) and 5 years as director NEPA. If these 3 posts and 12 years are taken away, it is my 23rd posting in a total period of 12 ½ years. Every time, the transfer was on a principled stand, which I took without bending.

2. During last few days, I have been hearing that during the period of last one month, when you decided to disassociate me and the Special director from the Hawala case, you have been mentioning that nothing was done in the Hawala case till the last month when yourself directly took over the case which precisely is on 26.6.1995. This mention was made before the IOs even.

3. Fact remains that it is I who introduced PC Act angle in the Hawala case, I brought the concept of kickbacks in projects much before interrogation of Jains' as I developed my information sources in various institutions dealing with power projects and got lots of information. My staff fully cooperated and worked day and night including all ranks from DIG down to constable or a clerk. I myself, examined Kawas project first of all, supervised the interrogation of Jains' which yielded valuable information. I am referring in particular to the statement of S.K. Jain, which has been thoroughly corroborated to the extent we could look into for further verification. I am always very frank while discussing with my juniors as also the seniors, but at the same time, carried out all the orders and jobs assigned to me and my organisation by yourself. I was however, in favour of looking into the massive record first before we convert the PE into an RC so that we have the evidence of payments and receipts, which is something primary for making out a case. But somehow we could not wait because of the pressure of Supreme Court and had to convert it into an RC a little premature but that was beyond our control.

4. It is also correct that the Supreme Court every time came heavy on us but for that the responsibility squarely rests with S.G.I. who as our Counsel should have had complete knowledge of Law and should have been a master of facts but he has neither the knowledge nor the understanding of criminal laws and nor the capability to project whatever is told to him. He would not marshal all the facts before the Hon'ble court. The other factor has been no investigation for a little over 2 years between

1991 to 1993, for which Supreme Court holds CBI responsible. Though CBI as an institution is indefensible for this delay, but actually none of us is individually responsible as none of us was there at the scene at that time in this case.

5. It is correct that scrutiny of records was rather slow and I was myself not satisfied, but it was because I had very limited staff and during last almost an year, despite my requests verbally and in writing, not even one person could be added to Anti-Corruption II though it is normal for investigation of such a scam. Now full one DIG with an SP and 6 IOs were added through ACB/Delhi. I could not supplement from ACI as they are also deep in investigation of Assam LoC scam which also has huge dimensions and for that also I got only one extra IO. All through this time, I worked with 50 to 60% vacancies of Inspectors in my charge. I could never spare more than 2 to 3 IOs, except when S K Jain, JK Jain etc. were being interrogated, when I put the entire AC II on this job. Chronologically earlier as directed by the Supreme Court from September to December, the staff was busy in interrogating the 115 persons whose names were found entered in diaries. From January, the exercise of collecting the documents of various projects in which Jains' had worked and subsequently, the verification into the PE started and after conversion of PE into RC, on 4.3.1995, the searches, arrest and interrogation of Jains' started which continued round the clock till 20.3.1995. After that, we prepared for the Supreme Court where matters relating to bails and arrests of Jains, came up and we started running into courts and arranging for arrest of N K Jain and BR Jain. There were Supreme Court hearings on 27.3.95, 2.4.95, 18.4.95, 2.5.95, however, we kept on working overtime collecting records, examining projects, verifying statements of Jains and also arrested N K Jain after getting him from UK. It was only after 2.5.95 that we could heave a sigh of relief, as ACII directly under Amod and closely supervised by me had been working for long hours into the night foregoing their leave and

holidays. How can one say that no work was done? We carried out every aspect of investigation as desired by yourself and also whatever occurred to us. Your further directions by that time were also received regarding conduct of investigations which was impossible if my team was not strengthened by diverting entire staff of ACII to this case. As such, on 4.5.95, leaving only 4/5 IOs in the other 3 branches, I diverted entire strength of ACII to Hawala case and divided them into 3 teams each under an SP, Shri M.P. Singh and Shri Mukesh Sahay were to examine the projects and team under Shri HS Sandhu, SP was to collect field information and conduct field enquiries into various persons mentioned in diaries in order to fix their identity and to collect the evidence of payment/receipt by them, including the evidence regarding their assets, their families, etc. Work picked up very fast and we located evidence in Kawas, questionable nexus in Uri and Dulhasti projects but which still required deeper probe. Slowly, we were progressing to close on some of the big guns in particular as statements of S K Jain and J K Jain were getting verified. In May when Amod was suddenly repatriated from the scene it did slow down the work as the feeling went round that he has been removed. I talked to the IOs and SPs and brought them out of their frustration, but about a week was lost. Amod K. Kanth was perceived by the staff as an honest and straightforward officer, but by sudden repatriation, whereas earlier his willingness and my recommendations had been sought by Administration Division of CBI, the message went home that straightforwardness is at a discount even in CBI.

6. Yourself held detailed discussion, during the week with various SPs and discussions with Shri HS Sandhu were awaited when in last week of June, I was removed from the scene and yourself took over the work of supervising the IOs directly and started discussing about chargesheeting some public servants. Even the SDCBI was by and large ignored in subsequent discussions. The question of chargesheet had come up with me also but I brought it to the notice of DCBI that :

a. There was as yet no evidence regarding receipt of payments made to the persons named in Diary.

b. Evidence of motive was yet to come.

c. Evidence of favours shown and irregularities committed was coming in, which had to be developed and put in right perspective.

d. For unearthing further evidence and the assets searches were also required in particular of the big fish as they were emerging the main culprits.

7. All through, I have been of the opinion and still hold that if it was not possible to chargesheet the big fish, as different standards are supposed to be adopted in their cases, then we should forget about the small ones also. For, this scandal originated from kickbacks, which were created forced on this country and were perpetuated by the big ones including the Ministers and Prime Minister. Chargesheeting minor functionaries only, for receiving fringe benefits of the scam would amount to a cover up of the scam itself. I will come to this question again in detail a little later.

8. The DCBI started avoiding me and broke the hierarchical chain and I became a subject of denegration before my own subordinates. I may not bother for my own sake but, the chain of command was breaking, and the wrong signals were being transmitted. Incidentally, during 3 weeks since then till 18th, only the existing information has been compiled. It was something known, and established only the identity. The further scrutiny stopped, the experts who had been called, had to be dropped for the time being. I was planning this work some 10 days later, as sitting day and night where I would also have participated with the staff, this compilation would take 3-4 days only and in the meantime, I was searching for further evidence as early as possible to find some evidence regarding payments/receipt/motives/ favours. The contents of all the diaries and documents brought in the searches of March'95 were personally known to me as I had

glanced through most of them when these were initially brought. These contained only the routine information of telephone numbers. One diary had repeated mention to MPN and flat for MPN. It is from this diary that Jain in interrogation identified him as MP Narayan and we reached the Neyaveli Lignite and the Coal sector. These only helped in establishing identity. It was a minor matter as compared to evidence of motive, favours, payments etc. and moreover it required very little time. However, we work as a team according to the directions of the director. Had director told me about his priority, I would have got the compilation work done. There would be no need to ignore me or the Special director on this account, but to my mind, it appears that as myself and Special director both were not prepared for premature chargesheet and chargesheeting of small fish alone, and perhaps I was also to be removed from the scene after Amod, it was all preparatory to that.

9. Besides, the Hawala case, my information goes that there were pressures from outside for my removal because of Krishnamurthy case and the LoC scam case of Assam in investigation of which, Shri Hiteshwar Saikia, Chief Minister, Assam is emerging as the kingpin. Since April'95, in Krishnamurthy case, director had a lurking feeling that I kept him in the dark in the operation to restrain VK from going to Washington on the night of 19/20th April, 95. Kindly allow me Sir, to place it before you that there was absolutely no reason to keep you in the dark but there was no reason or occasion to inform you earlier than at the time I did. I had your mandate to file SLP then details are my business as JD. Since permission to file SLP was accorded by Government on your recommendation, the only possible conclusion was that Shri Krishnamurthy is to be prevented from going abroad as otherwise the entire exercise would be infructuous. Since morning on 19th April, we were trying to get the case fixed up for next morning which is done by the Chief Justice himself. We could not approach Supreme Court during day as copy

of judgement became available to us from the High Court only at 4.30 p.m. on 19.4.95. We were told that for urgent hearings, the cases are taken to his residence by the Additional Registrar General every evening. That day, perhaps there was no other case. Addl. Registrar General after hearing our case took the CBI team to the residence of the Chief Justice at about 8.30 p.m. but the Chief Justice left for dinner. They dispersed after deciding to meet him next morning at 8.00 a.m. and I was informed accordingly. Krishnamurthy had not told that he was leaving the same night, but at about 10 O'clock, the information came through his PA that he was leaving at 00.30 hrs, on 20.4.95 i.e. the same night. Amod K Kanth phoned me, we discussed that he will consult the Addl. Registrar General, if anything could be done to salvage the situation at that late hour as our efforts should be fully mobilised not to allow Shri Krishnamurthy to go abroad in the interest of our case. The other persons of staff were still in office. He collected them and went to the residence of Addl. Registrar General who asked them to come to the residence of the Chief Justice. Amod had now no occasion immediately to inform me that they had reached the residence of Chief Justice and till then, there was nothing that I could inform the director or the Special director. As they reached the residence of the Chief Justice, he also arrived and decided to convene the court there itself. Amod could neither leave the residence of Chief Justice and nor could he ring up from his residence to inform that the court had been convened. But still as a responsible officer, he managed to go to the telephone of the Chief Justice and informed me at 11.40 p.m. at night that the Hon'ble Chief Justice had decided to convene the court and I immediately informed the DCBI. I informed the director at the first and the earliest opportunity when anything worth mentioning occurred. As JD, I am responsible to control and to supervise the movements of my staff and inform my seniors only when there is something worth informing. If it had any political fall-out, that is not a circumstance which I will take into account. If some politicians in power or out of power or anybody else gets angry, that is a non issue so far as I am concerned as a professional who goes only by facts and truth. To me, any mixture even of tact, in truth, deflects the truth from straightforwardness. You have given me a crime for investigation and I am a collector of facts. I collect facts in the rightful, legal and truthful way, to whomsoever it may hurt is no concern or consideration with me and in this case, I did not falter in informing you or I did not keep you in dark deliberately or otherwise nor did Amod. He informed me at the first available opportunity and same did I. If for travelling the path of truth, I am sent back to state or repatriated from centre or sent out from CBI, I am least bothered, as I have seen 23 transfers in 12 years and every time, I was transferred because of the principled stand that I took and it applies this time also.

10. Case of Krishnamurthy is a big scam by itself and its dimensions are very large and so are the pressures. Government of India have not allowed us investigations in Japan and Switzerland from where the kickbacks originated and were channelised through banks. Though, request for permission to issue L.R. was sent on 14.5.93, the permission has not come till today despite lapse of over 27 months. Earlier we used to apply to court for issue of L.R. under the law, and at the same time request G.O.I. to issue declaration of reciprocity, which was fairly a routine matter, but pursuant to Krishnamurthy's case, as my information goes, executive instructions curbing the law were issued by G.O.I. and we have consequently been restrained by Policy Division Circular No. 21/44/89-PD dated 17th August, 1994 from filing request in the court unless G.O.I. permit us to move such application under section 166 A Cr.pc. It all speaks of the great influence and pressure Shri Krishnamurthy commands and exercises. As DCBI is aware, his influence and intervention did not stop at this. He could successfully dictate us through his contacts in government to file a

lame duck Affidavit in the High Court where his application was heard on 18.4.95. it was on this point that we had arguments before filing the affidavit and again on 18.4.95, when his petition was allowed and he was permitted to go abroad.

11. Compromising a little here on there is perhaps more pragmatic in the prevailing circumstances where a civil servant feels himself helpless, but people perceive us as an agency comparable to FBI. We are supposed to investigate crime in high places. If we get bogged down for whatever reason, it does us discredit. While investigating the corruption in high places, our subjects normally have to be high ranking politicians and officers, if we start bending the law for them or interpreting differently, my conscience does not accept it. Will nobody or no agency in this country look into the corruption by high and mighty?

12. However, there may be some lapse or error, as a human being, which did happen once, and which I acknowledged immediately before you when I was late by a few hours in informing the disclosures of SK Jain. I was convinced of his disclosures on the night of 12.3.95 only, when I assigned the work of final compilation late at night, but it was just a slip that I did not inform about the disclosures then. The next morning at about 10.30 a.m. in your office when I informed, you naturally told me that I should have informed earlier, perhaps you would have liked to talk to Jains'. Whereas my lapse remains, but God is kind that on that day, we got remand to police custody of S K Jain extended by one day, which gave ample opportunity for yourself or Special director to have interrogated him. It salvaged the situation so far as the case is concerned or delay in information is concerned, but I agree that my lapse remains, though it was purely bonafide and only a chance slip.

13. I have the feeling that because of various pressures mine and AK Kanth's straightforwardness in both these cases, i.e. interrogation of SK Jain and recording of his statement

and our role in reconsideration of Krishnamurthy case for proceeding abroad are not palatable at Government level. No individual is indispensable but I think the term of AK Kanth could have been extended as is normally being done in CBI. To my knowledge, no reference was made to Government at all which is a fair routine in CBI and for which in case of Amod his willingness to stay and my comments were asked for in February, but the situation changed in March and changed drastically in April. He was removed first and it was clear to me that I also had very limited time as JD.AC(HQ). I have no regret in being changed as I could not have been a party in leaving out the big and the influential while chargesheeting the small even if that is the interpretation we take of Supreme Court order.

14. The worst malady that ails our nation is the corruption and that too corruption at high places by high and mighty. Hawala case is a classic example where as per the accounts, we have so far, about Rs.80 crores were generated through kickbacks in which big people right up to the Prime Minister were involved. If we now concentrate only on minor functionaries, are we not aiding and abetting corruption? Catching Jains' is the starting point only. There is no confusion that corruption occurred because of these high functionaries, Jains' are only the peddlers who could do nothing if the authorities did not conspire and abet. Since nation has reposed its destiny in their hands and entrusted investigation of betrayal by them to us, to my mind we would be betraying our nation if we do not concentrate on big people. I strove for complete investigation into the power sector, which is draining this country. As kickbacks may be 3 to 10%, of the project cost, but up-valuation is anything between 40 to 100% of the basic and real project cost. It is in this context that I sent a report on Chamera Project to you where against an estimated cost of Rs.1393 crores in 1992, the negotiations for allotment are on for Rs.3300 to 3600 crores i.e. @ Rs. 12 crores per MW whereas in the world

over rate of only around Rs. 6 crores per MW is considered reasonable for Hydro Electric Projects. Even if this figure were to be Rs. 2000 crores for 300 MW Chamera Project, should we not look into it when Rs.1000 to Rs. 1500 crores of the nation are being squandered for kickbacks of Rs. 100 crores. This is the part which I was proposing to investigate and present a clear picture irrespective of the fact that who comes in. Certainly, some members of Union Cabinet both the present and past would come in and evidence against some of them was being uncovered. It does not matter if the name of former PM or the present PM figured or figured in a big way. As a professional, charged with the duty of collection of facts, I would not hesitate even if a big name comes in. Once we chargesheet the small, even if we do not intend to close the case, we would be forced to close the same, as happened in Dharmendra Deo Mishra's case and as per my information efforts are afoot in Assam LoC Scandal as the line has reached the Assam CM.

15. I am a low profile civil servant who seeks no publicity. But so far as the right action is concerned, I try to be absolutely straight and that is what I did during my stay as JD.AC (HQ) for 15 months and will continue to strive.

Yours sincerely,
Sd/-
(B.R. LALL)

Shri K Vijaya Rama Rao,
Director CBI
CGO Complex
New Delhi.
A copy is forwarded to Shri N N Singh, Special director (A) CBI.

Sd/-
(B.R. Lall)

Annexure B

Part Statement of Shri Surendra Kumar Jain S/O Shri Jyoti Prasad Jain, R/O A-13, Friends Colony, New Delhi.

I have reconsidered the entire issues again and again during the past over several years and I have taken a decision to reveal the whole truth in connection with the entries made in the diaries and files which have been seized from the house of JK Jain on 3.5.1991. I am volunteering the truth of my own free will in order to relieve myself of the burden of secrecy which I have been carrying on with me so far.

The sequence of events of receipt and disbursement of the payments mentioned in the diaries and files are as under:

1. Jainendra Kumar Jain has been my close confidant and I have been taking his services in keeping money on my behalf which pertained to accounts other than official accounts of my business. He has been collecting money and also distributing the same to different persons on my instructions from time to time.

2. I came in contact with Mr. Quattrochi, an Italian who was the representative of Snam Progetti in India sometime towards the end of the year 1982 or in the beginning of 1983. He was introduced to me at Delhi by Mr. Gerni who was the Manager of Onsaldo, a government Undertaking of Italy. He was based in Delhi during those days. Both Mr. Gerni and Mr. Quattrochi were living in Friends Colony, New Delhi. I met Mr. Gerni for the first time at Delhi in connection with discussions of a tender

which he had quoted for erection and supply of steel structure and boiler etc. for Rourkela Steel Plant. He had come to know that my company BEC had good name in this field. I and Mr. Gerni had discussed the said contract with the intention that if the work of Rourkela Steel Plant was allotted to Onsaldo, the erection and fabrication work would be given to my company BEC. We started working jointly on this project. Onsaldo got the contract of Rourkela Steel Plant but within a few days or a few weeks, this contract was cancelled after the issuance of Letter of Intent. It was subsequently allotted to BHEL. The reason for cancelling the contract on Onsaldo and for giving to BHEL was to give preference to the public sector undertaking of the Government of India instead of awarding the same to any foreign company.

3. After about a year or so, I met Mr. Gerni and Mr. Quattrochi together at the residence of Mr. Gerni in Friends Colony. There was no body else except Mr. Gerni and Mr. Quattrochi. From then onwards, I developed friendship with Mr. Quattrochi also. We frequently used to meet from time to time.

4. Mr. Quattrochi was interested in taking up the contract of supply, fabrication and erection of boiler at Vizag in the Captive Power Plant, Visakhapatnam. It was a 60x3 MW Project. It was an understanding between me and Mr. Quattrochi that if they got the contract, they would give me sub-contract for erection and fabrication of boiler etc. Mr. Quattrochi had submitted tender for this Project in the name of Snam Progetti. The prices quoted by Snam Progetti i.e. the company of Mr. Quattrochi were very high and that is why we did not pursue this contract. This was ultimately allotted to BHEL. Mr. Quattrochi was involved in many businesses like fertilizers, ONGC, pipelines etc. There was one more work in either of these lines which I had done with Mr. Quattrochi, but I am not able to recollect the same. It was a sizeable contract but it did not pertain to erection, supply or fabrication. This was not a contract which our company did for Snam

Progetti but I had assisted Mr. Quattrochi at certain levels. I shall try to recollect the same and tell the details later.

5. In or around 1987, the contract of Hydro Project of NHPC at Dhulhasti in Jammu & Kashmir came up. It was awarded to M/s Ceglec Company of France. I and Mr. Quattrochi had assisted Ceglec company to get this contract from, NHPC. During those days only, another Hydro Project of Uri also came to be tendered. M/s Scanska of Sweden which was a consortium of several companies had also tendered for the same. ABB was also one of the companies in the said consortium. Mr. Benbourn, the Executive Vice President of ABB in India was known to me from before. He was introduced to me by Mr. Arun Nehru at the residence of Sh. Shivshankar, Minister, who was a close friend of mine. I took Mr Benbourn and introduced him to Mr. Quattrochi. Mr. Quattrochi thereafter put Mr. Benbourn in touch with Mr. Rajiv Gandhi for discussing the finalisation of the said contract of Uri. Mr. Quattrochi worked as a middleman for getting the Uri contract awarded to Scanska and Dhulhasti to Ceglec by Shri Rajiv Gandhi, the then Prime Minister of India. The Project of Dhulhasti was for about Rs. 800 crores and that of Uri was for Rs. 1200 to Rs. 1300 crores as I roughly remember. As per my understanding with Mr. Benbourn and Mr. Quattrochi, I was to get the work of erection and fabrication in the Uri Project for Rs. 300 to Rs. 400 crores. In the meantime, terrorist activities started in Uri and, therefore, I lost interest in the said jobs. The said works were also, thus done by ABB themselves or through some other contractor. For the help which I and Mr. Quattrochi had rendered to ABB in getting the contract of Uri, I was to get my commission of 3% and Quattrochi was to get his commission of 7%. For the work of Dhulhasti also, I was to get commission of about 3% from Ceglec of France. I am not able to remember the name of the person who passed on the commission of Ceglec to me but he belonged to the said company. With regard to the

> payment of the commission pertaining to Uri project, I had insisted upon Mr. Quattrochi to give me the payments in Indian Rupees in India and, therefore, he had brought one Ameer Bhai to my office and had introduced him to me saying that he would make the payment to me in Indian Rupees. He had told me that Ameer Bhai was residing in Bombay. JK Jain had also met him in my office at that time. Ameer Bhai was aged about 45 years. He was about 5'6" height, medium built, medium complexion. He used to speak English and Hindi both. He was a very close confidant Mr. Quattrochi. The said Ameer Bhai had met at Bombay also once in Hotel Oberoi. JK Jain had also met him once or twice there. I do not know his telephone number or address as JK Jain used to contact him for collection of money etc. As far as I know Mr. Ameer Bhai has left India about 3 years back and his location is not known.

After the work of Uri project was allotted to Scanska, my share of the commission was settled at about 18 to 19 million dollars as I can now recall and Mr. Quattrochi had transferred the said 18 to 19 million dollars in the account of Ameer Bhai who was living in Bombay to be delivered to me in Indian Rupees as and when I asked for the same. Mr. Quattrochi had a bank account in ABN Bank at Antwerp (Belgium) or Genevea/Zurich in Switzerland and possibly Ameer Bhai had also his bank accounts in the said banks. Ameer Bhai had been passing on the money to me through JK Jain as and when I used to ask for the same from him through JK Jain. Whenever Ameer Bhai used to pay the money to JK Jain, he used to tell him to account for the receipts against the secret heads 'A', 'AB' and 'K'. I had been thus getting my share of the commission in Indian Rupees through Ameer Bhai of Bombay in the manner stated above. JK Jain was maintaining the account of the same accordingly.

I had a desire to become the biggest industrialist of India and to grow on the lines of Dheeru Bhai Ambani of Reliance. I had known that Dheeru Bhai Ambani had risen with the help of his close contacts with politicians. I also, therefore, wanted to come in close contact with the politicians and highly placed public servants by paying them money. Since I had got a lot of easy money by way of commissions from the works of Uri and Dhulhasti as mentioned above, I started giving money to several politicians and highly placed public servants from the year 1987 which I continued upto the year 1991.

During the year 1989, the file of Kawas Project of Gujarat, which was retendered, was pending for clearance in the Ministry of Power and Energy. Mr. Arif Mohd. Khan was then the Power and Energy Minister in the Government of India. GEC Alsthom were the lowest bidders in the said contract. Mr. Revvillon was the Vice President of GEC Alsthom who was looking after the export works in India. Mr. Revvillon met me and requested to get clearance of the Kawas Project file expedited. I had, thereupon, requested Mr. Arif Mohd. Khan, Power Minister to expedite the clearance of the said contract file which ultimately had to go to GEC Alsthom. After the allotment, a sub-contract for about Rs. 20 to 22 crores pertaining to erection and fabrication works was to be given to me by GEC Alsthom but ultimately when the contract was awarded, they gave me a sub-contract of about Rs. 4 to 4.5 crores only. For the consideration of the work of my expediting the contract of Kawas Project with Mr. Arif Mohd. Khan and also in compensation of the less work given to me as sub-contactor in the said Project, I told Mr. Revvillon to give Rs. 10 crores to me which he transferred to the account of Ameer Bhai with ABN Bank, Antwerp or Geneva. I had introduced Mr. Revvillon to Ameer Bhai for the said purpose. Ameer Bhai had taken this amount also in the common pool of my earlier credits which he was holding on the transfer of the commission for Uri and Dhulhasti Projects as mentioned above. Out of the said amount of Rs. 10 crores, I had paid a sum of Rs. 6.5 crores in three installments to Mr. Arif Mohd. Khan during May to August 1990 which he had probably utilised in setting up the hospital for handicaps in Bahraich. I had made these payments to Mr. Arif Mohd. Khan after receiving money from Ameer Bhai through JK Jain from the amount held by him on my behalf as mentioned above. The remaining amount of Rs. 3.5 crores was held by me in the same common pool which I utilised for my own purposes subsequently.

During the year 1989 itself, the work of Cintering Plant of Durgapur Steel Plant was awarded to M/s Tyaza Permo Export, a Govt. of Russia Undertaking. I have been in contact with the said company from before because of my old contact with Bhillai Steel Plant with which they were also associated from long time before. Mr. Egrovf of Russia was the President of the said company. While awarding the contract of Durgapur Steel Plant to M/s TP, there was a demand of Rs. 10.5 crores towards political expenses at Delhi. Since TP was the govt. undertaking of Russia, they could not make any direct payment to anybody towards the said political expenses and, therefore, they suggested that they could make the payment to our company, i.e., Bhilai Engg. Corporation from where the required amount could be given towards political expenses. The understanding in between us and the TP was that TP would compensate us in the export orders at the inflated price which we would be quoting to them. With this background, TP gave an advance of Rs. 15 crores by cheque to my company which I deposited in my company's accounts. Against the said payment of Rs. 15 crores I paid Rs. 10.5 crores in instalments to Shri Satish Sharma in Hotel Holiday Inn at New Delhi. Sh. Satish Sharma told me that he had got the money taken down through the lift upto the parking place in the underground from where the same was sent to the house of the then Prime Minister of India, Shri Rajiv Gandhi. I knew Shri Satish Sharma since 1986. I had met him in the house of Shri Rajiv Gandhi, the then Prime Minister of India. Sh. Satish Sharma had told me that instead of showing his connection with the said amount to anybody, its payment may be connected to Shri Lalit Suri in whose Hotel the payments were made. I had accordingly directed JK Jain to show the said payment in the name of Lalit Suri while accounting for the same even though I had paid the amount to Sh. Satish Sharma as mentioned above. As regards the adjustment of Rs. 15 crores given to me by TP, the said amount was adjusted against the export order of about Rs. 30 to 40 crores which TP had placed on us and we had exported the castings etc. against the said order to Russia for manufacturing the components for Durgapur Steel Plant. The above noted sum of Rs. 10.5 crores which I paid to Sh. Satish Sharma from my black money thus became white through the process mentioned above.

During the year 1990, my friend Pradip Chopra, a British National, who stays in London (address not remembered) had sent me Pounds 32,000 through Hawala channels which I had received at Delhi in Indian Rupees at the rate of Rs. 40 per Pound. The entry of the said Pounds and the receipt of Rs. 12.8 lakhs mentioned in September and October 1990 against KI (9.00) and KII (3.80) pertain to the said payment. I do not remember the telephone number and the address of Pradip Chopra but I would be able to furnish the same after consulting my diaries. He had paid the above mentioned Pounds to me from my money which I had kept with him in foreign exchange for meeting my expenses whenever I visited abroad. I do not remember as to how much amount I have kept with him but these were also from the commissions which I had received from foreign companies as mentioned above and from my own earnings abroad from the export business etc.

The other receipt of money through the Hawala channels is Rs. 1.90 lakhs which I had received in US Dollars at Dubai during January 1989 when I had visited Dubai for 3-4 days with my wife Poonam and daughter Geetika during the New Year's celebration of 1989. I had received this amount through the above mentioned Ameer Bhai's channels at Dubai and that is why it is accounted for in the diary against his account only under code 'A'.

The first two pages of the diary contain the receipt of Indian Rupees from Ameer Bhai against the conversion of US Dollars at Hawala rates prevalent during the relevant period. This gives the account of about 22.65 million US dollars which were received by us from Ameer Bhai which I had distributed to different persons and business organisations as mentioned in detail in the two diaries and two files in coded words and figures.

The other receipts shown in the names of my family members and other contractors etc. are the receipts of black money from my business earnings or the intra-family transactions which also include refund of some amounts received by them from the amounts received by JK Jain from the channel of Ameer Bhai etc. My brothers NK Jain and BR Jain knew about such receipts from the channel of Ameer Bhai as mentioned above and also they know the sources of the said funds. The amount of Rs. 13 lakhs shown as received from one Abbi is the receipt of black money through one contractor PN Abbi for sale of steel scraps etc. at Bhilai. I do not know the exact whereabouts of PN Abbi even though I tried to ascertain it for quite some time.

With regard to the disbursements made from the amounts received by me through the above channels, I have to state as under.

1. I had paid Rs. 4 crores to Shri Rajiv Gandhi during March and May 1991 because he had demanded the said amount for making payment to Smt. Jaya Lalitha of Madras. The sum of Rs. 2 crores was collected by Mr. George, Private Secretary to Sh. Rajiv Gandhi from my residence in the month of March, 1991. I had kept the said amount with me after collecting the same from JK Jain. JK Jain, however, knew that his amount was going to Sh. Rajiv Gandhi and, therefore, he had entered the said disbursement in the Diary under code name 'RG' during the month of March 1991. The other sum of Rs. 2 crores was given by me and JK Jain to Shri Sita Ram Kesri, Treasurer of Congress Party, at his residence in Delhi in two instalments. One instalment of Rs. 1 crore was given to him on 2.5.91 and the other 1 crore was given about 10-15 days thereafter. Since these diaries had already been seized by CBI by that time, there is no entry in respect of the payments made to Shri Sita Ram Kesri as mentioned above in the month of May, 1991.
2. After the assassination of Shri Rajiv Gandhi, Shri Narasimha Rao, present Prime Minister of India, became the President of Congress Party. Shri RK Dhawan, Member of Parliament, who is known to me from the time of Sh. Rajiv Gandhi's Government, took me to Sh. Narasimha Rao at his residence at Motilal Nehru Marg, New Delhi. Sh. RK Dhawan told me in the presence of Sh. Narasimha Rao, to give Rs. 50 lakhs for party fund saying that I would be compensated adequately somewhere else. I had agreed for the same. Sh. RK Dhawan, in the meantime,

further told Sh. Narasimha Rao that I would be giving Rs. 5 lakhs for his (Sh. Narasimha Rao's) expenses also on the elections etc. I agreed to make the said payment also. Since I already had the flowing money from the channels of Ameer Bhai, I had no difficulty in making these payments. After about 2 or 3 days, I paid Rs. 5 lakhs to Sh. Narasimha Raoji at his residence at Motilal Nehru Marg on or around 27th May, 1991. I also paid Rs. 50 lakhs to Shri R.K. Dhawan for the party expenses when Sh. Narasimha Raoji was to leave for Uttar Pradesh for electioneering etc. After about a month or so when Sh. Narasimha Raoji became the Prime Minister of India Sh. Satish Sharma called me to his own farm house where Chandraswami was already present. I left my car at the farm house of Sh. Satish Sharma and went along with Chandraswami in his car to PM's house at Race Course Road. Sh. Narasimha Raoji talked to me separately and told me to pay Rs. 3 crores for the party out of which I was supposed to pay Rs. 50 lakhs to Shri Satish Sharma who, at that time, was not in the Cabinet, Rs. 50 lakhs to Sh. Narasimha Rao himself and Rs. 2 crores to Shri Chandraswami. I had agreed for the said payments. At that time, some large scale modernisation work was likely to start at Rourkela Steel Plant. I expected some work in the said plant to be given to me also and I agreed to pay Rs. 3 crores as mentioned above. I met Shri Narasimha Raoji on 9 occasions during those days. Shri Chandraswami was not checked and his car had free access to PM's residence. I was also, therefore, not checked and my name was not recorded at the reception whenever I accompanied Chandraswami in his car. When I went separately on 2 or 3 occasions my name was recorded at the reception and I was checked also by the security staff. In one of the meetings, Sh. Narasimha Raoji told me that I may pay his money of Rs. 50 lakhs also to Shri Chandraswami. I thus paid Rs. 50 lakhs to Satish Sharma and Rs. 2.5 crores to Chandraswami at their respective residence in instalments. These payments were required for the purposes of effecting defections of some MPs in support of Congress Party which was being planned during those days by Sh. Satish Sharma and Sh. Chandraswami. These amounts were also from the same channel of Ameer Bhai which I have been receiving through Shri JK Jain as mentioned above. Since the diaries had been seized by the CBI by then, none of these payments are entered in the said diaries etc. I went to the residence of Sh. Narasimha Raoji in the evening prior to Holi of 1992. He again asked me to pay Rs. 3 to 4 crores more for the party works which I could not pay.

With regard to the other payments shown in the diaries and files, I state that the entire accounting has been made in lakhs and not in thousands as I had stated earlier. I had taken the plea of the amounts being in thousands only with the motive of saving taxes. I have taken the same position in the petitions filed by me on my own behalf and also on behalf of my companies before the Settlement Commission at Bombay.

Annexure C

Central Bureau of Investigation

D.O. No. 63/JD(N)/CBI/96
GOVERNMENT OF INDIA
C.G.O. COMPLEX. BLOCK NO.3
LODHI ROAD
NEW DELHI-110003

Dated February 27, 1996

B. R. LALL
JOINT DIRECTOR (NORTH)

Dear Shri Rao,

I am enclosing a photocopy of a clipping from 'Indian Express' dtd. 22.2.1996, the underlined portion of which states that the statement of Sh. SK Jain as recorded in March,1995 was unreliable. Somewhat similar news had earlier appeared in the 'Pioneer' also where the veracity of recording the statement of Jain was doubted and something similar has also appeared in 'Frontline' of 9.2.1996 and everywhere it is with reference to a source from CBI and in inverted commas. Nothing could be farther from the truth, as this statement was recorded after taking utmost precautions and I had myself verified with Jain what he was saying. Every part of this statement which has been verified, has come out to be true, but his statement in relation to Prime Minister present and the past, Shri Rajiv Gandhi was not allowed to be verified by yourself. It was one of the major issues on which I was transferred from investigation of Hawala Case. I have already put it on record vide my DO letter No. 79/(A)/JD(N)/CBI/95 dtd. 1.8.1995 delivered on 11.8.1995, which was addressed to you and a copy of which was sent to Shri NN Singh, Special Director.

The day it appeared in the 'Pioneer', I had spoken to the Special Director, but he was of the opinion that lots of versions are in the air, and he did not agree for my request for issuing a contradiction. But, now that it has appeared in various papers and magazines carrying the same language by and large, prima facie, it appears to be based on official briefing.

As a faceless civil servant, after writing my DO Letter to you, I have talked neither in public nor in press anywhere for the simple reason that I stick to civil service morality. But, if such official briefings are carried out, it reflects badly on the team, that I led, two (myself and Amod Kanth, my DIG) senior most members of which have already been transferred out. Accompained with such statements and attributed to CBI and going unchecked and uncontradicted, go against me. I will request for a clarification to be issued in the Press as I feel very strongly about any comments being made or such sweeping judgements being passed on a matter, which I presided over and for which I take responsibility and I feel proud that my action was the most truthful, straightforward and professional.

Yours sincerely,

Sd/

(B.R.Lall)

SHRI K. VIJAYA RAMA RAO

DIRECTOR,CBI

CGO COMPLEX

NEW DELHI

A copy is forwarded to Shri N.N. Singh, Special Director, CBI
ENCL : As above

Sd/- 22.2.1996

B.R. LALL

Annexure D

Central Bureau of Investigation

D.O. No. 296/JD(N)/CBI/96
GOVERNMENT OF INDIA
C.G.O. COMPLEX. BLOCK NO.3
LODHI ROAD
NEW DELHI-110003

Dated October 18, 1996

B. R. LALL
JOINT DIRECTOR (NORTH)

Dear Shri Singh,

When you took over as director/CBI, you had advocated and promised complete transparency in the functioning of CBI, but unfortunately it is the hush-hush atmosphere, which is prevailing. There is no certainty about anything. The deep thought which should precede any action in this sensitive Organisation both in operation and in administrative fields has given place to sudden impulsive orders. The system of transfer of charges instead of presenting transparency is leading to dark alleys.

On 7.10.96, there was a usual weekly meeting, which lasted till past 12 noon. There. was no mention about chopping off my charge, but in the afternoon sometime between 3 and 4 p.m., DIG, Chandigarh rang me up why I was being divested of the charge of Chandigarh. Since I had no official information despite the fact that I was with director till 12 O'clock, I declined any knowledge, which shocked the DIG. At the tea table when I mentioned this to my colleagues they were also surprised at the manner.

I tried hard to figure out the possible reasons. I could not guess any except that (believing that working in CBI should be free of fear and be transparent) I have been commenting freely on certain decisions, which to my mind have been against the CBI culture of truthfulness and have been affecting vitally the organisation and its reputation. I also made comments on Biswas affairs on the narration of Shri R.C. Sharma, which was unfortunately in your absence otherwise I would have commented on that in greater details there itself. When you re-entered the room, the meeting was dismissed as you had some immediate commitment in courts/with A.G.

Such hush-hush transfers are becoming a tool of punishment to the so-called inconvenient who work and speak truthfully. The mechanism is also designed as a pressure device for others to fall in line. If my transfer was a part of re-organisation, it should have been discussed or at least I should have been sounded in advance, I authentically came to know of it only on the 8th (A.N.) i.e. next day. When facts are suppressed rumours take over. Already lots of rumours are afloat. While promising transparency, why these hush-hush orders were made leading to rumours is not understood. Rumours or guesswork are detrimental to this sensitive Organisation.

There has to be some reason for every action and there must be some reason with you, but if that reason cannot be told, cannot be transparent, it naturally leads to the conclusion that there is something fishy.

Similar things have happened in case of the Special director when immediately on your taking over he was practically divested of all the work. Subsequently the telephone tapping case was given to him, which even a naïve would realise was only a cover up and the real intention was that DCBI wanted to sideline the Special director as his advice in some cases could have been a stumbling block. Similar is the impression that has gone down in CBI with two time transfers of Shri U.N. Biswas confining him to Patna only and stranding his family or taking him off from Patna altogether.

I have always followed the dictum that "act well thy part and there all the honour lies". But I find that the tinkering with the system, breaking it at will gives the impression down the line that director does not want straight forward functioning and those who do not fall in line, are being divested and harassed. My reputation actually gets a boost by such actions as I have established my reputation here during 2½ years and in state and Government India during last 2½ decades, but if my organisation, which is so dear to me, suffers, it pains me. This unpredictable action, for which no reason or rationale has been shown takes the morale of CBI cadres down, which hurts me. I shall feel grateful if I could kindly be informed why this chopping off was done and why in a hush-hush manner without any transparency. I believe that I and whole of CBI openly is entitled to know that.

Yours sincerely,
Sd/
(B.R. Lall)

Shri Joginder Singh
Director, CBI

A copy is forwarded to Shri R.C. Sharma, Special director. I am sending this copy as I have made a mention of the name of my senior, so, I feel morally bound to endorse a copy.

Sd/
(B.R. Lall)

Annexure E

How to Make CBI a Free Agency

By B.R. Lall

(An article published in Hindustan Times on March 1, 1996)

JACOB G. Grossberg, deposing before the commission on graft and organised crime in 1933 in the US, said: "Politics is the business of the party organisation, party organisation is the business of the mercenary criminal, the racketeer. The political boss is usually the well-paid agent or manager for the latter, and the men he puts in office are usually puppets... the policeman on the beat or the plainclothes man does not bring in the big shot, whose gang controls his ward committee chief, who controls his captain, who controls him. It is the party organisation which furnishes the Governor, the Judge, the Prosecutor, and which gives orders to the police. In other words, it furnishes the law-enforcing organisation. It is manifest that that organism suffers paralysis.. .and a paralysed body cannot function properly."

In place of the word 'police' in the above quote, we can read administration in entirety. It is the administration in totality which is suffering from paralysis.

In this country we have specialised agencies in all the States and the Central Bureau of Investigation (CBI) at the Centre. We must understand its dynamics before the crucial questions are answered. Corruption is a game and prerogative of people in power.

Basically corruption is nothing but conversion of power (both political or administrative) into money. The anti-corruption organisation to be effective should be capable of taking action against persons in power but the bureaucratic functioning including these agencies suited the times of British rule where it was a master-servant relationship. The slave cannot question the actions of the master or disobey his orders.

Even an upright official, when faced with orders from his political masters, turns helpless in effort to uphold rules and values. He is seen to be disloyal as if loyalty is not to the system but to the individual. Even wise people have become players in this sordid drama. The investigative agencies do real good work, otherwise, but when it comes to exposing a person in high office, be he a political master, or a bureaucrat, they shake and tremble. They are used to functioning under the political masters' directions only.

The rules and procedures under which the registration, the investigation, the enquiry or verification of criminal misconduct are to be initiated against the high and mighty, dissuade the agency and stonewall all the legal processes. The safeguards enjoyed by these persons offer near-immunity from any action by these agencies against those in power. This applies to the highest agency of the land, the CBI. It is a well-known fact that the CBI has to seek the permission of the Government for every step it takes.

Persons in power who indulge in corruption can be expected to make every effort to block the investigation. Even if some cases have to be taken up as a result of a public outcry, investigating officers who function under these very masters keep weighing the political fall-out and consequences.

There are executive instructions overriding the laws of the land to seek permission for making enquiries, for registering criminal cases, for conducting searches, in case of persons beyond a certain level in office which reminds one of that strict warden who prescribed: "Nobody will move out of the hostel without my permission and be sure that permission will not be granted."

The job of the agency is to find and collect facts in the most truthful manner without any consideration other than the law and without any fear, favour or pressure. The CBI or any other authority that may be created needs to be placed under a board of control. The job of the government is to maintain law and order which is not the job of the CBI. If taken out of the government's control, the normal functions of the government will not be affected in any way except that corrupt public servants will not be able to indulge fearlessly into this all degrading nefarious activity.

The mechanism of appointment of the CBI control board (or whatever other name we may give to this autonomous highpowered body) should not be dependent upon any recommendations or a selection process. The members of the board should come up in their own right rather than being appointed and be beholden to anyone. The board should be headed by a retired Chief Justice or a judge of the Supreme Court and include a retired Comptroller and Auditor General of India (CAG) and a former director, CBI as members with the serving director/CBI as its non-participating secretary. The term of each member and the Chairman shall be for two years. The Chairman shall have the same status, perks and salary as the Chief Justice/ Judge of the Supreme Court and the other two equivalent to that of the Comptroller and Auditor General of India. They should be removable only through the process of impeachment as provided for judges and the CAG.

The board will exercise all the operational functions of the Government in the context of all the CBI cases against corruption. The CBI board should be treated as appointing authority for all the suspects against whom the agency proceeds or proposes commencement of enquiries, investigations, and grant of permission for prosecution under the PC Act. The Government will cease to have any operational control over CBI. Since the position of DCBI will become very crucial, his appointment will also vest in the board and it will be a term posting. The rules governing him will have to be worked out in detail, but in brief, his term could be three years like the chief of a defence force. An IPS officer with a very good track record and having put in at least 30 years of service should be eligible. The Government of India could sponsor five to seven names but there will be no bar on considering other names by the board.

The board members and the DCBI shall be prohibited from undertaking any job under any Government or private sector, barred from following any business or profession after a term on the board and also there shall be no extension as a member of the board or DCBI under any circumstance. The status of the DCBI should be raised to that of service chiefs.

The above will free the chief investigating agency from undesirable extraneous controls and also from the allegations that it follows the dictates of political masters or that it acts to serve their political ends. It will restore the confidence of the people. The prospect of action against the high and mighty is going to deter and prevent the high-ups from indulging in unlawful activities.

(Mr. B.R.Lall is a serving, senior IPS officer)

Annexure F

Address of Prime Minister HD Deve Gowda on Nov. 22, 1996 at CBI Conference

Friends, I have spent nearly two and a half hours to know your views, but I am not fully satisfied. The reason being that several officers have not been able to express their views because of the shortage of time. I request those officers who have not got the opportunity not to feel that I have let them down. If you have got any valuable suggestions, you can directly write to me at my personal address. I will listen to those suggestions so that improvement can be made by considering those suggestions.

Three organisations have assembled here today and yesterday. CBI, the Vigilance of Public Sector Undertakings, and the Vigilance Commissioners of the States. I was enriched by the valuable suggestions made by several of your officers with regard to the lapses in our system. I am really happy. Most of the Prime-Ministers cannot spend two and a half or three hours normally. They will come and deliver their speech and go. Even when I was CM of Karnataka, when I addressed the police officers, I used to spend half a day with them. I did not give them a speech at the initial stage: I wanted to hear them first.

Now I would like to ask a question. This is a family affair. Do not try to feed the press. Let me ask the straight question: which country is free from corruption? Can anybody stand up and say before me? I am posing a question; I have given freedom to you.

There is no question of reservation from anybody, even if you were SPs and DIGs. Which country is free from corruption? Please tell me. Is Japan free from corruption? Is America free from corruption? Which country today is free from corruption?

I have got some experience from public life and I have served the nation for around 35 years in various capacities. Why has such a situation developed recently and are there no patriots in the politics or the bureaucracy? Certainly there are. Don't be under the impression that everything has gone wrong. Yes, there are some black sheep. But they are not only among politicians. They are not confined only to the bureaucracy. The black sheep are there in the very system of our governance. Our Constitution framers have taken sufficient care. They have given us such a Constitution where checks and balances are there. If there is any accountability today, it is for the politicians that there is accountability. It is for the bureaucracy that there is accountability. The politician should go once in five years before lacs and lacs of people. Whether he has got a good image or a bad image, he will be subjected to scrutiny by the people of the nation and those politicians have scrutinized the bureaucracy. There are certain areas where they do commit mistakes, in a democratic system like this.

But at the same time, the only area where there is no accountability is judiciary. Don't be under the impression that the judiciary today has got an opportunity to improve the system. If anybody is under the impression that corruption is going to be removed by this activism, they are in fools' paradise.

Lokpal or Lokayukt. If you are going to bring it by passing a legislation in the Parliament, then we can remove corruption! In Karnataka, we passed the Lokayukt Bill. The then CM said, on the day of introduction of the Lokayukt bill, in the Assembly, henceforth, there will be no corruption in Karnataka. If anybody finds any corruption in any department in Karnataka, they can straightaway go to the Lokayukt. And they are free to frame the charges. The guilty will be punished. In May, 1984, the Lokpal system was introduced in Karnataka. Are you reading through newspapers? Is Karnataka free from corruption?

The Lokayukt was established in Karnataka. I was the only man who on a flimsy complaint went before the Lokayukt. I did so because I wanted to respect the law of the land. I appeared in one case and after my case was over, there have been complaints against several politicians, ministers and chief ministers. No politician appeared before this Lokayukt. They tried to attack the Lokayukt. They tried to dilute the institution. And today nobody bothers. Don't be under the impression that the Lokayukta or the Uplokayukta brought a revolutionary change. When the Bill was introduced in the Assembly. I was hearing that, I was just laughing. Here also this United Front Government will introduce the Lokpal Bill. Let the Bill be passed. I will also live for another 10-15 years. Let me see how much corruption is going to be reduced in this country. You all will watch.

Let us touch our conscience first. Instead of preaching to others, let us touch our own conscience. Let us work according to our conscience first. Instead of blaming each other, finding fault with each other please try to set yourself right. Are we not able to understand where we are committing mistake? Is anybody required to advise us when I am making certain decision? I myself will be able to know. Whether I am doing wrong. If that realisation is going to come forward, the person who is at the helm of affairs can know what is required and where things went wrong. Yes, it may be cost consideration, it may be any other considerations. We commit mistakes. But we cannot say that the entire organisation or the entire system has totally collapsed.

What impression are we creating today? The whole world today thinks, our country is full of corrupt people: the whole bureaucracy is full of corruption. In a country of 950 million population, day in and day out, if you read all the newspapers, barring corruption there is nothing! Some spokesmen of CBI, or the sources within CBI can they bring any credit to this organisation? Please tell me. We are all family members. You want to denigrate the image of each other? Demolish the image of another? Do you want to feed reports that are accurate or inaccurate, or exaggerated? Tell me is this not going on? You must understand, an institution which has got the highest prestige, the CBI today has become a mockery. Even a Munsif Magistrate is issuing the directions to the CBI/director.

Forget the Supreme Court, I am not going to comment. But an ordinary Metropolitan City Magistrate is going to issue directions to the top officers of the CBI. Forget the person, he is the head of the institution. Are you collectively prepared to fight to retain the image of the organisation? Today it is going to happen to him and tomorrow, it may happen to you. And if a politician is summoned before the Court, the politician is lost.

I will just come to one point. A politician with about 50 years in public life, after he took over a new office, there is a Public Interest Litigation, and that litigation was referred to CBI for enquiry. In 50 years, there is no complaint. For 50 years he was an honest politician, and for 50 years nobody questioned his integrity. Because he is occupying an important position, a petition is filed in the High Court. The High Court asks the CBI to enquire about his property or his grandson's property or his relatives property. When he was serving in public life for 50 years nobody cared about his relatives' property, or about his assets or liabilities. So, the political atmosphere today has given a handle to the judiciary to take revenges against politicians.

When was there no corruption? When Partap Singh Kairon was the Chief Minister and Jawaharlal Nehru was the Prime Minister, was there no corruption? The Haridas Mundra's case was raised in the Parliament by Firoz Gandhi, was it not corruption? Let us be cool and calm and try to improve. If there is any area of mistake, let us try to rectify it. But today, wherever we go, the media is also playing the same thing. Is the country going to progress in such type of atmosphere? Personal ambition, personal gains and short-sightedness is going to destroy the very system. Are not the courts divided? I don't want to elaborate; I know so many things.

Somebody has mentioned how in Public Sector Undertakings the Chairman and Directors, misused their office. If the Public Undertakings Committee and the Public Accounts Committee discharged their duty properly, can it not be minimised at least? It may not be possible to totally eradicate it. But it is possible. And I will tell you very frankly today, even today in our system, more than 90% of our officers are honest. Otherwise the system would have totally collapsed. There are a few black sheep in every walk of life but everywhere more than 90-95% people are honest. Otherwise with this population in this country, we would have totally collapsed. Please, for God's sake, don't be under the impression that the whole thing has gone out of control. But the only thing is, the atmosphere is totally vitiated by the media. Day in and day out they try to give such a distorted version. Some people say circulation of some papers is going down, but that is a different matter, they have their own freedom. But such distorted information is being fed to the media by our own colleagues. I am the Prime Minister. The DIG, or the Joint director, even the director, we are all part of the system. If you have got some grouse, sit within the four walls and discuss among yourselves. You want to quarrel, quarrel—but within the four wells. This is a wrong thing you are doing. Discuss, debate, then come to a consensus. I am not going to say to protect. I will never say that A or B. I am not concerned with that. If I have no interest to at least acquire some knowledge from your experience I would not have sat here for two and a half hours. I am equally anxious how best we can improve system. The system is good, but it is eroding. Even today, I love my system. But unfortunately, each wing is not functioning within its earmarked area. They are crossing their boundaries. I tell you very frankly, this is going to destroy the system.

Yes, there are a lot things to be done. But,let us sit collectively, think over it, apply our mind. Where things went wrong — we will all try to share the burden. Judicial activism for some time that people will feel outside that they are doing something, because of the media. When once the true colour of the events that are going to take place in the judicial system, comes out, then again people start doubting. I do not want to cast aspersions against anybody. As a CM or PM, normally we are going to meet the Chief Justices. I met only two times the Supreme Court Chief Justice. One paper writes that the Prime Minister met him at 2.00 a.m. early in the morning. At 2.00 a.m. by covering my face. This is why this country is ruined. And your Supreme Court's advocates, they want to make a big rally in protest. Are you loyal to the Constitution? Either you are loyal to one political party or loyal to your particular community. Something is there, otherwise why a Prime Minister of a country has to go and meet at 2.00 a.m. This is how this country is denigrated.

This country has got some cherished values, and we people for our selfish ends, want to spoil the atmosphere. Everybody has to work under the Constitution. One official, a senior bureaucrat, was sent to jail for one month. I was the Chief Minister. Hundred per cent I know, he was an honest officer. Everything has got its limitation. Even tolerance has got its limitation. Even patience has limitation. If 3 or 4 DIGs are straight-away sent to jail, then from whom I will get my work executed. If all of you friends say tomorrow that yes, you are the Prime Minister, but we cannot do any thing, if the non-cooperation is started by the bureaucracy, as the policy maker myself, can I get the work done? Can I deliver the goods? My masters are the people. There must be some mistake I do agree, but while exercising certain discretion, the overall picture of the country should be borne in mind. Today we are fighting because of sharp political differences. Do not be under the impression that everything is functioning under the ambit of the Constitution. Things are moving outside the purview of the Constitution. Even the CBI without the permission of the State Government, on the direction of the sitting Municipal Magistrate, has to go for investigation against an elected leader who is head of the elected Government. Then why should we believe the State machinery? The State machinery may want to please their political bosses. Now the matter will be referred to CBI. When Rajiv Gandhi was there, the then Prime Minister, my own Chief Minister said in the Assembly that CBI was only a Government Agency. It is his master's voice. It is not Narasimha Rao period. It has gone, when Rajiv Gandhi was there, when Indira Gandhi was the Prime Minister, in 1983-84, when Jalappa's case was referred, it is not CBI, it is Congress Bureau of Investigation. Because of this dirty politics and for their own political ends they tried to demolish the image of the CBI, the investigation organisation which has got the highest reputation in the country. The judiciary also draws the threats from the politicians when they want to make you in the eyes of the public very small. Don't give room for this. It does not mean you fight against judiciary I don't say. But you all apply your minds. If there is any area of difference among yourselves try to sort out among yourselves and give some valuable suggestions. It is the team of officers sitting together where certain improvement has to be made in the existing service conditions or where certain changes have to be made. I am just prepared to call the senior officers, if need be I will sit with them and will discuss with them. I am prepared to give a solemn assurance to improve the image of this organisation and I will give you an assurance that I am prepared to interfere but at the same time nobody should try to cross the boundaries. For fifty years a politician who served the nation has not come across any complaint of corruption. But once he became something at the national level, within one week a Public Interest Litigation is filed. And next morning, one CBI officer says, I will go and enquire and arrest.

Where do you stand if the atmosphere today is so much spoiled. Let us all collectively think over on these matters. It is not the question of A,B,C or X,Y,Z. The executive powers cannot be taken away by judiciary. Can judiciary start investigation of its own without your help? Or can the executive force it independently without the Parliament or legislature? Now where are we leading to? You are meeting in a crucial period, very crucial period. Without any bias, think over, apply your mind collectively, how best we can improve the present system. If there are any omissions and commissions, how best the image of this organisation should be improved. The Government cannot sleep over all these matters. You should also see and try to cooperate. As long as I am the Prime Minister and I don't want to encroach upon the powers of anybody. Who am I? It is for you.

I took so much of your time. Thank you very much for your valuable advice and those people who have not participated, please write to me about your experience where things have to be improved and how best this organisation can be made free from any interference. If it is possible to work, I am prepared to consider all those things. Only thing is because of some short gain please don't be a party to the destruction of the image of this reputed organisation of the country that is CBI.

Annexure G

List of Major Scams/Scandals in Free India

This list is not exhaustive, but only indicative. As it has been compiled impromptu it may have left out many more scandals/ scams.

1. T. Prakasam episode of misappropriating public money in 1946 while heading the interim government of Madras province.
2. Jeep Scandal of V.K. Krishna Menon 1948
3. Plates Scandal of V. K. Krishna Menon 1949
4. Haridas Mundhra or the LIC Scandal — early Fifties.
5. Mines and Fuel (or Serajuddin) Scandal of 1956.
6. Scandal against ministers of Madras Government (enquired 1949-50). It was treated as a party affair and no action was taken except that the ministers were made to resign.
7. Scandals surrounding the Amin Chand Pyarelal firms.
8. HBJ Pipeline Scandal
9. NagarwalaScam
10. Kendu Leaf Scandal

*11. **Commission of Inquiry, New Delhi, 11 June 1964. S.R. Das' Report on Sardar Partap Singh Kairon.**

*12. Commission of Inquiry, Jammu and Kashmir Government, Srinagar, 30th June 1967. N. Rajagopala Ayyangar's Report on Bakshi Ghulam Mohammed.

*13. Commission of Inquiry, Government of Orissa, Mr. Justice H R Khanna's Report on Biju Patnaik and others.

*14. Committee of Inquiry (Steel Transactions) Department of Iron and Steel, Government of India, New Delhi, February 1968.

*15. Commission of Inquiry constituted by the Government of Bihar to inquire into charges against K B Sahay and others, 5th February 1970.

*16. Commission of Inquiry, Report on the charges against fourteen ex-United Front Ministers, Superintendent Secretariat Press, Bihar, 19th November 1969.

*17. The Hon'ble Justice J R Mudholkar, Special Judge for Inquiries, Government of Orissa, 26th September 1968 (Re. H K Mehtab)

*18. The Orissa Inquiry Commission 1971-72, Government of Orissa, 25th May 1972, Sarjoo Prasad's Report on Dr. HK Mehtab.

*19. Commission of Inquiry consisting of S Velu Pillai (Re. Mrs. K R Gourim, E K Imbichi Bava and M K Krishnan) Parts I to IV, Government of Kerala Press, Trivandrum, 1971.

*20. Commission of Inquiry consisting of A N Mulla (Re: M N Govidan Nair and T V Thomas) Government of Kerala, 1971.

*21. Commission of Inquiry, the Hon'ble Justice M U Issas (Re: allegations regarding acquisition of land for the Kerala Agricultural University), Ernakulam, 12th October 1971.

*22. Commission of Inquiry to inquire into allegations against B. Wellingdon by P Govinda Menon, Government of Kerala, 24th March 1972.

23. M O Mathai Case

24. HDW Submarine Case

25. AN-12 Purchase Case

26. Airbus – 320 purchase Case
27. Sugar Scam
28. Fairfax Case
29. Bofors Scam
30. St. Kitts Scandal
31. Harshad Mehta or the Banking Securities Scam
32. Housing Scam
33. S U 30 Purchase Scam
34. Indian Bank Scam
35. Dhoti Saree Scam of Bihar
36. Sugar Scam II
37. Jain Hawala Case
38. Lakhubhai Pathak Case
39. Assam LoC Scandal
40. JMM Bribery Case
41. AHD Bihar Scam
42. Urea Scam
43. Petroleum Ministry's Oil selection and LPG depot allotment Scam.
44. Telecom Scandal
45. Medical Equipment Scandal
46. Goldstar Steel Allows Ltd. Case of Prabhakar Rao—Hiten Dalal
47. U P Ayurveda Scam
48. ITC FERA Violation Case
49. CRB Scam
50. MS Shoes Scam
51. Bailadilla Mines Sell Out Scam
52. TN CM Jayalalita's Cases
53. UTI Scam
54. Tehelka Scandal

55. Punjab Public Service Commission Recruitment Case
56. Maharashtra Public Service Commission Recruitment Case
57. Taj Corridor Case
58. Judeo Scam
59. Jogi Bribery to MLAs' Scam
60. Telgi Scam
61. Postal Stamps (disclosed by Telgi)
62. Ketan Parikh Scam
63. Fairgrowth Case

---

*Scandals in which commission of enquiry were set up, but no action was taken in spite of the fact that the persons at high places were found to be guilty.

Index